SEX AND STYLE

Sex and Style

LITERARY CRITICISM AND GENDER
IN EARLY MODERN ENGLAND

ELIZABETH SCOTT-BAUMANN

PRINCETON UNIVERSITY PRESS
PRINCETON & OXFORD

Copyright © 2025 by Princeton University Press

Princeton University Press is committed to the protection of copyright and the intellectual property our authors entrust to us. Copyright promotes the progress and integrity of knowledge created by humans. By engaging with an authorized copy of this work, you are supporting creators and the global exchange of ideas. As this work is protected by copyright, any reproduction or distribution of it in any form for any purpose requires permission; permission requests should be sent to permissions@press.princeton.edu. Ingestion of any IP for any AI purposes is strictly prohibited.

Published by Princeton University Press
41 William Street, Princeton, New Jersey 08540
99 Banbury Road, Oxford OX2 6JX

press.princeton.edu

GPSR Authorized Representative: Easy Access System Europe - Mustamäe tee 50, 10621 Tallinn, Estonia, gpsr.requests@easproject.com

All Rights Reserved

Library of Congress Cataloging-in-Publication Data

Names: Scott-Baumann, Elizabeth, 1982– author
Title: Sex and style : literary criticism and gender in early modern England / Elizabeth Scott-Baumann.
Description: Princeton : Princeton University Press, 2025. | Includes bibliographical references and index.
Identifiers: LCCN 2025013047 (print) | LCCN 2025013048 (ebook) | ISBN 9780691272023 paperback | ISBN 9780691272016 hardback | ISBN 9780691272030 ebook
Subjects: LCSH: English literature—Women authors—History and criticism | English poetry—Women authors—History and criticism | English poetry—History and criticism—Theory, etc. | English poetry—Early modern, 1500–1700—History and criticism | Women and literature—England—History—16th century | Women and literature—England—History—17th century | BISAC: LITERARY CRITICISM / Poetry | LITERARY CRITICISM / Modern / 17th Century
Classification: LCC PR113 .S355 2025 (print) | LCC PR113 (ebook) | DDC 820.9/92870903--dc23/eng/20250501
LC record available at https://lccn.loc.gov/2025013047
LC ebook record available at https://lccn.loc.gov/2025013048

British Library Cataloging-in-Publication Data is available

Editorial: Anne Savarese, James Collier, and Emma Wagh
Production Editorial: Ali Parrington
Jacket/Cover Design: Drohan DiSanto
Production: Erin Suydam
Publicity: William Pagdatoon and Charlotte Coyne
Copyeditor: Catja Pafort

Jacket/Cover Images: Courtesy of James Marshall and Marie-Louise Osborn Collection, Beinecke Rare Book and Manuscript Library, Yale University; Bodleian Libraries, University of Oxford, MS Rawl Poet 90, fol. 5v.; and Burke Library at Union Theological Seminary, Columbia University in the City of New York.

This book has been composed in Arno

10 9 8 7 6 5 4 3 2 1

For Edward, Will, and Phoebe

"My joy, my bliss, my happy story" (anonymous, *Eliza's Babes*, 1652)

CONTENTS

List of Illustrations   ix
Acknowledgements   xi
Note on the Text   xiii

1 Criticize   1

2 Feminine   26

3 Original   49

4 Irregular   75

5 Smooth/Soft   105

   Conclusion: A new history of style   148

Notes   155
Bibliography   175
Index   189

ILLUSTRATIONS

1. Manuscript of Lucy Hutchinson, *Order and Disorder* — 88
2. Copy of Katherine Philips, "Retirement" — 97
3. Copy of Katherine Philips, "In praise of a Countrye Life" — 99
4. Anne Wharton, "Answer to Mr Waller", *Poems by several hands, and on several occasions collected by N. Tate* (London, 1685) — 124
5. Anne Wharton, "To Mr Waller", *The Gentleman's Magazine*, Vol. 85, pt. i (June 1815) — 126
6. Anne Wharton, "To Mr Waller", Osborn MS b408 — 128
7. Anne Wharton, "The inconstancy of Woman Kind", Osborn MS b408 — 142
8. Anne Wharton, "Unchangeable", Osborn MS b408 — 144

ACKNOWLEDGEMENTS

THE EARLY RESEARCH FOR this book was conducted during a James M. Osborn Visiting Fellowship in English Literature and History, at the Beinecke Library, Yale University, and I am grateful both to the Library and to Dr Kathryn James, formerly Curator for Early Modern Books and Manuscripts at the Beinecke Library. I am grateful to the Leverhulme Trust for an Early Career Fellowship, 2012–15 (ref. ECF-2011-389), initially under the mentorship of Professor Sarah Knight at the University of Leicester, and then at King's College London. Thank you to King's College London for supporting work on this book, especially through teaching remission and research assistance provided by the Parents and Carers Fund. I would like to thank Clare Whitehead and Cen Li for research assistance at key moments. At Princeton University Press, many thanks to Anne Savarese, Ali Parrington, and James Collier for shepherding the book through the press. I am indebted to my anonymous readers for Princeton for their invaluable suggestions and their belief in the book.

An earlier version of Chapter 1 was published as '"crittickize uppon the smallest word": Anne Southwell and the place of gender in early modern criticism', in *The Places of Early Modern Criticism*, edited by Gavin Alexander, Emma Gilby and Alexander Marr (Oxford University Press, 2021), and a version of Chapter 4 in 'Lucy Hutchinson, Gender and Poetic Form', *The Seventeenth Century*, 30 (2015), 265–284. I am grateful for permission to reprint this material. Many thanks to the libraries and databases who have allowed permission of images: the Beinecke Library, Yale University; the Bodleian Library, Oxford University; The Burke Library at Union Theological Seminary, Columbia University in the City of New York; ProQuest British Periodical Series and ProQuest Early English Books Online.

I have been fortunate in the many conversations I have had with early modernists over many years which have fed into this book, including Gavin Alexander, Liza Blake, Vanessa Braganza, Vicki Burke, Ben Burton, Danielle

Clarke, Margaret Ezell, Colby Gordon, Kit Heyam, Lorna Hutson, Christina Luckyj, Dianne Mitchell, Joe Moshenska, Victoria Moul, Katie Murphy, Jennifer Richards, Sarah C.E. Ross, Rebecca Rush, Paul Salzman, Gitanjali Shahani, Emma Smith, Ros Smith, Courtney Weiss Smith, Adam Smyth, Robert Stagg, Elizabeth Swann, and Will Tosh. For generously sharing unpublished research on Anne Wharton, many thanks to Gillian Wright, Gillian Manning, and Michael Londry. Thank you to David Norbrook and Sharon Achinstein for starting me on the early modern path and for their inspiration, rigour, and friendship. I have been very fortunate in my early modern colleagues at King's: John Lavagnino, Sarah Lewis, Jemima Matthews, Lucy Munro, Gordon McMullan, Emily Rowe, and, until recently, Sonia Massai and Farah Karim-Cooper. Thank you to Rowan Boyson and Adelene Buckland for writing workshops and camaraderie, and to Sue Wiseman for strong coffee, humour, and wisdom. And in memory of Hannah Murray, leading clinical psychologist and awe-inspiring friend. Thank you always to Caroline Holdsworth, with whom I've been talking about feminism and poetry for twenty years, even while building train sets and toasting marshmallows. To Hannah Crawforth, who has read every word of this book and without whose insight, wit, and friendship I would never have finished it, or had nearly so much fun along the way.

My parents, Alison and Mike Scott-Baumann, have made everything possible, and are the finest role models any teacher and writer could have; my brother Jimmy, the best friend and uncle. Finally, thank you to my husband, Benjie, and our children, Edward, Will, and Phoebe, who have made every day an adventure, and whom I love infinitely.

NOTE ON THE TEXT

FOR EARLY MODERN TEXTS, I have either used modernized editions or modernized myself. This includes spelling and punctuation.

Early modern typography, punctuation (or lack thereof), and even spelling can contribute to a text's meaning. Their material histories of production and transmission are often evident in these markers (as I explore in Chapter 4). But the majority of texts by women on which this book focuses still exist in manuscripts, while proportionately more of the men's works are in printed books. Retaining original spelling and punctuation in this book, therefore, would have generated an unhelpful and inaccurate sense of stylistic difference between male and female writers.

Where early print or manuscript features pertain to the argument, as in Chapter 4, I have quoted from manuscripts and identified this in the notes.

SEX AND STYLE

1

Criticize

> Dare you but write, you are Minerva's bird,
> The owl at which these bats and crows must wonder,
> They'll criticize upon the smallest word:
> This wanteth number, case, that tense and gender.
> > Then must you frame a pitiful epistle,
> > To pray him be a rose was born a thistle.
>
> Could you, as did those Sibyls, prophesy,
> Men will but count you witches for your skill,
> Or be endowed with any quality,
> They'll poison it with some depraving ill.
> > Envy is barren and yields nought but weeds
> > And fears lest better ground have better seeds.
> > —ANNE SOUTHWELL, "PRECEPT 4"[1]

THE FIRST USE OF the English verb "criticize" was probably by a woman. In this witty, angry, and finely-crafted poem, Anne Southwell uses the term to describe how men censure women's language use, excluding them from the sphere of literature. The *OED*'s first usage for "criticize" is Milton's *Eikonoklastes* (1649), while Robert Burton used it in his 1621 *The Anatomy of Melancholy*. It was not defined in dictionaries until the eighteenth century.[2] We do not know exactly when Southwell wrote this poem, which was only printed in the twentieth century, but it was probably in the early decades of the seventeenth century. And Southwell's use is telling: she uses "criticize" to mean judgment of language and even specifically grammar—"this wanteth number, case, that tense and gender"—and also its broader, later sense of "censure" that could even be moral and social—"men will but count you witches for your skill". Criticism, then, is a means of exclusion, and specifically, of prohibiting women's writing, and curtailing their place in society. Criticism is a tool of oppression: of educational exclusion (pointing out incorrect usage of number, case, tense, gender), of stigma and superstition ("count you witches") and of insecurity ("Envy is barren and yields nought but weeds"). Yet it is also, this book argues, a place where women have shaped literary culture, innovated in style, and defined the terms in which poetry is read and valued.

Southwell's vivid, angry poem motivates the questions that *Sex and Style* asks: what is criticism? Who gets to be a critic? Who gets to criticize? These are fundamental questions about authority, discernment, and taste, of which tastes prevail and are recorded in history. Moreover, this book argues that women like Anne Southwell did in fact write literary criticism. In poems, letters, commonplace books, prefaces, and many other forms that are not explicitly treatises on poetics, women were writing at the origins of literary criticism. As we will see, Southwell's criticism in poetry and prose, which remained in manuscript until the twentieth century, explicitly engages with canonical forebears of literary criticism: Sidney, Daniel, Shakespeare. Southwell provides the central case study for this introductory chapter because she herself was an early user of the verbs "criticize" and "play the critic", and because her work is critical in many senses. The place of women theorists like Southwell in the history of literary criticism has been obscured, and this exclusion is in fact one that motivates their writings, such as Southwell's ferocious satire on envious and superstitious men. Here "criticism" comes also to mean critique, a protest against prevailing norms. *Sex and Style* is, too, then a work of criticism and critique, and offers the possibility of a new history of literary criticism—one with women's voices throughout.[3]

The History of Literary Criticism: Where are all the Women?

I began thinking about the history of women critics as I was trying to become one. My own doctoral research was on seventeenth-century women poets, at an exciting time to be working in this field. With many discoveries and rediscoveries in archives had come a growing acceptance in both teaching and publishing that an all-male literary canon was both unethical in the present and inaccurate to the past. Digitization projects were making manuscripts and rare books newly accessible, alongside a burgeoning in expertise in book and manuscript history that allowed deeper understanding of the place of handwritten works, in particular, in the literary marketplace. It felt as if premodern women's poetry was gathering the attention needed to change the canon. And yet, when I looked for scholarship on how women theorized the poetry that they were producing so prodigiously, I drew a blank.

I was not the only one. "Why Are There No Great Women Critics and What Difference Does It Make?"asked Susan S. Lanser and Evelyn Torton Beck in 1979, riffing on Linda Nochlin's famous 1971 essay "Why Have There Been No Great Women Artists?".[4] As Lawrence Lipking noted, the standard *Critical Theory since Plato* "does not find room in its 1,249 double-columned, small-printed pages for a word by [...] any woman".[5] He extrapolates elegantly from this absence: "Unlike Shakespeare's sister, Aristotle's sister has yet to break her silence".[6] Lanser, Beck, and Lipking made these observations over thirty years ago, and yet they have remained curiously—and dispiritingly—relevant; there is still no acknowledged tradition of classical or early modern women literary critics. Even much more recent collections of early modern theory commonly fail to identify a single female critic.[7] Anthologies which focus exclusively on women critics find little before 1800.[8] We know that early modern women produced major literary works, but we do not know whether or how they theorized and criticized literature, and especially—the focus of this book—poetry. To explain this apparent absence, let us look to early modernity, the period in which these divisions between gender and criticism took root, and yet also a time when (I will argue) women were writing against these prohibitions.

Poetry itself has long been associated with women. Montaigne wrote that poetry is "a study fit for [women's] purpose", which seems promising. But he goes on to explain why: "being a wanton, amusing, subtle, disguised, and prattling art; all in delight, all in show, like to themselves".[9] Whether this represents Montaigne's own views or a satirical reflection on those of his peers, his terms here are revealing: both women and poetry are associated with unregulated sexuality (wantonness); unregulated volubility (prattling), and also duplicity (subtle, disguised). George Puttenham's eccentric yet influential *Art of English Poesy* also imagines women both reading and writing literature. Puttenham professes to write for women, describing some of the techniques in his book as "pleasanter to bear in memory: specially for our ladies and pretty mistresses in court, for whose learning I write".[10] Sasha Roberts argued that *The Arte of English Poesie* functions, not least, as "an exercise in the promotion of women's cultural capital": dedicated to Elizabeth, written for gentlewomen readers.[11]

Yet Puttenham's terms, like Montaigne's, are painfully ambivalent.[12] While he claims to write "for" the learning of courtly ladies, he does not aspire too highly for them. In his chapter on "vices or deformities", Puttenham concedes that some stylistic lapses might be allowed "in the pretty poesies and devices of ladies, and gentlewomen makers, whom we would not have too precise poets least with their shrewd wits, when they were married they might become a little too fantastical wives".[13] Women are, then, allowed to lapse from accepted stylistic ideals when they compose poetry because to write too well might compromise their wifely decorum.

Montaigne's and Puttenham's statements also draw together the two interconnected strands of this book: women as theorists, and gendered theories of poetry. Most early modern rhetoricians do not consider the former: poetry is only "a study fit" for women insofar as men criticize both women and poetry for their wantonness and disguise. Puttenham's particular description of women's poetry as "pretty poesies and devices" is revealing. As Danielle Clarke points out, "[v]irtually all Puttenham's apostrophes to female readers occur in Book III, 'Of Ornament', which suggests their supplemental status".[14] In one of his "senses of style", Jeff Dolven captures the double bind (multiple, even), in the relationship between gender and style:

> [W]hat is the difference between style and substance? One answer, always at the ready, is that one is masculine and one is feminine. That is, style is feminine, ornamental, yielding, while substance is masculine, anchoring, authoritative. Unless, of course, style is the masculine signature inscribed by the stylus upon impressionable, feminine matter. Gender has its preferences with style, but they are not always predictable.[15]

By ventriloquizing the associations made by early modern theorists like Puttenham, Dolven shows up their misogyny by juxtaposing the multiple (and even contradictory) uses of poetics to exclude: femininity is insubstantial, except when it is useful substance for masculine impression. Definitions of style often reach for binaries and, as Dolven suggests, in these binaries the element of the pair coded as feminine is always downgraded.

If the feminine is coded as supplemental, then it can just as easily become either unnecessary detail or excess. Contemporary feminist critics have taken these negative associations and redefined them: both detail and excess have been reclaimed as vitally and, importantly, feminine stylistic traits. In the context of nineteenth-century women writers, Ellen Rooney, reflecting on the work of Naomi Schor, argues that "insistence on reading the detail—as the particular, the ornamental, the marginal, the feminine, the contingent, the useless—undermines traditional hermeneutics", while Karen Jackson Ford has championed excess as a strategic rejection of the decorum imposed on twentieth-century women writers.[16] By exploring the early modern roots of such slights and prohibitions we can in fact locate the women writing against them. And indeed Margaret Cavendish was already embracing and reshaping the sexist charge that women's style was decorative and excessive in the mid-seventeenth century:

> Poetry, which is built upon fancy, women may claim, as a work belonging most properly to themselves: for I have observed, that their brains work usually in a fantastical motion: as in their several, and various dresses in their many and singular choices of clothes, and Ribbons; [...] in their wrought works, and divers sorts of stitches they employ their needle, and many curious things they make, as flowers, boxes, baskets [...]; besides all manner of meats to cure: and thus their thoughts are employed perpetually with fancies.[17]

We have seen how Puttenham defined women's poetry as "pretty poesies and devices", amidst many similar statements of dismissal or exclusion. With Cavendish, though, we see a woman theorist intervene in this debate about gender and poetics. Cavendish here seems perversely to embrace the idea of poetry as decorative and ornamental, yet uses these to forge a feminist poetics of craft, variety and imagination. She makes a powerful claim for individual agency too: while women might not choose to spend their days in needlework, poetry (she suggests) might be a sphere in which they can manifest autonomous "choice", rejecting the "rule and method" from which their lack of education excludes them anyway. With her distinctive wit and faux modesty, Cavendish blends stereotypes of women's nature as innate ("their brains work[...]") and as social (needlework, cookery as feminine activities). She takes these connections between femininity and the domestic, ornamental or decorative, and attributes them instead to a potent feminine aesthetic. Cavendish engages a tradition of critical poetics that takes femininity as its conceptual engineering; in doing so, she practises a critical poetics.

In writings by Montaigne, Puttenham, and their peers, the literary sphere is feminized only for this feminization to be used against women, to exclude. These moments proliferate as you read, as each invitation twists into a prohibition. Dictionaries, and glossaries of hard words in English, were often addressed to women. Yet Juliet Fleming has shown that these works aimed not to educate women, but instead to interpolate them as lawless language users who needed regulation.[18] In her analysis of classical and early modern rhetoric, Patricia Parker makes this a question of *place* for women: "It was the public nature of rhetoric—talking outside their proper 'province' or place—which disqualified them".[19] As with dictionary-makers' concern for women's place within or outside regulated language use, Parker finds rhetorical works anxious about moveable, wandering, or errant women—women out of place. Parker's brilliant analysis excavates the sexism embedded in the classical rhetorical tradition, and its inheritance by the English Renaissance. In several works, she finds classical and early modern rhetoric suffused with anxiety about the possibility of unregulated female speech. One of the key manifestations of this anxiety is the assertion of a "virile style":

> [...] it is precisely this influential Roman tradition that pervades early modern European praise of a stylistic (but also much more than stylistic) *virilitas*—not only on the Continent but in the articulation, in England, of a style that would have (as Ben Jonson put it) a "manly" strength and vigor, a reaction against an "effeminate" Ciceronianism that privileged words over deeds or things, and ultimately the "plain" style of a nascent early modern science described as a "*masculine* birth of time"[20]

Ideas about linguistic order were harnessed to issues of social control, sexual regulation, and gender hierarchy, as for instance rhetorician Dudley Fenner demanded that metaphor be "shamefast, and as it were maidenly".[21] He explains that for a trope to be "maidenly", means that it can be "led by the hand to another signification" rather than "driven by force". Fenner's explanation of his own metaphor suggests the violence which underpins such images of female identity for language use. Lorna Hutson has explored this area further in relation to English writers, especially Ben Jonson. In *Timber, or Discoveries*, Jonson paraphrased and amplified Quintilian's famous analysis of virile and effeminate styles.[22] In Katharine Craik's words, "the ordered, masculine, temperate body signified excellence in verse, whereas the curious, effeminate, asymmetrical body betokens literary indecorum".[23] Simply put, good style is sinewy, muscular, and virile, while bad style is soft, effeminate, or submissive. Lacking sinew, women do not—should not—write stylishly, let alone *about* style.

Parker, Hutson, Fleming and others reveal a history of the sexualization of language, of supplemental, ornamental, even dangerous or deviant language being labelled as feminine. Does this explain the absence of women from the history of literary criticism? Certainly it played a part. Women perceived themselves as barred from literary culture by the inherent sexualization of rhetoric—and its fundamentally misogynistic (as well as homophobic) implications—so aptly identified by Anne Southwell and Margaret Cavendish in the seventeenth century, and Patricia Parker and Lorna Hutson in the twentieth. Were there, then, in fact many women critics writing in places which have become less visible over time? If only we look in the right places we can find women writing criticism alongside the classically-derived poetic theory by men, and their distinctive—to us, deeply troubled and troubling—gender politics. Moreover, revelatory work in early modern trans studies helps us think beyond the assigned genders of authors, and to locate variously oppressive or liberating possibilities in the complex gendering of early modern poetics. As Joseph Gamble argues in defining a practice of trans philology, exploring the etymology and genealogy of words might take us both into their history and our own lived future. I hope that this book, in asking what poetics can tell us about premodern categorizations of gender, can similarly point in two directions. It seeks both to reveal the damaging, exclusive uses of language to define identity, and also to unearth a history of unrecognized potential, of meanings of words, in Gamble's terms, "that lie dormant in the language that sets the conditions of our possibility".[24]

Yet gender politics are not the only cause and context for women's absence in the history of criticism. Questions around periodization, genre, and material form have also played a part. Scholars of women's writing have noted the poor fit of accepted period boundaries with writing by women, from Joan Kelly's famous question "Did women have a Renaissance?" to Michelle Dowd and Lara Dodds's argument that it is the "critical belatedness" of scholarship on early modern women's writing which has allowed women's writing to remain marginal to early modern studies more broadly.[25] Scholars of Premodern Critical Race Studies have articulated a similar yet different experience, also kept at a distance from the "mainstream" of early modern studies. PCRS work has often also been at the forefront of gender analysis, in the work of Kim F. Hall, Margo Hendricks, Sujata Iyengar, Joyce Green MacDonald, Urvashi Chakravarty, Bernadette Andrea and many other scholars.[26] The study of premodern women's writing as a subfield has much more work to do in integrating the concerns of gender and of race, while respecting the different trajectories of these fields and the fights for social justice they reflect in the present.

Models of periodization, then, based on a white, male canon, have been challenged by multiple scholarly movements which attend to writers marginalized by gender, race, sexuality, ability, politics, or class. The study of criticism faces the same challenge, not least given the technical training, institutional affiliation and educational access often needed to write and publish a defence, art or treatise of "Poesy" in the early modern period. Existing collections and studies of early modern criticism are usually either labeled "Renaissance" or "Augustan". This is a function of accepted period labels, and also points to an intriguing gap in the early- to mid-seventeenth century. Few stand-alone works of literary criticism were published between Samuel Daniel's *Defence of Rhyme* in 1603 and Dryden's Restoration works. Gavin Alexander refers to these years as a "pause for thought" and this absence remains unexplained.[27] But I will show that this period represents a transition rather than a lacuna in literary criticism. Writers like Donne, Herbert, Carew and Milton were commenting on the purpose and style of literature in their own poetry rather than in explicit works of criticism. Moreover, it is no coincidence that the early years of the seventeenth century which have been seen as a gap in male-authored criticism, were also a brief moment in which "women found themselves at the center of the nation's new cultural enterprise".[28] However temporary and circumscribed, Anne of Denmark's reign saw a flourishing of women's agency as writers, performers and patrons. Instead of accepting the narrative of the early- to mid-seventeenth century as a pause or silence in critical writings, then, this book will reveal the many writings by women, in print and (especially) manuscript, that can be read as critical.

Far from disappearing, writing about writing becomes paratextual in the mid-seventeenth century. Prefaces and poems-about-poems become even more central in defining the period's debates than stand-alone essays. The civil war and Restoration also saw women formulating new concepts of literary purpose and practice in prefaces and other paratextual critical works, at the same time that male writers like Davenant and Cowley were doing so. In bringing together such writings by women as "criticism", *Sex and Style* creates a new literary history as well as revealing the biases of existing seventeenth- and twenty-first century canons of criticism. The perceived gap or pause in criticism between Jonson and Dryden is in fact a plenitude. Women like Anne Southwell were both challenging the exclusions of criticism and writing criticism of their own. The landmark analyses by Parker and Hutson that I have discussed focused on the gendering of rhetoric by male writers, and its sexist underpinnings. Building on both their work, and a half-century of recovery of women writers, especially in manuscript, *Sex and Style* reveals and analyzes a little-known wealth of manuscript writings by women as criticism. The scholars writing foundational works in the field of early modern women's writing several decades ago were also writing about how women placed themselves in the literary sphere: writing *by* women was often also *about* women writing.

Getting to the point of authorship was a major project for early modern women, and one on which they often commented. But as long as this remained of interest only to scholars of women's writing—crucial and major as that field is—these ideas and texts were not being read as theory, not being brought into dialogue with male theorists, not allowed a place within the history of literary criticism. The increasing understanding of women's works had, therefore, not yet managed to change that history, in the way it was dramatically changing histories of poetry. Placing these women critics alongside and in dialogue with those of their famous male peers, we can see that women were in fact at the vanguard of poetics, pioneering ideas like originality and techniques like feminine rhyme often ahead of their male peers.

Anne Southwell: "I play the critic"

Women poets were acutely aware of the prohibitions against them, as we can see from Southwell's account of the vitriol and abuse directed at women who "[d]are [...] but write". Her poem defies the injunctions it describes; it shows that women responded not with silence, but by developing potent voices, both as poets and as critics.

Southwell imagines hostile readers criticizing women's use of the fundamental components of composition: number, case, tense, and gender. Her use of "criticize" here, then, suggests her knowledge of both grammatical intricacies and the work of philological "critics" in analysing these. While little is known of Southwell's own education, her writings show an extraordinary breadth and depth of knowledge across a range of spheres. Southwell's poem is in the genre of Decalogue poetry, specifically on the fourth commandment, the injunction to keep the Sabbath day, "Precept 4". In this poem, Southwell refers to the seven liberal arts, invoking the "four springs", the quadrivial arts of arithmetic, geometry, music and astronomy, which are in turn graced by the trivium of "rhetoric", "grammar" and "logic" (ll. 309–314). Her title of "Precept" means "Commandment" but it was also used to describe rhetorical rules and she plays with this dual category: biblical injunction as rhetorical manual.

Southwell's poem is also a work of textual criticism in another sense: her interpretation of Ovid. She adopts a striking image for her representation of writing women, in the form of the owl of Minerva:

Dare you but write, you are Minerva's bird,
The owl at which these bats and crows must wonder [...]

Minerva had long been associated with an owl, and both goddess and bird broadly associated with wisdom. Southwell's image, though, engages more specifically with Ovid's retelling in *Metamorphoses* 2. Her reference to the envious "wonder" of "bats and crows" recalls Ovid's crow complaining he had been usurped by the owl in Minerva's favor. In evoking Ovid for her image of the abuse of female writers, Southwell also evokes a story of sexual scandal and exclusion. Ovid's owl has a dark back-story; she is Nyctimene, a princess who is raped by her father, the king of Lesbos. Fleeing in shame, like so many other survivors of sexual aggression in the *Metamorphoses*, Nyctimene is transformed. She is offered a partial, and still stigmatized, new identity; Minerva turns her into the owl, daring only to show her face in darkness. Southwell situates her reader in Ovid's intensely-charged world of transformations, using myth to evoke the conditions which generate women's silence: sexual violence, shame, social isolation.

As well as characterizing the attacks on women writers, Southwell derisively suggests one way to deflect these: adding a "pitiful epistle". Both women and men poets of the seventeenth century frequently added epistles before their text, either by themselves or by others. Dedicating the work to a patron or would-be patron whose connection to the text, however, tenuous, might protect it from censure. Such epistles and prefaces are one of this book's key repositories for poetic criticism, showing that early women's criticism is often found in unexpected yet conspicuous places: it hides in plain sight. Southwell here seems to scorn such defensive epistles, in lines which may daringly refer to King James as the Scottish thistle who becomes an English monarch, a pseudo-Tudor rose.[29]

And Southwell herself also knew when to "frame an epistle", not only as a preface (as she gestures to in "Precept 4"), but as a critical form itself. Several of Southwell's letters are themselves works of criticism.[30] While her "Precept 4" poem has one of the earliest uses of the verb "criticize", one of her letters also has an early usage of the term "critic":

> Thrice honored Lord
> Will you vouchsafe a pardon if I play the critic with this one word in your letter?[31]

What might seem a brisk, even rebuking start to the letter, gives way to an elegant gesture of flattery in Southwell's own erudite and playfully philological style:

> Wherein you say you are deprived of all. Is the sun bereft of his beams because a cloud interposeth betwixt him and our watery balls? Could a banished philosopher say unto himself, Omnia mea mecum porto? (p. 5–6)

Writing to her friend Lord Falkland who is about to leave Ireland, Southwell playfully rebukes and corrects his use of the word "deprived" in a flattering and affectionate quibble. He seems to have said that he will be deprived of her company when he leaves. She counters that their friendship will remain an objective truth, despite distance. The sun is not less bright because a cloud obscures it from our eyes, a philosopher might be banished, but would still say (in Ciceronian allusion) "all that is mine I carry with me". Here Southwell uses the phrase "play the critic" in the sense more of philologist, an attentive correspondent but also one who claims authority over the interpretation of language. In this letter, too, which includes Latin quotations, references to unusual imported dance practices, and words such as "aequipollent", to be a critic implies deep learning and verbal dexterity. Women act as critics in ways which expand our sense of what criticism is.

Anne Southwell's critical writings often feel unusual: her range of genres, the abrasive, learned, witty texture of her writings, and her early coinages of the terms for criticism themselves. Yet even in their seeming extraordinariness, her writings may well be representative of the wealth of critical writings by women that has remained outside the reach of histories of literary criticism, despite their clear common ground with the most influential male early modern theorists. While Patricia Parker focuses on women theorists being out of place metaphorically, this book will reveal how women's critical writings have been out of place because of the genres they write in, and often also the material form their works take. Southwell's work brings together many of the places in which we find criticism by women: manuscripts, miscellanies, letters, poems, and paratexts. It was not only women who chose to write critically in these modes; men did so too, as well as in stand-alone treatises and defences. But as women did not usually write in the more familiar critical genres, it is in the neglected places of manuscript compilations and printed paratexts that we must look to find women critics. Reading across these forms of women's critical writing yields multiple insights and surprises, which can be captured in six key provocations.

Sex and Style: Six Provocations

The language of style has always been gendered

Original ideas. Muscular prose. Heroic couplets. Virtuosic performance. Smooth lines. Feminine rhyme. What do the words we use to describe poetry tell us about our literary history? How do these terms make that history? How is the story of style also one of bodies? Principles which still dominate our language of literary value, such as originality, are often seen as developed by a lineage of male poets, from Chaucer to Shakespeare to Milton and on into modernity.

Women's style has been read through their bodies

While key tenets of poetic practice are often seen to have originated in men's writing, women's writing is frequently read through culturally-informed (or misinformed) ideas about their bodies. When Abraham Cowley writes in praise of his peer, Katherine Philips, he does so by projecting her style onto her body:

> I must admire to see thy well-knit sense,
> Thy numbers gentle, and thy fancies high,
> Those as thy forehead smooth, these sparkling as thine eye.[32]

While Cowley's terms are strongly positive, the ineluctable connection between style and body meant that women poets were read as women, more than as stylists or critics. Moreover, Philips's poetry could be praised through comparison with her body because she was young, and died young. As women were defined through their bodies, they could only write smooth or sparkling verses while their bodies were perceived as such—not a problem faced by poets famed for their late style, a phenomenon largely reserved for male poets, for instance.

Women weaponized the language used against them

Yet women writers frequently took such exclusionary and stereotyping language and transformed it into a distinctive strand of women's poetics. Margaret Cavendish transformed the language used to depict women writers as anomalous into a gendered principle of originality; Aphra Behn and Anne Wharton transformed gendered slurs on the softness of women's bodies, morals, and poems, into a claim for a uniquely feminine poetic affect.

Women theorized literature as much as men did

Women theorized literature in a variety of genres and material forms. In fact, men wrote in those forms too, but their works have often been extracted and canonized in ways that make their criticism speak as if they had written standalone treatises. One example of a genre of criticism that appears throughout the seventeenth century is letters. From epistolary artefacts that were actually sent to fictional letters written-for-publication, this sociable form is a rich seam of women's critical writing that has not hitherto been recognized as dialogue with men's theoretical writings. It is a realm of firsts (however cautious we may wish to be about identifying such milestones while further texts are still coming to light): Anne Southwell's letter to her friend Lady Ridgeway may be one of the first critical discussions of Shakespeare and Marlowe. Margaret Cavendish's collection of *Sociable Letters* (1664) includes what is arguably "the first critical essay ever to be published on Shakespeare".[33] These are not just firsts for women, but milestones in the history of literary criticism.

Women engaged in debates we see as key to seventeenth-century poetics

In a letter to her friend Charles Cotterell, Katherine Philips discussed a translation of Pierre Corneille's *La Mort de Pompée* by a group of her contemporaries: "the expressions are some of them great and noble, and the verses smooth; yet there is room in several places for an ordinary critic to show his skill." Her use of "an ordinary critic" seems to suggest any old critic. By suggesting that anyone can be a critic she takes down this role from a position of inaccessibility. And it is a critic who shows *her* skill (not his) discussing this play, as Philips herself goes on to analyse features including its rhymes ("frequently very bad"), its texture ("flat or rough"), the nature of the work as a paraphrase rather than a translation (given "the great liberty they have taken in adding, omitting and altering the original").[34] Philips's critical faculties may have been sharpened by her own current project: she was also translating the same play, and her version of *Pompey* would be performed in Dublin in 1663. While Cavendish often defines a poetics that is specifically feminine, Philips's technical concerns are exactly those of male poets and critics in the period: of accuracy, decorum, and form.

Practice is theory

Gavin Alexander has argued for the inextricability of literature and criticism in the early modern period: "where we now tend to see the scholarly study of literature and literary theory as inhabiting a different world from the writing of literature, and expect there to be little communication between the two, Renaissance literary criticism is usually the work of writers of literature, and is aimed at readers and authors alike: it shows how to write, and how writing ought to be read."[35] Women's style, including their adherences and deviations from certain tastes and norms, processes of composition and correction, prefaces, dedications, and expressions of intent to circulate their works or (more often) not do so, might be drawn together as a form of poetic knowledge. This is a poetic knowledge which challenges contemporary and historical male-authored theories of literature, which have come to be seen as the sole originators of our own in the present.

Anne Southwell's Defence of Poetry: "give me your hand"

As we have seen, Southwell's poetry is profoundly critical, and this book will argue throughout for poetry as a locus of women's theory. If we continue to look beyond print and beyond the obvious theoretical genres (treatise, manual) we find a vibrant body of critical writings by women in prose, such as this eloquent vindication of poetry, also by Anne Southwell:

> How falls it out (noble lady) that you are become a sworn enemy to poetry? It being so abstruse an art, as it is, that I may say, the other arts are but bases and pedestals, unto the which this is the capital. The mere herald of all ideas; the world's true vocal harmony, of which all other arts are but parts, or rather, may I justly say, it is the silk thread that strings your chain of pearl; which being broken, your jewels fall into the rushes; and the more you seek for it, the more it falls into the dust of oblivion.[36]

The images for poetry here range from architectural, decorative, and musical to biblical. The common image of jewels or pearls is nuanced by the idea of poetry as the thread joining the gems, rather than the gems themselves. The description of the "dust of oblivion" might seem particularly loaded in the work of a woman whose works, largely in manuscript, have been barely known until the last few decades, resting not exactly in dust, but in the Folger's collections. The range of arts invoked, though (jewels, buildings, song) defies straightforward gendered categorization. Southwell's critical prose engages with that of her male peers, those we are used to identifying as the origins of criticism: Puttenham, Sidney, Daniel.

This passage appeared neither in print, nor in a manuscript treatise but in a letter. It opens "To my worthy muse, the Lady Ridgeway. that doth these lines infuse". Southwell's letter is a defence of verse, addressed to her friend Lady Ridgeway who has apparently claimed the superiority of prose, for various reasons including its prior existence. Southwell disputes this idea of authority by precedence, arguing that primacy does not equal correctness: "You say, you affect prose as your ancestors did; error is not to be affected for antiquity" (fol. 3r). And here we can see a twofold move characteristic of much of the criticism by women that this book will uncover: Southwell looks both backwards and forwards. Her arguments engage with Biblical and medieval as well as sixteenth-century critical modes, drawing on grammar as a divine model and God as the ultimate poet. Yet her assertion that "error is not to be affected for antiquity" is also a bold rejection of precedent as the ultimate form of authority. Instead, she implies, we have to look forward and anticipate—or even forge—alternative models of writing. In Chapter 2 we will see how seventeenth-century women poets rejected earlier stereotypes of "feminine rhyme", instead using it to create a resistant poetics. In Chapter 3 we will see how Margaret Cavendish pioneered an idea of originality as newness rather than recourse to a past "origin".

In advocating verse over prose, Southwell adopts a similar defence to that of Samuel Daniel, who had defended English over continental systems of versification in 1603. Daniel cautioned against giving too much authority to historical models: "we should not so soon yield our consents captive to the authority of antiquity".[37] And Southwell offers her own, rather different, narrative of precedents:

> Therefore (noble and witty lady) give me your hand, I will lead you up the stream of all mankind. Your great-great-grandfather had a father, and so the last, or rather the first father, was God; whose never enough to be admired creation, was poetically confined to four general genuses: earth, air, water and fire. The effects which give life unto his verse, were: hot, cold, moist and dry; which produce choler, melancholy, blood and phlegm. By these just proportions, all things are propagated. Now being thus poetically composed, how can you be at unity with yourself, and at odds with your own composition?[38]

With a physically evocative rhetorical device, Southwell takes her interlocutor through the stages of her argument by imagining literally leading her by the "hand". The lineage is father to father, yet Southwell clearly sees herself and her female correspondent intervening in this patrilineal descent of authors and creators. Here again, Southwell forges a critical poetics which is Sidneian yet also Biblical, and revisionist.

There is a lovely flourish with the logic of her conclusion: God wrote you like a poem, so how can you oppose the conditions of your own creation? Like Sidney and Puttenham, Southwell refutes the idea of literature as *blasphemous* because an act of creation with the retort that literature is *godly*, because an act of creation.[39] Her use of biblical precedent goes much further, however, than the argument that God is a creator and we should create in his image. She creates an analogy between the writer's materials and God's: God "was poetically confined to four general genuses, earth, air, water and fire". Here the word "genus", an overarching class or kind of thing, might also suggest the specifically literary "genus" or "kind" (what we now call "genre"). The four basic qualities hot, cold, moist, and dry "give life to his verse" and produce the four humours. Tetracolon (patterning in fours) is indeed one of Southwell's favourite techniques in what is a highly structured piece of prose. She writes that "By these just proportions, all things are propagated" and connects pattern, structure, proportionality, and decorum, saying: "All exorbitant things are monstrous, but bring them again to their orbicular form and motion, and they will retain their former beauties [...]" (p. 5). By pairing it with "orbicular" (round, circular), Southwell draws attention to the etymological meaning of "exorbitant", diverging from an orbit or track, and metaphorically a rule.

Samuel Daniel had characterized the imagination as "an unformed chaos without fashion" which with the transformative power of divine poetry, could "be wrought into an *orb* of order and form" (my italics).[40] Both Southwell and Daniel use the image of the orb or orbit to argue that it is not just the fundamental creativity of poetry that makes it divine, but its technical elements: Daniel sees rhyme as coming from "the divine power of the spirit" to create poetry with the "closes" required by nature, "that desires a certainty, and comports not with that which is infinite".[41] Southwell takes the cosmological image further than Sidney and Daniel in her version of the analogy of God's creation for poetic creation. Her "exorbitant" and "orbicular" evoke the perfectly circular (pre-Kepler) orbit. To be "exorbitant" is therefore to be irregular, out of proportion, "monstrous". As we will see in Chapter 4, irregularity was often used to stigmatize feminine or effeminate identities and writing styles (while, conversely, by the twentieth century it was often used as a term of aesthetic adventurousness, and instead used to praise rule-breaking male poets). Here Southwell describes not prosodic rule-breaking, but the distortion of poetry by erotic subject matter, especially in recent epyllia (she mentions *Venus and Adonis* and *Hero and Leander*, as we will see later). But the idea of poetry having an innate, cosmological, or natural proportion also draws on recent arguments about meter. In a poem in her Lansdowne manuscript Southwell asserts that rhyme can "from an ingot form a curious Jewel" (p. 152). Rhyme can be shaping and purifying. Southwell's own rhetorical patterning, too—especially tricolon and tetracolon—testifies to the importance she places on other kinds of ordering. This is elegant, densely rhetorical, and etymological, critical prose.

As she champions poetry over prose, Southwell develops Sidney's ideas and images:

> Poesy seems to do more for nature, then she is able to do for herself, wherein, it doth but lay down a pattern what man should be; and shows, that imagination goes before reality. (p. 4)

For Southwell, poetry is both a way of creating an ideal, better than nature (doing "more for nature, then she is able to do for herself"), just as in the *Defence of Poesy*, Sidney had famously argued that nature's "world is brazen, the poets only deliver a golden".[42] Southwell argues that poetry can inspire mankind to virtue and also dwells on it as a form of creation with biblical poetry as the authorizing precedent:

> [...] will you behold poesy in perfect beauty. Then see the kingly prophet, that sweet singer of Israel, explicating the glory of our God, his power in creating, his mercy in redeeming, his wisdom in preserving; making these three, as it were the comma, colon, and period to every stanza. Who would not say, the musical spheres did yield a cadency to his song, and in admiration cry out; O never enough to be admired, divine poesy. (p. 5)

Sidney and many others had called upon the poetic origins of the psalms to defend their art.[43] Puttenham had also laid out the different functions of the comma, colon, and period, but does not use them metaphorically as Southwell does; indeed, this harnessing of grammar to God is one of the most striking features of her writing.[44]

As well as laying out an underlying framework for a virtuous poetics, Southwell evaluates contemporary poems. Guessing that Lady Ridgeway has been put off poetry by "wanton" contemporary poems, she writes a critique of erotic epyllia, alluding to Shakespeare's *Venus and Adonis* and Marlowe's *Hero and Leander*:

> I will take upon me to know what hath so distasted your palate against this banquet of souls, divine poesy. Some wanton Venus or Adonis hath been cast before your chaste ears, whose evil attire, disgracing this beautiful nymph, hath unworthied her in your opinion [...] . To hear a Hero and Leander or some such other busy nothing, might be a means to scandalize this art. (p. 5)

Southwell rejects the erotic here. Elsewhere she satirizes the clichés of Cupid, suggesting "a forceful anti-Petrarchanism that is centred on the female subject", as Danielle Clarke and Marie-Louise Coolahan argue.[45] And yet, Southwell also absorbs and adapts the very poems she criticizes—specifically, *Venus and Adonis*—in her own devotional poetry.[46] Southwell's comments are relatively rare, amongst both male and female critics, for evaluating named works—here *Hero and Leander* and *Venus and Adonis*.[47] Southwell shares strands of her argument with writers like Puttenham, Sidney, and Daniel, yet the letter to Lady Ridgeway has its own distinctive texture: the evocative phrases "busy nothing" and "banquet of souls" are unusual, if not unprecedented. While the letter to Ridgeway delineates Southwell's theory of a virtuous poetics, we see a different kind of critical writing in her poetry itself. Indeed, the poetry in both Southwell's manuscript collections demonstrates a quite different tone: a technical and specific critical language, by turns witty, abrasive, and optimistic. Southwell's corpus reveals the multiplicity of early modern criticism by women. She engages with the major debates of the day yet her arguments are her own: distinctively gesturing towards modernity and change, questioning past rules and precedents. Hers is a critical poetics; it is both poetry and criticism.

Sex and Style

This book is structured around five key gendered terms describing poetic style: Original; Feminine; Irregular; Smooth, and Soft. Each of these terms has a complex history in the early modern period, both in terms of its meaning for poetic practice, and of its freighting with gendered and sexualized connotations. With one of these terms as its starting point, each chapter will show how certain labels and styles were used to exclude women. It will also show how women were in fact forging or challenging these ideals alongside their male peers. In this way, *Sex and Style* draws on the technique of cultural inquiry modern critics have been more likely to read women's poetic irregularities as errors, and men's as intentional, masking women poets' aesthetic innovation. In the mid-seventeenth century, Lucy Hutchinson produced the first full translation of Lucretius's famously difficult Latin poem, *De rerum natura*. Two hundred years later, scholar Hugh Munro suggested that Hutchinson has been distracted by her children and miscounted "the syllables of her translation."[54] Munro read Hutchinson's metrically deviant lines as error rather than intention, and this assumption is echoed in interpretations of early modern women's poetry, from the seventeenth century, to Victorian readers like Munro, and right up to the present.

We saw in the previous chapter how metrical irregularities in women's poems were often seen as accidental and rough, disrupting the reader's experience. **Chapter 5: Smooth/Soft** explores a related story of gendered style: the rise of smoothness. I will argue that smoothness, a term and feature which had previously been seen as feminine, becomes a masculine poetic attribute in the Restoration. The chapter reveals how women challenged this narrative in two key ways. First, Anne Southwell and Lucy Hutchinson write devastating critiques of smoothness, condemning it as the style adopted by poets and politicians to conceal their political crimes. The chapter then moves to the 1680s, a decade when Edmund Waller's smoothness was highly praised as an ideal. It shows that as smooth was co-opted by male royalist poets, "soft" and "tender" became the terms used for women poets. These terms shifted the grounds of description from style to body, and were built on a misogynistic tradition of depicting the female body as inherently soft, malleable, and fickle. In a cluster of poems by Anne Wharton and Aphra Behn, several of which remain unpublished, I show how these writers claimed and redefined a poetics of softness. Building on work by Jenny C. Mann on sixteenth-century softness, I show that the idea developed a different yet connected politics of style and gender in the Restoration, and as used by women themselves.[55] This chapter reveals both a misogynistic tradition of associating women with bodily softness and moral inconstancy and a radical counter-tradition of women embracing softness as a mark of their superior moral and poetic capabilities. In both the roughness of Southwell and Hutchinson, and the softness of Wharton and Behn, we find women challenging the famously dominant smoothness of male, royalist poets such as Edmund Waller and, in doing so, writing a different literary history.

This book shows how different English criticism looks when we reintegrate women at its origins. The last half century has seen the canon of early modern English poetry expand from Sidney, Donne, Shakespeare, Milton, and Dryden to include Mary Sidney, Wroth, Philips, Cavendish, and Hutchinson. *Sex and Style* reveals that our canon of theory now needs to feature Southwell, Cavendish, and Wharton, and many other women, virtuosic theorists of originality, irregularity, rhyme, smoothness, and softness.

———

Throughout her devotional poetry, Anne Southwell demonstrates what we might think of as a profoundly textual imagination: she repeatedly represents the divine through images of writing, from the grammatical and rhetorical, to the physical and material. Across her various letters and poems, she imagines that God's power, mercy, and wisdom are a comma, colon, and period; that the devout person is graced with rhetoric; that his thoughts are a grammar; that his reason possesses all the art of logic, that his deeds and moods are tropes and figures. She forges "a purposeful female aesthetic that takes its cue from the divine".[56] Compared to poets of either sex, Southwell deploys textual metaphors densely and extensively. She brings to the surface the rhetorical or poetic meanings of words with other primary meanings: precept, colour, congruity. Her writings demonstrate an immersion in the technical elements of rhetorical and literary composition, metaphors from which suffuse and structure her imagining of the world. While the letter to Lady Ridgeway is a persuasive refutation of attacks on poetry as a virtuous art, "Precept 4" plays both sides of the argument.

We may have to look in unexpected places for criticism by early modern women, but we will usually find male critics writing in these modes too. As I have suggested, the first half of the seventeenth century was a transitional period for the genres of literary theory more widely. Between the defences and manuals of the sixteenth century and the major essays of the Restoration (Puttenham's and Sidney's among the former, Dryden's and Atterbury's the latter), criticism took place in all sorts of genres. The relative paucity of stand-alone critical essays by women has allowed them to be absent from histories and anthologies of criticism, yet this shows not that they were outside the critical tradition but in fact that they were within it. Like their male peers, women "played the critic" (in Southwell's phrase) in prefaces (Margaret Cavendish), dedications (Aemilia Lanyer), letters (Katherine Philips), elegies (Aphra Behn), panegyrics (Anne Wharton), commonplace books and miscellanies (Anne Southwell, Lucy Hutchinson), in manuscript and print. In many instances, these are responsive forms (letters, prefaces, commonplace books), with a real or imagined interlocutor providing a sort of wager, a spur to speak about things which are, in Patricia Parker's terms, outside women's proper province. Southwell would not have been surprised by Parker's conclusions both that women were excluded from rhetoric and that rhetoric was gendered so as to devalue the feminine. But her writing proves that such an awareness provoked rather than muffled her critical voice, and that its serenity, fury, wit, abrasiveness, and technical texture show deep engagement with her peers and predecessors and demonstrate her own vigorous model of criticism. Women's own use of the term "criticism", its origins and its derivatives, reveals their alertness to the use of criticism to censure and silence, yet also their part in its history. While the term itself may have changed in meaning, women's use of it draws us to moments of profound engagement with the history of criticism, and women's place at its origins.

Alternative Chapter List: Keywords and Writers[57]

Chapter 2. Feminine

Feminine (rhyme)
Masculine
Sweet
Weak
Strong
Foreign
Excessive

*

Philip Sidney
Samuel Daniel
John Harington
Edmund Spenser
Mary Wroth
Edward Denny
Hester Pulter
Anne Southwell
Katherine Philips

Chapter 3. Original

Original
Singular
Matchless
Exceptional

Copy
Changeable
*

Margaret Cavendish
Walter Charleton
Anne Bradstreet
Lucy Hutchinson
Ben Jonson
Ovid
Katherine Philips
"Philo-Philippa"

Chapter 4. Irregular

Irregular
Regular
Loose
Correct
Incorrect
Liberty
Lawless
*

Lucy Hutchinson
Lucretius
Katherine Philips
Abraham Cowley
John Milton

Chapter 5. Smooth/Soft

Smooth
Rough
Hard
Soft
Loose
Tender
Constant
Ease

*

Anne Southwell
Lucy Hutchinson
Edmund Waller
Anne Wharton
Aphra Behn
John Wilmot, Earl of Rochester

2

Feminine

And as for two syllabled meters, the French call them the feminine rhyme, as the sweeter, and the one syllable the masculine. For as men use to sow with the hand and not with the whole sack, so I would have the ear fed but not cloyed with these pleasing and sweet falling meters.

—JOHN HARINGTON, PREFACE TO *ORLANDO FURIOSO* (1591)[1]

But since she pricked thee out for women's pleasure,
Mine be thy love, and thy love's use their treasure.

—WILLIAM SHAKESPEARE, SONNET 20 (1609)[2]

But stay, weak female, whither does thou wander?
How dares thy waxen plumes approach the sun?
Thy better sex are lost in this meander
In which thy ignorance presumes to run;
Pardon, dear saviour, pardon my presumption
And let my faith rely on thy assumption.

—ANNE SOUTHWELL, "THOU SHALT KEEP HOLY THE SABBATH DAY"[3]

SWEET; EXCESSIVE; EXOTIC; foreign; comedic; mournful; bathetic; philosophical; rich; semantic; sensory; pleasurable; uncomfortable: feminine rhyme has been interpreted in all these ways, from the sixteenth century to the present. Masculine rhyme, in which the final, rhyming syllable is stressed, and feminine rhyme, in which the final, rhyming syllable is unstressed, are terms that often embarrass modern critics and teachers. Some writers choose instead to use the terms "strong" and "weak" (or even perfect and imperfect) which are problematic in different ways, though perhaps less clunky than stressed and unstressed hyperbeats. Even recent scholarship seems to reinforce gendered conceptions: feminine rhymes are, we are told, "softer, less forceful, more pliable".[4] But before we reject or replace the term feminine rhyme, much remains to be understood about its history and usage. Feminine rhyme remains under-studied and under-theorized. What was the relationship between the term and the actual practice of the feature it named? Were these terms perceived as misogynistic, or even as necessarily gendered, in the early modern period? And finally—a question that has barely been asked, let alone answered—how did female as well as male writers use and respond to "feminine rhyme"? This chapter will suggest some answers to these questions, through analysis of writing by Samuel Daniel, John Harington, Ben Jonson, Katherine Philips, Hester Pulter, William Shakespeare, Philip Sidney, Anne Southwell, and Mary Wroth.

'Feminine rhyme' encapsulates how the terms and taxonomies we use affect our interpretation of literature and how embedded this language is in its historical and ideological contexts. Is feminine rhyme labelled as such because it sounds inherently feminine, or do we hear it as feminine because it is called feminine rhyme? This chapter will look at male writers' prose about feminine rhyme and then practice of it, followed by women writers' poetry and then prose: a chiasmatic or, if you like, rhyming structure. While we might think of prose works as theory and poetry as practice, this chapter will also (as the whole book does) challenge the distinction between theory and practice; it will argue that both men and women theorize poetic form through usage, and that women's use of feminine rhyme, in particular, should be read as works of poetics. First I will explore the term's origins and history as it entered English poetics in the late sixteenth century, investigating whether it functioned as a tool of patriarchal control and misogyny or more simply an unfortunately-termed aesthetic device. Secondly, the chapter will explore male poets' practice of feminine rhyme in the light of its already-vexed definition. Thirdly, this chapter will look at the use of feminine rhyme by women poets, focusing on Anne Southwell and Hester Pulter. This will suggest both that women wrote in the awareness of misogynistic traditions of feminine rhyme and in direct resistance to these. Moreover, it will show that close attention to women's rhyme patterns also allows us to identify aspects of their distinctive styles—wit, confrontation, technical knowledge, scepticism—and which we are perhaps more likely to look for in male writers. Finally, in its fourth part this chapter will look at how women writers theorized feminine rhyme, considering the letters of Katherine Philips as a neglected corpus of female-authored literary criticism.

1. John Harington, Philip Sidney, Samuel Daniel: Theory

The use of feminine rhyme was debated from the moment when the term entered English usage in the last decade of the sixteenth century. John Harington used feminine rhymes in his translation of *Orlando Furioso* in 1591, and he explains in his preface:

> And as for two syllabled meters, they be so approved in other languages that the French call them the feminine rhyme, as the sweeter, and the one syllable the masculine.
>
> (FOL. [XIII]R)

In Harington's formulation, sweetness is feminine rhyme's defining feature. This may seem straightforwardly gendered and he does seem to suggest that it is feminine rhyme's sweetness that led to its French label. But is rhyme feminine because it sounds sweet, or do we think it sounds sweet because we call it feminine? He goes on:

> Now for them that find fault with polysyllable meter, me think they are like those that blame men for putting sugar in their wine, and chide too bad about it, and say they mar all, but yet end with God's blessing on their hearts.
>
> (FOL. [XIII]R)

This seemingly casual comparison demands that we try to understand taste, Harington's own metaphor for poetic preference, in its historical moment.[5] Sweetness is neither straightforwardly positive nor negative. There are multiple connotations here: adding sugar to wine may have been seen as lowbrow, and also as particularly English, perhaps a source of embarrassment to well-travelled and highly-educated Englishmen.[6] Kim F. Hall and Gitanjali Shahani have shown that sugar was a building block in the identity of elite white English men and women, not in adding sugar to wine, but in showcasing colonial produce.[7] But Harington is not himself criticizing adding sugar to wine, but in fact those who judge others for doing so. And Harington's discussion goes on to use an even stranger set of taste-related metaphors:

> For indeed, if I had known their diets, I could have saved some of my cost, at least some of my pain, for when a verse ended with civility, I could easier

after the ancient manner of rhyme have made see or flee or decree to answer it, leaving the accent upon the last syllable, then hunt after three syllabled words to answer it with facility, gentility, tranquility, hostility, scurrility, debility, agility, fragility, nobility, mobility, which who mislike may taste lamp oil with their ears.

(FOL. [XIII]R)

Harington says that if he "had known their diets", meaning the preferences of his contemporaries, he could have saved some of his "cost" or "pain" by pairing feminine with masculine as well as feminine endings. He goes on to characterize those who dislike this mixed rhyming with a striking synesthetic metaphor: they "may taste lamp oil with their ears". Harington seems to suggest that mixed masculine and feminine rhyme might seem fusty and archaic. Perhaps he also recalls the medical practice of ear-cleaning to evoke an oil that you really would not want to eat. The three strands of the metaphor here—tasting, lamp oil, and hearing—combine to create an unpleasant imagined sensory experience. Harington himself can see the advantage of this approach, and again he imagines this experience as both aural and gustatory: "For as men use to sow with the hand and not with the whole sack, so I would have the ear fed but not cloyed with these pleasing and sweet falling meters."

A decade later, Samuel Daniel also uses the metaphor of appetite in his discussion of masculine and feminine rhyme. His 1603 *Defence of Ryme* traces Daniel's theory of poetic style, with an appealing self-awareness about its fungibility.[8] In defending vernacular poetics, Daniel argues that literary taste changes across time and across cultures. He also admits that his own practice has changed during his career. Daniel asks "who knows not that we cannot kindly answer a feminine number with a masculine rhyme, or (if you will so term it) a trochee with a spondee, as weakness with confess, nature and endure, only for that thereby we shall wrong the accent, the chief lord and grave governor of numbers?" Like Harington's "fed but not cloyed", Daniel uses a metaphor of excessive consumption for feminine rhyme. He is concerned "to avoid this over-glutting the ear with that always certain and full encounter of rhyme".[9] Feminine rhyme poses questions of good usage, of good *taste*; the gustatory metaphors used by Harington and Daniel are not accidental.

The metaphors of aesthetic preference used by these theorists reveal a complex picture of taste, sexuality, and control. Daniel's reference to "the chief lord and grave governor of numbers" brings poetics into the realm of social and national governance. Critics have shown how aesthetic treatises also acted to reinforce social structures or national and class hierarchies.[10] When Daniel suggests that we cannot "*kindly* answer a feminine number with a masculine rhyme" (emphasis mine), he implies that the mixing of feminine and masculine rhymes goes against naturalness, completion, and propriety. To mix rhymes of a different "kind" is seen by some as unnatural and improper. When puzzling over the difficulty of rhyming trisyllabic words, the example Harington gives is "civility", a loaded term in discussions of both imported poetic practice and social decorum. Again, the question here is whether it is only permitted to find a full rhyme (such as the equally loaded "facility, gentility"), or whether he could pair this feminine ending with a masculine one (such as "see, or flee, or decree"). What is at stake here is civility, propriety, and regulation.

These metaphors of use and rule are often gendered and sexualized. Harington recommends a manly abstemiousness, an economy of rhyme: "For as men use to sow with the hand and not with the whole sack, so I would have the ear fed but not cloyed with these pleasing and sweet falling meters." So a poet's use of feminine rhymes is like a good farmer's use of seeds: more generative when sparing. It is not only Harington who connects feminine rhyme to seeds. In his *An Apologie for Poetrie* (1595), Philip Sidney gives a brief account of three kinds of rhyme in European vernacular poetry:

> Lastly, even the very rhyme itself, the Italian cannot put in the last syllable, by the French named the masculine rhyme, but still in the next to the last, which the French call the female; or the next before that, which the Italians term *Sdrucciola*. The example of the former, is *Buono, Suono,* of the *Sdrucciola*, is *Femina, Semina*. The French, of the other side, hath both the Male, as *Bon, Son,* and the Female, as *Plaise, Taise*. But the *Sdrucciola*, he hath not: where the English hath all three, as *Due, True, Father, Rather, Motion, Potion* [...] with much more which might be said, but that I find already, the triflingness of this discourse, is much too much enlarged[11]

Maureen Quilligan suggests that Sidney's examples here provide a microhistory of gendered rhyme.[12] And indeed, alongside his example of "Buono, Suono" and "Plaise, Taise" for feminine rhyme, he chooses a fascinating example for Italian three-syllable rhyme: "Femina, Semina". The pairing of femininity and seed here echoes Harington's image of the man judiciously sowing feminine rhyme. These wayward rhymes need to be used carefully, mastered, and regulated. Sidney expresses his unease here by cutting himself short, embarrassed at the "triflingness of this discourse", commiserating with those who read his "inkwasting toy". And while he may mean the whole *Apologie*, it seems pertinent that these particular apologies appear here, connected to the sweetness, triflingness of feminine rhyme itself, perhaps, which Daniel also claims is itself "fittest for ditties", rather than epic or heroic poetry.

Daniel writes of the practice of mixing feminine and masculine endings, "which ever since I was warned of that deformity by my kind friend and countryman Master Hugh Samford, I have always so avoided it, as there are not above two couplets in that kind in all my poem of the Civil Wars" (sig. H7r). So mixed gender rhyme might be a "deformity" but it is one in the opinion of Daniel's particular, named, friend. Daniel stresses this point about the contingency of an individual's and a period's taste:

> for indeed there is no right in these things that are continually in a wandering motion, carried with the violence of uncertain likings, being but only the time that gives them their power.
>
> (SIG. H7R-8V)

The discussion of feminine rhyme in these defences represents the comparative nature of literary criticism in English, comparing poetic practice across time, and across cultures. Harington, Sidney and Daniel all compare English to classical and vernacular poetics, and not only (though often) in order to claim its superiority. Daniel also explains that he changed his opinion as his career progressed, and this is borne out in his own editing of his poems, as he rewrote some of his sonnets in *Delia* to remove their feminine rhymes.[13] Both Sidney and Daniel are careful to distinguish good from bad practice. Sidney says of various kinds of rhyme: "the cause why it is not esteemed in England, is the fault of poet-apes, not poets".[14] Daniel goes further in asserting the contingency and historical embeddedness of these formal features' meaning: it is "only the time that gives them their power". The issue is not that feminine rhyme is undesirable of itself, but that there is a certain skill and decorum involved in its practice. So feminine rhyme is associated with sweetness and foreignness; it requires moderation, regulation and structure, in ways that change across time and according to taste.

In *Timber, or, Discoveries*, Ben Jonson discusses various pitfalls of poetic style and, as Chapter 1 argued, these are gendered and sexualized in ways that are central to establishing a gendered hierarchy of style. Jonson uses sound and touch to define "women's poets":

> Others there are that have no composition at all, but a kind of tuning and rhyming fall in what they write. It runs and slides, and only makes a sound. "Women's poets", they are called, as you have "women's tailors".

> They write a verse, as smooth, as soft, as cream;
> In which there is no torrent, nor scarce stream.
>
> You may sound these wits, and find the depth of them, with your middle finger. They are cream-bowl- or but puddle-deep.[15]

Jonson's reference to "a kind of tuning, and rhyming fall" draws on terms used to describe feminine endings; Harington, for instance, calls them, "these pleasing and sweet falling meters". Jonson's verb "slides" in fact, echoes the Italian term for polysyllable rhyme "sdrucciola" used by Sidney, which literally means sliding or slippery and is used as a feminine-inflected adjective for polysyllabic rhyme. If Jonson does have feminine rhyme in his sights, he may be thinking of Samuel Daniel who was clearly self-conscious about their use, editing out many feminine rhymes from *Delia*.[16] And Jonson deploys Quintilian here to make much wider connections between gender and style. Jonson's comments ask to be read with a pinch of salt (or sugar?), of course, but they also provide some fascinating insight into the gendering of style in the seventeenth century. Being "only [...] sound" is the epitome of gendered insult and the acoustic quality of feminine rhyme becomes part of this gendered hierarchy. Feminine rhyme is sound, and as such it is gendered and devalued. We will see how Jonson deploys feminine rhyme in his own poetry to, and about, women.

Edmund Spenser, Samuel Daniel, William Shakespeare: Practice

How do these troubled theories of feminine rhyme inform (or reflect) poets' actual practice? Critics have shown how feminine rhyme creates all sorts of effects in poetry: failed closure; the action of thought; impressively "rich" aural effects and bathetic ones.[17] Philip Sidney's influential usage implemented a strict decorum. He used them structurally (rather than for local effect), so for instance "each quatrain of *Old Arcadia* 57 has a feminine rhyme in its second and fourth lines; and each stanza of *Certain Sonnets* 23 maintains a pattern of alternating feminine and masculine rhymes."[18] Usage is also dependent on genre or form: Sidney and Wroth use them in their songs but not in their sonnets.

The few recent analyses of feminine rhyme have focused on its place in the practice of individual (male) poets. Brian Cummings argues that for Fulke Greville, the use of feminine endings is "a markedly mental process, with a characteristic Grevillean lugubrious downbeat edge", manifesting philosophical thought in action.[19] David Scott Wilson-Okamura sees Spenser's use of feminine rhyme as part of a systematic and acoustic project which combines "rich, feminine, and visual rhymes" to create what he terms fat rhymes ("rime grosse or, better still, rime grasse") or costly rhymes: "Spenser, when he opened the floodgates of feminine rhyme, was not trying to make a statement, or even be sexy; he was trying to make a big, fat sound".[20] Defining these rhymes as fat, rich or costly, rather than feminine, Wilson-Okamura shifts these rhymes from gendered to other kinds of social connotation: wealth, prestige, value, scale. But the sensory connotations endure, albeit somewhat transmuted, through the ideas of taste and excess.

Wilson-Okamura's argument about Spenser diverges from that of Maureen Quilligan, one of the very few critics to explore the possibility that this gender-labelled feature was used in gendered contexts. Quilligan argued brilliantly both that Renaissance theorists of feminine rhyme use gendered examples, and that Spenser and Sidney use feminine rhyme specifically for poetic treatments of femininity, usually problematic femininity.[21] She argues that the sudden influx of feminine rhyme in *The Faerie Queene* books 4–6 (over 160 in these books after only one in 1–3) suggests Spenser's increasing focus on threats of effeminacy and emasculation, and on female rule.

Quilligan's argument for the gendered use of feminine rhyme has largely not been developed or adopted, and this may be because of the interpretive difficulties of locating meaning in local and occasional uses of a particular feature, such as feminine rhyme. Poets' use of feminine rhyme to write about gender and sexuality is most evident when the rhymes dominate an entire poem.

Shakespeare's Sonnet 20 is notoriously the only sonnet in the sequence to use all feminine rhyme.

> A woman's face with Nature's own hand painted
> Hast thou, the master mistress of my passion;
> A woman's gentle heart, but not acquainted
> With shifting change as is false women's fashion;
> An eye more bright then theirs, less false in rolling,
> Gilding the object whereupon it gazeth;
> A man in hue, all hues in his controlling,
> Which steals men's eyes and women's souls amazeth.
> And for a woman wert thou first created,
> Till Nature as she wrought thee fell a-doting,

And by addition me of thee defeated,
By adding one thing to my purpose nothing.
   But since she pricked thee out for women's pleasure,
   Mine be thy love, and thy love's use their treasure.

It seems clear that Shakespeare uses feminine rhymes here in conscious reference to their gendered label. Even here, though, the particular force of the feminine rhymes is not self-evident. Is Shakespeare using feminine rhyme to emphasize the stereotypical faults of women: false women's fashion; their false rolling eyes? The possible sexual puns on "acquainted" and "nothing" might support this misogynistic reading of rhyme. Alternatively, Helen Vendler argued that "the feminine rhymes enact the originally intended feminine sex in Nature's creation of the young man", while Michael Schoenfeldt suggests that the extra unstressed syllable of the feminine rhyme offers a metrical equivalent of the "thing" Nature *adds* to the youth.[22] Unlike Cummings on Greville's philosophical feminine rhyme or Wilson-Okamura on Spenser's ostentatious feminine rhyme, these interpretations depend on the reader recognizing not only the sound effect but the label of "feminine rhyme". In Sonnet 20 the use of feminine rhyme does seem to be clearly connected to gender and biological sex, and specifically the relationship between the two. It has a narrative as well as symbolic effect, as both enacting feminine stereotypes (changeability of "fashion"), adding the arbitrary extension (as Nature gives to the beloved).[23] In Colby Gordon's terms, the poem enacts a process of "trans technogenesis", and rhyme is one of its technologies.[24]

If Shakespeare toys with misogyny in his feminine rhymed sonnet about transition, Ben Jonson goes even further in his song on the misogynistic saying "That women are but men's shadows". And here he combines masculine with feminine and mosaic (multi-word) rhyme:

"Song. That women are but men's shadows"

Follow a shadow, it still flies you;
   Seem to fly it, it will pursue:
So court a mistress, she denies you;
   Let her alone, she will court you.
Say, are not women truly, then,
   Styled but the shadows of us men?
At morn and even shades are longest;
   At noon, they are or short, or none:

> So men at weakest, they are strongest,
>   But grant us perfect, they're not known.
> Say, are not women truly, then,
>   Styled but the shadows of us men?[25]

This poem of course expresses misogynistic assumptions: these are its starting point. But its implications are perhaps more complex. What is the force of "styled", in "are not women [...] Styled but the shadows of us men"? Jonson writes not that women are men's shadows but they are depicted as such. To style is to call or give a name to, so here Jonson is distancing himself from the misogynistic saying, albeit in a poem which repeats and extends it. The poem swiftly creates a persona who, we suspect, is over-claiming, his use of "truly" betraying some doubt in his own misogynist assertions. It explores how women are styled or *presented* as men's shadows, not actually their shadows. And here the possible sense of "stilled" resonates too, in the 1616 print spelling of "stil'd": by styling women as men's shadows, we still or constrain them, even as we slander them as being mutable and fleeting. In this sense, the poem is about the saying and the speaker, not women's innate identity. It is about the representation of gender difference as a power struggle, in which the advantage of one is always to the detriment of the other: "So men at weakest, they are strongest", the "so" here introducing a dubious correlation. Apparently outright misogyny gives way to something more reflective, even if just as harmful: a performance of these views, as in *Timber*'s characterization of "women's poets". Women's poets are not women poets but men trying to write for women; women are not men's shadows but are "styled" as such. And, importantly here, Jonson's interest in the construction of gender identity through style is aptly expressed in the poem's self-conscious use of rhyme. Jonson uses majority feminine rhyme in a poem about women. There are only two masculine rhymes in this poem, and one of them occurs on the word "men" itself:

> At morn, and even, shades are longest;
> At noon, they are or short, or none:
> So men at weakest, they are strongest,
> But grant us perfect, they're not known.[26]

He also uses the rhyme word "strongest" in a feminine (or "weak") rhyme position. The context of this poem's composition suggests an intriguing connection to the Sidney family, the period's most famous feminine rhymers. In his *Informations*, William Drummond presents this poem as the product of a conversation between Jonson and the Earl and Lady Pembroke (William Herbert and Mary Talbot) during which Lady Pembroke tasked Jonson with writing a poem on this saying.[27] William Ringler argued that Philip Sidney's "great innovation was to bring feminine rhyme back into English verse" and Jonson's poem suggests his use of them in the context both of misogynistic writing and writing commissioned by members of the Sidney family.[28] Even more strikingly, Jonson used them in his witty, praising, ambivalent sonnet to Mary Wroth, cousin and lover of William Herbert as well as accomplished practitioner of feminine rhyme:

"A Sonnet: To the Noble Lady, the Lady Mary Wroth"

I that have been a lover and could show it,
    Though not in these, in rhymes not wholly dumb,
    Since I exscribe your sonnets, am become
A better lover, and much better poet.
Nor is my muse or I ashamed to owe it
    To those true numerous graces, whereof some
    But charm the senses, others overcome
Both brains and hearts, and mine now best do know it:
For in your verse all Cupid's armoury,
    His flames, his shafts, his quiver, and his bow,
    His very eyes are yours to overthrow.
But then his mother's sweets you so apply,
    Her joys, her smiles, her loves, as readers take
    For Venus' ceston every line you make.[29]

From its complimentary punning anagram on Wroth's name as Worth, this poem is the opposite to "That Women Are But Men's Shadows"; this is a poem lavishly praising a woman poet, so lavish that some have conjectured that it was commissioned as a prefatory poem.[30] It is unusual for Jonson to write in the sonnet form, and he ensures this connection between form and addressee is noted, both in the title and in the poem itself: "I exscribe your sonnets [...]". But while the recent Jonson editors for Cambridge read this as a "delicate compliment" to Wroth, it is also, in Gavin Alexander's words "at least a wrong reading of *Pamphilia to Amphilanthus*".[31] The sonnet is double-edged, as commendatory poems almost always are, and especially Jonson's. The poem exhibits a kind of brilliant modesty which detracts from, or at least complicates, the praise of Wroth. Jonson plays down his own poem but says he can write better and does so elsewhere, turning a compliment into something close to a slight. Perhaps this is Jonson's way of styling Wroth as but the shadow of a man, to

> True love such ends best loveth,
> Unworthy love doth seek for ends
> A worthy love but worth pretends
> Nor other thoughts it proveth:[36]

Wroth adapts a Sidneian framework in which feminine rhyme is structural (repeated in the same position in the poem, for instance the third and sixth line of each stanza, though here also more often as well), musical, and used only in certain genres. These feminine rhymes are often used in certain places and genres, and the feminine rhyme itself is often created through a verb ending, all patterns that we will see eschewed in the work of Anne Southwell and Hester Pulter.

Anne Southwell's use of feminine rhyme is very different from Wroth's. We can see some patterns of Southwell's practice, for instance, in "An Elegy written by the Lady A. S. to the Countess of London Derry supposing her to be dead by her long silence".[37] This is a witty poem, playfully teasing her correspondent who has not written to her for some time:

> Good lady, friend, or rather lovely dame,
> If you be gone, from out this clayie frame,
> Tell what you know, whether th'saints' adoration
> Will stoop, to think on dusty procreation?
> And if they will not, they are fools (perdye) [*By God; indeed*]
> That pray to them, and rob the Trinity,
> The angels joy in our good conversation,
> Yet see us not, but by reverberation [...]
>
> (LL. 61–68)

Southwell also uses four feminine rhymes, here all of them are complex abstract nouns, rather than the verbs more commonly deployed in Sidney's and Wroth's songs, for instance. Elsewhere in this poem, Southwell pairs other complex nouns in feminine rhyme: tapestry/epitome; hierarchy/felicity; fantasy/destiny. These feminine rhymes are not lilting or fading or sweet. They draw attention to themselves. These nouns are harnessed to a playful, witty game where Southwell imagines her slow-to-respond correspondent has ascended to heaven and might therefore provide privileged information about the workings of the angels. Subsequently the manuscript shows that this game of words turned darker, as Southwell's correspondent in fact did die. Southwell's epitaph for Ridgeway opens with the pain of having joked about this possibility:

> Now let my pen be choked with gall
> Since I have writ prophetical[38]

And where the previous poem's feminine rhymes were audacious and difficult, the epitaph's feminine rhymes are melancholy. She asks astronomers:

> Or can you by your art discover
> Her seat near the celestial mover?
> She is gone, that way, if I could find her,
> And hath not left, her match behind her,
> I'll praise no more, her blessed condition,
> But follow her, with expedition.
>
> (EPITAPH, LL. 11–16)

The multi-word rhymes ("find her / behind her") and feminine rhymes ("condition/expedition") are here anguished. These two poems, one playful, one elegiac, pick up societal tropes of female silence: "supposing her to be dead by her long silence"; "I'll praise no more". Southwell herself speaks in the absence of her silent, then deceased, friend.

Southwell also deploys feminine rhymes specifically to write about female authorship. And it is in a somewhat surprising genre, her Decalogue poetry (poems about the Ten Commandments). Her poem on the fourth commandment, or "precept" (Thou shalt keep the Sabbath day) exists in two different copies in her British Library and Folger Library manuscripts. And in both she explores the vexed status of women's writing, and women writers:

> For me, I write but to my self and me
> What God's good grace doth in my soul imprint
> I bought it not for pelf, none buys of thee
> Nor will I let it at so base a rent
>   As wealth or fame, which is but dross and vapor
>   And scarce deserves the blotting of a paper[. . .][39]

> Dare you but write, you are Minerva's bird,
> The owl at which these bats and crows must wonder,
> They'll criticize upon the smallest word:
> This wanteth number, case, that tense and gender.

Then must you frame a pitiful epistle,
To pray him be a rose was born a thistle.[40]

But stay, weak female, whither does thou wander?
How dares thy waxen plumes approach the sun?
Thy better sex are lost in this meander
In which thy ignorance presumes to run;
Pardon, dear saviour, pardon my presumption
And let my faith rely on thy assumption.[41]

These three examples show Southwell reflecting on the act of writing. She uses feminine rhyme to accentuate the spiritual conflict involved in writing, and perhaps especially in writing as a woman. The awkwardness of "presumption/assumption" and prominent couplet "vapor/paper" might suggest that however much we may want to sublimate the writing self to God, we cannot help but draw attention to our own art—or lack thereof. But even more strikingly, in the latter two of these stanzas Southwell uses feminine endings to write about hostility to being a *woman* poet. She ventriloquizes attacks on women "But stay, weak female". Here she uses the rhyme pair "wander/meander", a summary-in-rhyme of the risks of female creativity in early modern culture, of being wayward, outside regulation. Again ventriloquizing the censure of woman writers she imagines critics as the bats and crows who "criticize upon the smallest word", with another pertinent rhyme pair "wonder/gender" and gender here referring specifically to grammatical usage.[42]

Southwell's poetry is often both devotional and satirical. Her "Precept 4" (the commandment on the sabbath day) becomes a work of critical poetics.[43] And in this poem, feminine rhymes are a marker of resistance: she evokes the misogynistic use of feminine rhyme by Shakespeare, Jonson, and Denny, and writes against it. Southwell's rhymes are also resistant in a more aesthetic sense. She does not adhere to the Sidneian decorum of structural feminine rhyme, nor the Spenserian rich sound version, nor Harington's dying fall. Southwell uses feminine rhyme to stop the reader short, ask more of them, to question and provoke. We turn now to another poet, writing slightly later in the seventeenth century, who also used feminine rhyme to write against the grain.

Hester Pulter—royalist, writer of poetry about death, alchemy, politics, and myth—uses feminine rhyme in more than half of her poems. These are not usually structurally positioned, nor used for whole poems, but appear in single or multiple instances amongst masculine and other kinds of rhyme. Like Southwell's usage, Pulter's feminine rhymes are usually not common polysyllabic words (such as the verb endings -ing and -ed; noun endings -ion and -ment). They are often technical nouns, as in "The Eclipse" where she rhymes "conflagration/contentation" and "dissolution/revolution", the latter is a rhyme also repeated in "My soul, why art thou full of trouble", there paired also with "salvation" and "transmigration" in a virtuosic quadruple feminine rhyme. "The Revolution" rhymes "radiances/outvies/splendencies" and "rarefy/circularly/magnify"; "View but this tulip" (Emblem 40) rhymes "fermentation/segregation". These words are not only difficult to rhyme but semantically difficult, and were perceived as such in the seventeenth century: many of them appear in contemporary guides to difficult words, such as Thomas Blount's *Glossographia, or a Dictionary Interpreting all such Hard Words* (1656).

Like Southwell, Pulter uses feminine mosaic (multi-word) rhyme in both comic and elegiac modes. In the emblem poems especially, feminine rhymes are witty, adding to the poems' reflexive texture and playful tone, relishing their own wordplay: "doxy/proxy" ("The Dolphin", Emblem 39), "pedester/master" ("An old man, a stripling and an ass", Emblem 54) and her poem on Davenant's loss of his nose due to syphilis, "To Sir William Davenant", rhymes "gnomon/no man". At the other extreme of emotion, her devastating poem "Upon the death of my dear and lovely daughter" rhymes "mantle by / tapestry".

Far from the gentle, fading fall often ascribed to feminine rhymes, Pulter's feminine rhymes (like Southwell's) foreground themselves. They create a bravura effect. This is especially the case with classical names which require imaginative rhyme pairings: "Aphrodite/Amphitrite" ("My love is fair"); "salamander/slander"; "took on / Phaeton" ("The Complaint of Thames"); "Epiphanes/Epimanes" ("Vain Herostratus", Emblem 28). This is not accidental: Pulter chooses to put these names in a rhyme position. Feminine rhymes (and polysyllable, and multiword rhymes) are very common in her work and used for a whole range of effects; she does not shy away from difficult rhyme and even revels in the challenges of difficult rhyme (unlike Harington who, we say earlier, grumbled that he "could have saved some of my cost, at least some of my pain" if he had thought it was acceptable to rhyme a polysyllabic word with a monosyllabic one, such as "civility" with "flee").

There is one rhyme pair which Pulter uses above any other, and it is feminine. "Story/glory" appears as a rhyme pair in a total of 26 poems (out of 120). This is partly about Pulter's tendency to return to and develop certain key themes.[44] She has several poems with the same title, such as four poems called "The Circle", or several called "Upon the same" (as the previous poem). These particular rhyme words are also specifically important to Pulter. These rhymes amplify Pulter's connection between female authorship, fame, legacy. There are not, of course, many options to rhyme with story or glory, yet Pulter chooses to use them as rhyme words much more frequently than other poets, and more frequently than she uses any other rhyme pair. Moreover, she is often using "story" as synonymous with "life" for which there are many more rhyme words: it is significant that she choose story rather than life, and that she uses it in a rhyme position. Using particular words in a rhyme position (at the line ending) is to give particular weight to these words. Story is almost always sad (often "my sad story") so that "story/glory" registers the hardship of earthly life, for which the reward is the spiritual glory of God. But it is also about legacy, and about the history and recording of (female) life. In "Aletheia's Pearl" the speaker's life is written in the book of fate, for instance, part of a woman's life story being written by multiple female characters. She writes of Aletheia, the speaker's spiritual guide,

> Turning the volumes of the book of fate
> To see what might advance th'eternal's glory,
> She happ'd to cast an eye on my sad story,
> And by my destiny she saw my life,
> At which she sighed: both infant, maid, and wife
> Would be involved and filled with inward trouble,
> But yet as brittle as the tenderest bubble[45]

One main use of this pair is to argue that while a woman's life "story" might be sad her "glory" will be in God (though Pulter also sometimes questions and challenges this promise of posthumous consolation). The repetition of these rhyme words so frequently also creates a relationship between poems, through repeated titles, repeated rhymes. Dianne Mitchell has written of the "alternate modes of temporality" evident in the poetics of women including Pulter and Southwell, connecting their repeated, painful experiences (child-loss, ill health, political disenfranchisement) to the temporal disruptions of their poems.[46] The rhymes across Pulter's poems might be read as both artful—a poetic fingerprint created through signature rhymes such as "story/glory"— and perhaps also resonant of the repetitions of early modern women's lived experience.

Amongst the many uses of feminine rhyme in early modernity, poetry about gender is a significant category; both male and female poets adopted feminine rhyme self-consciously in poems about gender. Moreover, Southwell and Pulter both use it to write explicitly about female authorship, with their striking ideological rhyme pairs such as "wonder/gender" and "story/glory". It is also often a distinctive element of certain women poets' style, both the acoustic and semantic effects of the rhymes themselves and what they tell us about their poetic vocabulary. Southwell and Pulter use feminine rhyme in quite ostentatious ways: instead of using common verb endings (-ing, -eth) and noun endings (-ion) as feminine rhymes, they use unusual, often technical words connected to philosophy, chemistry or religion. These words are aurally and visually arresting, and also intellectually demanding of the reader. Southwell and Pulter are both philosophical in quite different ways: Southwell's exploration of doubt, faith, and mental activity is signaled by her abstract verbal nouns, as are her rebarbative, witty attacks on misogyny. Her characteristic combination of the devotional and satirical is marked by these words and rhymes. Pulter's deep engagement with alchemy, astronomy, and natural philosophy finds its place in her abstract nouns of material transformation and movement (revolution, dissolution). Pulter's bravura polysyllabic rhymes on classical names showcase her witty and intimate knowledge of these stories, and also her reworkings, sometimes irreverently, of their narratives. And this focus on female storytelling, control of one's own written legacy finds its place in her signature rhyme: story/glory.

Southwell's and Pulter's use of polysyllabic words at the end of lines is part of their writing against the grain. It creates a particular texture: virtuosic, intellectual, sometimes spiky. Attending to feminine rhyme not only helps us trace the history of that particular feature, it also helps us see those features that are less commonly identified in women poets' work: wit; technicality; philosophy; satire. This is feminine rhyme not as fading, sliding, bathetic. This is "virtuosa rhyme".

Katherine Philips: Theory

Having looked at male-authored theory of feminine rhyme, male-authored usage, and female-authored usage, the final section of this chapter will look at female-authored theory. While there has been little analysis in the past of early modern women's use of feminine rhyme, there has been no analysis whatsoever of their theorizing of it. None has been thought to exist. But discussion of this feature can be found, not in treatises nor prefaces to poems, but in correspondence, one of the most important sources of early modern criticism by women. In the early years of the Restoration, the poet Katherine Philips corresponded regularly with her friend Sir Charles Cotterell, in letters which reveal her extensive and detailed aesthetic evaluation of other poets' work, as well as her own writing process.

Philips and Cotterell discussed the specifics of poetic style especially when she is translating Pierre Corneille's *La Mort de Pompée*. In December 1662, Philips solicits advice about a particular line ending:

> I was loath to use the word *Effort*, but not having language enough to find any other rhyme without losing all the spirit and force of the next line, and knowing that it had been naturalized at least these twelve years; besides, that it was not used in that place in the French, I ventured to let it pass [...][47]

Her concern is both about translation—"has *effort* been 'naturalized' into normal English usage?"—and about rhyme. In the lines Philips is discussing, "Effort" rhymes with "support", which in English pronunciation commits the stylistic offense noted by Samuel Daniel, of rhyming a feminine ending with a masculine one. This exchange, in the mode that Paul Trolander and Zeynep Tenger call "amendment criticism", allows Philips to solicit advice and avoid any errors.[48] It also allows her to assert her superior taste and judgement. We have only her side of the correspondence, so we do not know how Cotterell replied, but in a subsequent letter Philips thanks Cotterell "for altering the word *Effort*" and discusses other rhyme words that might be pronounced as one or two syllables, including "heaven" and "power".[49] These are both examples which had been discussed by George Gascoigne,

> This poetical licence is a shrewd fellow and covers many faults in a verse, it makes words longer, shorter, of more syllables, of fewer, newer, older, truer, falser, and to conclude it turkeneth [*changes; transforms*] all things at pleasure, for example, *ydone* for *done*, [...] power for *powre*, heaven for *heavn*.[50]

Gascoigne's metaphors of freedom, regulation ("poetical licence"), and his governing male personification ("shrewd fellow"), remind us of the ideological and social values at stake in prosodic theory. More particularly, Philips's concern over whether "heaven" and "power" are masculine monosyllables or feminine polysyllables shows that feminine endings were still problematic a hundred and fifty years after Harington, Sidney, and Daniel's uneasy explorations of the term.

Philips is also a vigorous critic of other writers, and one of the focuses of her criticism is their use of feminine rhyme. In September 1664 Philips has been reading another translation of *Pompey*, by a group of courtly poets including Edmund Waller. Writing to Cotterell again, she criticizes their method of translation, their use of couplets, and their use of rhyme:

> The word Roman blade shocks me very much, his frequent double rhymes in an heroic poem, his calling Pompey a consul, when that was not in the original [...].[51]

The middle of her three criticisms here is the use of "double rhyme". While some contemporary writers used this term to refer to internal rhyme, it seems more likely that Philips is aiming here at feminine rhymes, of which the rival to her translation of Pompey had many.[52] Philips does not use the term "feminine" for words such as effort, heaven, and power but she did have strong views about when they could be used. She stresses the decorum of feminine rhyme, that it is genre-specific and not suitable "in an heroic poem", recalling Daniel (and others) on it being "fittest for ditties". Not only does this demonstrate Philip's familiarity and confidence with prosodic theory, it also suggests that feminine rhyme was one of the features through which Philips positions herself as the critic, the arbiter of good taste.[53] So while Southwell and Pulter forge a poetic aesthetic of feminine rhyme that defies certain lyric decorum and regulation, Philips criticizes indecorous use of feminine rhyme in order to bolster her own cultural capital.

John Dryden writes of the constraints upon a poet:

> Neither can we give ourselves the liberty of making any part of a verse for the sake of rhyme, or concluding with a word which is not current English, or using the variety of female rhymes, all which our fathers practised[54]

Literary fashions had of course changed in the eighty years since Sidney, Daniel, and Harington. Where Harington saw feminine rhymes as novel, Dryden perceives them as old-fashioned and indeed uses them for conscious archaism. This chapter opened by identifying the unease with which theorists like Sidney, Daniel and Harington discussed feminine rhyme at the end of the sixteenth century, and here Dryden perceives the usage of feminine rhyme as having become even more difficult. Feminine rhyme continues to be both gendered and problematic into the eighteenth century. Samuel Wesley asserts "Nor loves our stronger *tongue* that tinkling *chime*, / The *darling* of the *French*, a *female rhyme*".[55] Hypermetric unstressed rhyme is still female, still foreign, still weak and uncomfortably dismissed as mere sound. Wesley's "tinkling chime", like Jonson's "tuning and rhyming fall" reminds us that poetry by "women's poets", like "female rhyme", "only makes a sound". The embarrassment and misogyny evident in early theories of feminine rhyme licensed dismissal of women's writing itself: the misogyny of the aesthetic term and its real-life implications cannot be separated.

The meaning of feminine rhyme has been re-ascribed again and again from the late-sixteenth century to the twenty-first. It is variously seen as sweet, melancholy, funny, uncertain, lingering, sexually ambivalent, rich, difficult, and ornate. This kaleidoscope of meanings suggests that a rhyme sound did not have one intrinsic significance for early modern poets, readers, and critics. It is clear, though, that both the rhyme itself and its label did accumulate gendered connotations through practice and criticism. Its use by Shakespeare, Jonson, and Denny in lyrics debating models of sex and gender or criticizing women suggests that the rhyme feature was often used *for* its label. But defining and using feminine rhyme was also a matter of decorum, foreignness, fashion—a matter of taste. Investigating women's use of feminine rhyme draws attention to the gaps in our knowledge of the interplay of theory and practice of poetics in the period more broadly, especially in the writing of women.

Almost every use of the term "feminine rhyme" concerns some judgement being made, from Harington's concern about being judged like those who sweeten their wine, to Philips's anxiety over the pronunciation of "effort" and "power" and censure of her contemporaries' "frequent double rimes in an heroic poem". But Harington and Daniel both stress the contingency of such judgements, that these are not a matter of widely accepted rules, but of historically specific preference: "indeed there is no right in these things that are continually in a wandering motion, carried with the violence of uncertain likings, being but only the time that gives them their power". The use and theory of feminine rhyme over a century, by both male and female, print and manuscript poets helps us understand the conflicting charge of "feminine rhyme" and to challenge any seemingly self-evident connections between sound, taste, and gender.

The theory and practice of feminine rhyme by both men and, crucially, women, suggest that it is not quite adequate to say of English poetry (as Wilson-Okamura does of French poetry) that feminine rhyme "gets used for everything and, in consequence, means nothing."[56] While feminine rhyme may not intrinsically mean one thing, it acquired through usage several meanings, and these were often gendered, as we can see in the misogynistic uses of

Shakespeare, Jonson, and Denny. The earliest theorizations of feminine rhyme in English are comparative and cautious, drawing on other European vernaculars for precedents in its usage and also suggesting an unease or embarrassment around this gendered feature that have persisted in modern criticism. The wariness about appropriate and moderate use of feminine rhyme is revealed through the gustatory metaphors of excess deployed by many theorists: Daniel on over-glutting; Harington on cloying; Jonson on verses "as smooth, as soft, as cream" and (in Wilson-Okamura's depiction) Spenser's "rime grasse". This is a matter of taste, demonstrating the vividly bodily use of that term to mean both gustatory and aesthetic taste. More than anything, perhaps, feminine rhyme was a test of skill and taste. This test was even more potent for women poets, against whom feminine rhyme was often used in misogynistic ways. Katherine Philips weaponized feminine rhyme to evaluate her contemporaries' translation of a French play she too was translating, demonstrating her command of poetic theory and the kind of detailed aesthetic judgment that is so far little known in women's writing. Reading Hester Pulter and Anne Southwell for feminine rhyme reveals their poetry as philosophical, critical, resistant, innovative, and virtuosic. Pulter uses bravura rhymes to foreground her witty, erudite reworkings of philosophy and myth, Southwell uses feminine rhyme to write about writing—it is central to her critical poetics. She also uses it to defend female authorship, bringing it to bear against the misogynistic tropes of Jonson and the embarrassment of Sidney:

> But stay, weak female, whither does thou wander?
> How dares thy waxen plumes approach the sun?
> Thy better sex are lost in this meander
> In which thy ignorance presumes to run.[57]

3

Original

Male authors have been read as agents of historical change more regularly than their female counterparts.

SARAH KUNJUMMEN, "READING MILTON LIKE A WOMAN" (2021)[1]

[...] as you have made your self an *original,* so are you likewise secure from being *copied.*

WALTER CHARLETON, LETTERS AND POEMS IN HONOUR
OF THE INCOMPARABLE PRINCESS, MARGARET CAVENDISH (1676)[2]

ALL EARLY MODERN women poets were unique, or so their male peers say. Mary Sidney Herbert is described as "peerless"; Katherine Philips is "matchless" and "incomparable"; Margaret Cavendish is "*Margaret* the First" and "singular", and Bradstreet has "sprung up", out of nothing.[3] They are exemplary, rare, anomalous, unlearned—all of them, ironically. Much early modern praise poetry can be read as epideictic, with the potential for critique as well as praise. Poetry in praise of women writers is especially marked by this double edge, and its effect: to exclude. As each woman poet is distinguished as the first and only, women's contribution to both poetry and poetics is limited. If a writer is first *and* last, she can neither take her place in a line of influence from earlier writers, nor in turn influence others: she has no literary history.

Literary historians largely agree that originality became key to poetic value during the later seventeenth and early eighteenth century: "It was not until the second half of the eighteenth century that the doctrine of literary imitation was overturned".[4] Critics agree that there were some earlier forerunners: Gavin Alexander sees Samuel Daniel as an "important precursor" to this trajectory; David Quint suggests the same of Cervantes.[5] Renaissance (male) writers found themselves divided between the desire to claim divine or classical authority and wanting to assert their own creativity. Women do not appear in this history, and this is characteristic of their exclusion from developmental narratives which still inform current ideas of literary value. Margaret Ezell has written about the idea of the anomaly in twentieth-century literary history: "as we continue to recover more and more handwritten texts, when does a person, a practice, or a text cease to be deemed "extraordinary" or "anomalous" and instead invite a restructuring, revision, or the creation of a new framework of understanding?".[6] This chapter will show that the language used to exclude women in the early modern period was one of anomalousness, exceptionality, firstness, and uniqueness. It also argues that early modern women were in fact important theorists of originality. These two seemingly opposed narratives are actually closely linked, as women's theories of originality co-opted the very vocabulary used to exclude them—that of exceptionality and firstness. Reading these women as theorists changes our chronology of originality, periodization models, and even scholars' ideas about modernity in literature: women embraced originality earlier than many male writers. In other words, women were original before men were.

Matchless Modesty

In Walter Charleton's letter to Margaret Cavendish, printed in a posthumous collection in her honour, the terms of the highest praise are those which also sharply delimit her impact: "you are the first great lady, that ever wrote so much and so much of your own: and, for ought we can divine, you will also be the last."[7] In one of his multiple definitions of style, Jeff Dolven teasingly claims that style is both "what makes someone unique and what is imitable about them".[8] This is a paradox of style, in Dolven's terms, and also one of originality, and it is a gendered paradox. For Walter Charleton, and many other early modern and more recent commentators, a man's originality places him at the head of a tradition, while a woman's originality is a dead end: as Charleton said of Cavendish, "you will also be the last".

This rhetoric of uniqueness contributes to a wider trope of praise-as-limitation, that of the gallery of worthy women. These collections, published from the sixteenth century onwards, gathered examples of idealized women.

The notoriety allowed women by their reputations as "worthies" has been described by Jane Stevenson as "contentless fame".[9] As one in a list of exemplary women, each woman's fame becomes one of moral worth rather than literary importance or influence. This can be seen in the rhetoric of women poets' uniqueness, too, where despite the source of fame being their writing, it is the woman's character and even physique that is praised. And this is one of the distinctive inflections of originality when it is applied to women writers in this period: the term "original" is often applied not to women's works, but to themselves, their bodies.

In the preface to Katherine Philips's poems of 1667, her anonymous editor blurs the line between body and page with an extraordinary, embodied analogy for textual ownership. This edition, attributed to Philips under her coterie pen name as "the matchless Orinda", claims to be authoritative, and is much concerned with textual originals and copies. It came a few years after the apparently pirated version of Philips's poems, and claims to be a far truer copy:

> But the small pox, that malicious disease [...] was not satisfied to be as injurious a printer of her face, as the other had been of her poems, but treated her with a more fatal cruelty than the stationer had them; for though he to her most sensible affliction surreptitiously possessed himself of a false copy, and sent those children of her fancy into the world, so martyred, that they were more unlike themselves than she could have been made had she escaped; that murderous tyrant, with greater barbarity seized unexpectedly upon her, the true original, and to the much juster affliction of all the world, violently tore her out of it, and hurried her untimely to her grave [...][10]

In a striking phrase, Philips is "the true original", but she is not the original who other poets imitate, instead her mind and body are the source while her works are copies. And the stress falls on body rather than mind through the extraordinary analogy drawn between the illicit printer of her poems and the smallpox disease, the one disfiguring her poems, the other her face.

Ben Jonson was one of the period's most important and influential theorists of poetic originality, and we will turn later to Margaret Cavendish's dialogue with his *Timber, or Discoveries*. He also wrote important praise poems to women writers which show how the language of originality could be used to limit, as well as praise, them. In the previous chapter we saw how Jonson's sonnet to Mary Wroth hovered over the line between praise and slight. In another poem for Wroth, he describes her as "Nature's index", a sort of store from which everything in the literary past could be recreated:

> Madam, had all antiquity been lost,
> All history sealed up and fables crossed;
> That we had left us, nor by time, nor place,
> Least mention of a nymph, a muse, a grace,
> But even their names were to be made anew,
> Who could not but create them all, from you?
> He, that but saw you wear the wheaten hat,
> Would call you more than Ceres, if not that:
> And, dressed in shepherds 'tire, who would not say:
> You were the bright Oenone, Flora, or May?
> [...]
> So are you Nature's index, and restore,
> I'your self, all treasure lost of th'age before.[11]

In Jonson's narrative, Wroth is so complete that "all antiquity" could be recreated from her, implying that she is the sum of all parts of learning. But the examples he gives are female characters, rather than particular texts: a Nymph, a Muse, a Grace, Ceres, Oenone, Flora, May. So "all antiquity" is scaled down to become fictional female figures from antiquity. Moreover, in this characterization Wroth is not original, she is *an* original. Literary history can be captured not in her writing, but "from you"; she is an "index" but one that derives from nature not learning (even though Wroth was, of course, extremely erudite). Joshua Sylvester's poem on Wroth also describes her as a "source" to poets:

> Accept these sighs and these few tears of ours,
> Which have their course but from the source of yours[12]

This idea of the source (often drawing on Virgil's fourth Georgic) was crucial to early modern writers' definitions of originality, as David Quint has shown.[13] The metaphor of the water source was influential and useful partly because writers could imagine themselves as streams flowing away from the source, fed by and inspired by it, but also themselves representing a different body of work. But here, in Sylvester's use, Wroth is a "source" of inarticulate tears and sighs, not poems.

Women poets in the seventeenth century were, then, often characterized as "original" through the word itself and its near synonyms: unique, first, only, exceptional, exemplary, matchless, peerless. But this characterization is often one of limitation, and even exclusion. The rhetoric of first-and-only was used to both praise and contain women's literary influence. Moreover, in a literary culture which privileges imitation, originality can be a form of modesty and even an insult. As Gavin Alexander puts it, "where we value originality and consider it as diametrically opposed to the imitation of previous authors and texts, Renaissance critics seem to value imitation above originality, or rather as a route to originality".[14] For a woman to be original might suggest she is outside the culture of poetics and rhetoric which deemed invention of equal, not greater, importance than disposition and elocution. In these senses, women are often characterized as original.

This pattern recurs throughout the century, most strikingly in efforts to delimit Margaret Cavendish. In the collection of praise published after Margaret Cavendish's death, Walter Charleton writes:

> [...] as you have made your self an *original,* so are you likewise secure from being *copied.* You have indeed, given the world an illustrious example; but you have given what it cannot take, the example being of that height, that it is hardly attainable [...][15]

While the message here is overtly one of hyperbolic praise, we might note that Charleton seems to have borrowed his praise from the outright insult of his peer, Mary Evelyn. In a letter, Mary Evelyn writes that she hoped that as Cavendish "is an original, she may never have a copy".[16] Evelyn may have had various reasons to dislike Cavendish, perhaps seeing a threat in Cavendish's interest to her own husband and his translation of part of Lucretius, or possibly an antipathy rooted in her own idea of how an intelligent writing woman should act. Evelyn weaponizes originality, using the idea of exceptionality to maintain the status quo, even one that excludes her own sex from public writing. And even as Charleton writes explicitly in praise of Cavendish, he borrows this potent image of exclusion to do so. These examples of contemporaries' praise of Wroth, Philips, and Cavendish reveal the critique and exclusion latent within the rhetoric of originality.

This is not the whole story, though. Women writers took this exclusionary form of originality and used it to put themselves at the vanguard of poetics. It was women writers who transformed the gendered principles of exemplarity, rarity, anomalousness, unlearnedness, and naturalness into the still-highly valued principle of originality. Anne Bradstreet's prologue to *The Tenth Muse* is a paradigmatic formulation of modesty as assertion[17]:

> Let Greeks be Greeks, and women what they are,
> Men have precedency, and still excel,
> It is but vain, unjustly to wage war;
> Men can do best, and women know it well.
> Preeminence in each and all is yours,
> Yet grant some small acknowledgement of ours.
>
> And O, you high-flown quills that soar the skies,
> And ever with your prey still catch your praise,
> If e'er you deign these lowly lines your eyes,
> Give wholesome parsley wreath, I ask no bays:
> This mean and unrefinèd ore of mine
> Will make your glist'ring gold but more to shine.[18]

Here Bradstreet fulsomely credits men as "preeminent", holding "precedency" and "excel[ing]". Yet as she shifts to the first-person plural voice, men/women to yours/ours, she articulates a counter-claim for women's place, one that might even be read as a different kind of "precedency" or "preeminence". By describing her own poetry as "ore", she claims purity, proximity to the source; ore is in fact the precedent for glittering gold. It may be "unrefined", but her poetry is the pure origin of other (more shiny) forms of gold. Here, as so often, a modesty trope becomes a claim for authority and purity, the source from which others might develop. The image of feminine potentiality has been strengthened in this edition of the poem from 1678. Bradstreet's 1650 version had the word "stuff" instead of "ore". The poem's imagery and syntax are thus changed to make it a more powerful image of female creativity: ore, rich with meanings in terms of raw materials, something that has not yet but will necessarily be cultivated or refined, holder of true value, and a claim to the extractive economy of men rather than the more domestic textile implications of "stuff".

Originality has indeed often been conceptualized in economic and commodity terms, most importantly the development of copyright. In Trevor Ross's dramatic formulation, "On 22 February 1774 literature in its modern sense began", with the copyright act in England.[19] Even much earlier, in the seventeenth century, authors' assertions of ownership over their works were often a site for articulating the author as origin. This was an especially vexed issue for women, intensified by their use of anonymous, pseudonymous, and manuscript forms. Women themselves were acutely aware of the risks of being known as a print author. Equally, they were aware of the risks of their works being attributed to others. Anne Bradstreet expresses an acute sense of vulnerability to accusations of plagiarism:

> I am obnoxious to each carping tongue
> Who says my hand a needle better fits;
> A poet's pen all scorn I should thus wrong,
> For such despite they cast on female wits.
> If what I do prove well, it won't advance,
> They'll say it's stolen, or else it was by chance.
>
> ("THE PROLOGUE", LL. 25–30)

Bradstreet sharply expresses the double bind facing women authors: those who do not like your writing will blame your gender; those who admire your writing, will argue that a woman could not have written it. This was a point of acute concern for Margaret Cavendish too, who even published a defence of her authorship by her husband: "An Epistle to justify the Lady Newcastle, and truth against falsehood, laying those false, and malicious aspersions of her, that she was not author of her Books".[20] Cavendish herself comments acerbically that when critics suggest she may not have been the author of her works, she can take this either as an insult or a compliment: "I am very much, or very little obliged to my readers, for my former books which I have set out, either by their approvement, or dislike, in not granting me to be the author".[21] As we will see in the next section, Margaret Cavendish defended herself against charges of copying or plagiarism through a defiant, bodily, yet also classicizing, rhetoric of poetic originality.

"Lumber stuffed with old commodities": Ben Jonson and Margaret Cavendish

These concepts of originality, anomalousness, and exceptionality could be exclusionary, then, but women writers also embraced them. Women poets used the rhetoric of originality often weaponized against them to forge a new poetics of originality that would influence the development of literary history. Alongside Bradstreet, Hutchinson, and Southwell, Margaret Cavendish turned modest unlearnedness into defiant originality.

We have seen that Cavendish's contemporaries like Evelyn and Charleton defined Cavendish by her singularity, and recent critics have done so too. In her landmark study, *Writing Women's Literary History*, Margaret Ezell argued that Cavendish fits into literary history only as the "anomalous aristocratic exception". Catherine Gallagher wrote of Cavendish's "total self-referentiality".[22] Another way of formulating "self-referentiality", I suggest, is originality. As I have shown elsewhere, these critics—both early modern and contemporary—are drawing on Cavendish's own self-representation as unique.[23] An engraved portrait of Cavendish which was printed in some of her works is accompanied by this poem:

> Studious she is and all alone
> Most visitants, when she has none,
> Her library on which she looks
> It is her head her thoughts her books
> Scorning dead ashes without fire
> For her own flames do her inspire[24]

This captures many of the key components of Cavendish's self-fashioned identity: scorning the "dead ashes" of learning and literary predecessors, she needs only "her head" and "her thoughts". Cavendish's claims not to have read anything have been amply dismantled by many scholars who have demonstrated her close engagement with literary, scientific, classical and historical sources.[25] But these claims remain very compelling, not as statements of biographical fact, but as the central tenets of Cavendish's poetics. And while she claims not to be influenced by any previous writers, Cavendish is clear about her desire to be an influence on others:

> whatsoever is new is my own, which I hope all is; for I had never any guide to direct me, nor intelligence from any authors, to advertise me, but write according to my own natural cogitations, where if any do write after the same manner in what language soever, that they will remember my work is the original of their discourse[26]

Cavendish wants to be "the original", whom others imitate in their own "discourse". Crucially here, Cavendish uses "original" and "copy" as terms for style: she is describing "discourse". Her usage here is closer to the modern sense of the term (given to independent exercise of the mind or imagination) than the predominant seventeenth-century usage (the original or source of something).[27] Cavendish's friend and waiting woman, Elizabeth Toppe, uses an embroidery image to place Cavendish triumphantly at the head of a lineage of writers:

You are not only the first English poet of your sex, but the first, that ever wrote this way: therefore whosoever writes afterwards, must own you for their pattern, from whence they take their sample [...].[28]

Like "discourse", here the apparently casual phrase "this way" is important in emphasizing Cavendish's style as well as the fact of her writing: it is important not just that she writes, but that she writes *in this style*. Toppe, like Cavendish elsewhere (as we will see in the next section of this chapter), adapts an image from needlework to defend female creativity. Here these become metaphors for originality: Cavendish is the pattern, whom subsequent writers treat as their example. This is not "contentless fame", but exemplarity as the head of a new tradition.

Cavendish's many essays and prefaces are works of poetics. While they focus on her own singularity, they do not do so in a vacuum; they are also direct engagements with contemporary debates in poetics. Specifically, Cavendish's essays in *The Worlds Olio* are in dialogue with Jonson's *Timber, or Discoveries*. This dialogue involves their respective use of gendered styles, attitude to the classical past, and literary originality. Jonson casts part of *Timber* as a guide to the education of sons, and this may well have been addressed to William Cavendish.[29] Regardless of biographical connections, it was in fact Margaret Cavendish who proved to be the true "daughter of Ben", her poetics in part forged through debate and challenge to her husband's friend and client.

Timber is a kind of printed commonplace book that builds a distinctively Jonsonian voice from a dense fabric of quotations and allusions. It is notoriously both strikingly modern and intensely backward-looking. To put it another way, Jonson reworks his sources—his timber—to surprising ends—discoveries—thus drawing on the latter word's meaning as things that have been "uncovered", in this case from the classical past, rather than actually creating new ones.[30] He also claims the classical past so as to assert himself over his contemporary rivals, and here his class-conscious self-assertions may have something in common with Cavendish's gender-conscious ones. Jonson's is a poetics of finely negotiated contradictions; he is "an imitative poet who was consistently preoccupied with his ownership of his writings"[31] who in *Timber* we find "performing his own direct emotional involvement [...] by manipulating, with consummate art, the utterances of other men".[32] Jonson claims the importance of plain-speaking from one's own experiences, as in the famous assertion "language most show a man: speak that I may see thee". And yet even here Jonson's apparent plainness of style and of character is underpinned by delicate allusions to Plutarch, Martial, and Erasmus.[33] It is also a work committed to masculinity. Patricia Parker has influentially described the "virile style" promoted by Roman and then early modern writers, one which claims to be unadorned and frank, and is often defined by metaphors of muscularity and masculinity.[34] And the establishment of a "virile style" involves evoking and dismantling both feminine and effeminate styles, as well as false manliness. The text is interlaced with misogynistic metaphors, from the "skirts of learning" to the "strumpet in good clothes", as well as homophobic slurs, via Martial and Quintilian, as Lorna Hutson has shown.[35]

Cavendish's collection of short prose pieces, *The Worlds Olio*, is a tantalizing exploration of the essay form. In genre, the pieces have more in common with essays by Montaigne and Bacon than Jonson, as Mihoko Suzuki has shown.[36] And like these writers, deeply learned as they are, Cavendish champions the opinions of the individual and challenges received wisdom. The title also captures some of the opposing pulls of the book, an "olio" (stew, OED 1.) evokes the domestic realm of the kitchen, in tension with the claim to speak for (and to) "the world". And even the kitchen term "olio" itself looks out to the world beyond, as it was an imported term from Spanish and Portuguese cooking. Cooking also generates a broader set of metaphors around taste and consumption, both culinary and aesthetic, throughout Cavendish's works. The recipe poems in her first collection establish a connection between the recipe and the poetic blazon, for instance, wittily undermining the Petrarchan convention of itemizing a woman's body by rewriting it into a recipe.[37] One contemporary woman reader adopted Cavendish's own food metaphors to describe *The Worlds Olio*. Susan Du Verger describes herself keenly consuming Cavendish's novel ideas: "my sharp appetite greedily took down those unaccustomed cates" (morsel or dainty, OED 1.a.).[38] "Olio" was also used metaphorically to suggest a mixture of heterogeneous elements (OED 2.a.), and this is not the only place where Cavendish deploys a culinary term to describe a literary genre. She also uses the related term "hodge podge" to describe pieces of writing which are also mixtures of ingredients or literary elements. And this is one distinctive element of Cavendish's originality, her "unaccustomed" style, as Du Verger describes it.

So what did Cavendish find in common with *Timber*, and its profound investment in both the classical past and in masculinity? Both *Timber* and *The Worlds Olio* are investigations of the materials and processes of writing, with both Jonson and Cavendish drawing widely on their reading yet developing a strong personal ethos and poetics. Central to this project, for both writers, is the question of originality—encompassing both originality as ownership and as singularity. The full title of Jonson's work is *Timber, or Discoveries Made upon men and matter: as they have flow'd out of his daily Readings; or had their refluxe to his peculiar Notion of the Times*, and we can see here that Jonson combines images of flow and flux, natural or organic movement of ideas, with his learning. For Cavendish, this would be a contradiction in terms. Thoughts "flow" only from her own mind, not from the forced and dusty recesses of educated men's minds:

> Scholars are never good poets, for they incorporate too much into other men, which makes them become less themselves, in which great scholars are metamorphosed or transmigrated into as many several shapes, as they read authors, which makes them monstrous, and their head is nothing but a lumber stuffed with old commodities, so it is worse to be a learned poet then a poet unlearned, but that which makes a good poet, is that which makes a good privy councillor, which is, observation, and experience, got by time and company.[39]

This essay, "Great scholars are not excellent poets", is a rebuttal of the learned texture of Jonson's style in *Timber*. Her "lumber" both aurally and semantically evokes "timber". The idea of "commodities" also engages with Jonson's central metaphor of reading and learning as "furniture". Jonson had chosen as epigraph to *Timber* a quotation from Persius's fourth *Satire*, "Tecum habita, ut noris quam sit tibi curt supellex", or, "Live with yourself, and get to know how poor your furniture is".[40] Hutson explains that *supellex*, the Latin word for furniture "positioned so prominently in this book on ethics and imitation, is one that has an important role in the history of the ethics and poetics of imitation for Christian humanists", and also an important concept for Jonson in particular as he writes about how to cultivate "critical independence of mind".[41] Cavendish, though far more well-read than she claims of course, developed a quite extreme poetics of unlearned originality, and the idea of borrowing others' furniture becomes "stuf[fing]" your head with "old commodities".

Jonson's epigraph from Persius also suggests, as so often, a gendered and even sexualized image to his metaphor for thought. In the motto "Live with yourself, and get to know how poor [or short] your furniture is", *supellex* (here, "furniture") could also be read as "sexual equipment".[42] If one's furniture is curt or short, this can also have the meaning of "gelded". Indeed, Jonson's theory of style is permeated with gendered and sexual metaphors, as we saw in

Chapter 1. In *Timber*, Jonson draws on Roman and early modern sources, yet creates an anxiously gendered poetics all his own:

> Others that in composition are nothing but what is rough and broken [...] They would not have it run without rubs, as if that style were more strong and manly, that struck the ear with a kind of unevenness. [They] are like men that affect a fashion by themselves, have some singularity in a ruff, cloak, or hatband, or their beards specially cut to provoke beholders and set a mark upon themselves. [...] And this vice, one that is in authority with the rest, loving, delivers over to them to be imitated; so that oft-times the faults which he fell into, the others seek for: this is the danger, when vice becomes a precedent.[43]

This passage has many gendered and sexualized images of language, most prominently the effeminacy and falsity of men who are over-interested in fashion, or who put on masculinity as an affectation or fashion, rather than embodying it fully in Jonson's ideal form. Cavendish responded closely to this passage in *The Worlds Olio*. She too describes writing as texture (whether aural or tactile), and clothing as a metaphor for identity, affectation, and inauthenticity:

> I desire those that will read this book, to read every chapter clearly, without long stops and stays: for it is with writers as it is with men, whose ill-affected fashion or garb, takes away the natural and graceful form of the person. To read lamely or crookedly, and not evenly, smoothly, and thoroughly, ensnarl the sense. Nay, the very sound of the voice will seem to alter the sense of the theme; and though the sense will be there in despite of the ill voice, or ill reading; yet it will be concealed, or discovered to its disadvantage. [...] So that writings sound good or bad, as the readers, and not as their authors are [...][44]

Both passages use metaphors of sound and touch for style, from Jonson's "rough and broken" style to Cavendish's imagined "ill voice" which makes a text "sound good or bad". They also use metaphors for the text as body, imagining the text/body's vulnerability or faults as its ill-chosen clothes. Jonson's target here is false manliness: he writes that affectedly rough writing is "like men that affect a fashion by themselves, have some singularity in a ruff, cloak, or hatband, or their beards specially cut to provoke beholders and set a mark upon themselves". Here we see that "singularity", one of originality's precursors, is desirable, but risky: those who seek it most assiduously are perhaps the least likely to achieve it. Cavendish's use of clothing metaphors is less clearly masculine or feminine, but instead the "ill-affected fashion or garb" which "takes away the natural and graceful form of the person". While Jonson sees these problems as inherent in certain styles of writing, however, Cavendish focuses on the possible future reading of a work. She transposes embodied metaphors of style from writing to reading, protecting her work from criticism by projecting any misreading onto the reader.

Despite the many differences between Jonson and Cavendish, here we see a shared object of censure: forced singularity. Both criticize a style that is not authentically original or inventive but an imitation of a standard of which it falls short. Jonson's remedy is what Hutson calls his "allusive plain style", a professed simplicity and honesty lying on top of a delicate tissue of quotation and allusion, identifiable to the fit (erudite, educated) reader.[45] Cavendish's solution instead is a poetics of nature, firstness, a rejection of classical learning on which Jonson's is founded. She rejects her peers who have

> an obstinate belief, that none but the ancients were masters of knowledge, and their works the only guides of truth, which is as ridiculous, as to think that Nature cannot or will not make any thing equal to her former works[46]

She rejects those learned writers whose heads are "stuffed with old commodities". At this very moment of rejecting his allusive style, though, Cavendish may be drawing on Jonson himself. He wrote in *Timber*:

> I cannot think Nature is so spent, and decayed, that she can bring forth nothing worth her former years. She is always the same, like herself: and when she collects her strength, is abler still. Men are decayed, and studies: she is not[47]

In the late nineteenth century, the poet-critic Algernon Swinburne said of this last line "Jonson never wrote a finer verse than that; and very probably he never observed that it was a verse".[48] Jonson's reputation was quite mixed at this time, and Swinburne's comment is itself curiously balanced between praise and scorn ("probably he never observed that it was a verse"). As we have seen, the idea that Nature herself is always generative is central to Cavendish's own poetics. And indeed two hundred years before Swinburne's comment about this line in Jonson, Cavendish had evoked it in *The Worlds Olio* where, as we saw, she writes that the idea of ancient authors' superiority to modern ones, is "as ridiculous, as to think that Nature cannot or will not make any thing equal to her former works".[49] This is a delicately double-edged allusion as Cavendish borrows Jonson's formulation and turns it back on him: for her, nature's endless novelty and generativity is used to topple ancient learning. Literature is as new and rich as nature, and we should not cede "master[y]" to the ancients. Cavendish's principle of change in nature is often a rebuttal of excessive learning. By depicting access to classical and institutional learning as in fact a burden, she clears a space for women to be original.

Both *Timber* and *The Worlds Olio* balance claims of novelty and of authority. For Cavendish these two principles are inherently combined: her novelty *is* her authority); for Jonson the latter is more connected to his ownership of the classical past. Cavendish's concept of originality is developed in dialogue with others. She rejected Jonson's elaborate tissue of allusion, his concept of the furnishings of the mind, and adapted his elusively disingenuous claims of plain style. As this suggests, Cavendish's engagement with Jonson was not solely one of antagonism—although there was plenty of that. It was also one of shared critical interests (false singularity or forced style) and metaphors (musical performance and clothing as analogies for writing and reading) as well as fundamental disagreement over the appropriate furniture or timber which "stuff" an unoriginal writer's head (in Cavendish's terms). Jonson was a crucial interlocutor as Cavendish developed her own influential poetics of feminized originality.

Original Change: Margaret Cavendish and Ovid

Cavendish's originality, then, often includes a rejection of the classical past. But there is one classical author who Cavendish claims as a collaborator in forging a natural, original poetics: Ovid.[50] In the hands of Cavendish, Ovid comes to represent naturalness, change, and variety. Moreover, Ovid becomes a key figure of feminine originality. "The Purchase of Poets", published in her first collection, *Poems, and Fancies* (1653), is a playful and satirical poem in which Cavendish brings classical poets to life. She sets up the witty premise that male poets want to buy Parnassus Hill and Helicon, the fountain of inspiration and source of originality:

> A company of poets strove to buy
> Parnassus Hill, upon which Fame doth lie:
> And Helicon, a well that runs below,
> Of which all those that drink, straight poets grow.[51]

In Cavendish's poem, the female figure of Fame, who owns Helicon, tells the poets that whoever can prove he has most wit can live with her. The poets "did dispute, which should Fame's husband be", competing over possession of her and therefore the well of inspiration, Helicon. As David Quint has shown, the idea of the source, deriving from Virgil and Plato, was in many ways the ultimate early modern metaphor for originality.[52] Cavendish's poem is a typically irreverent version of the myth of Heliconian inspiration and its fortunate inheritors. She satirizes an instrumental view of literature (with terms such as "company", "purchase") as the poets have to prove their worth, vying for cultural capital: "Then go you down, and get what friends you can, / That will be bound, or plead for every man". So the rival poets call in the debt of fame that their literary creations owe them: "Poets, which epitaphs o'th'dead had made, / Their ghosts did rise, and would Fair Fame persuade".

Cavendish's poem is itself original; it also explores the very concept of originality. Specifically, she satirizes male poets who act as if they can purchase the source of Heliconian originality. Putting poets literally in competition, Cavendish shows how mercenary they are, displaying misogyny and territoriality in competition for Fame's land and her virginity. Homer chooses his greatest hero to advocate for him:

> Then wise Ulysses in a rhet'ric style
> Began his speech, his tongue was smooth as oil;
> He bowed his head, and thus to Fame did speak:
> I come to plead, although my wit is weak [...]
> But since my cause is just, and truth my guide,
> The way is plain, I shall not err aside
>
> ("PURCHASE", LL. 65–70)

Cavendish here satirizes the adoption of plain style as a claim for honesty, perhaps even with Jonson's persona from *Timber* in mind. She undercuts the claim for plain-speaking, showing that the modesty of "my wit is weak" and the finely balanced syntax and reassuring monosyllables of "But since my cause is just, and truth my guide, / The way is plain, I shall not err aside" are as oily-tongued and rhetorical as any more overtly ornamental style. Plainness and modesty are styles adopted by smooth-tongued rhetoricians, and here Cavendish pre-empts most instances of the phrase "oily tongued" by a hundred years.[53] Overpowered by Ulysses's Homeric rhetoric, Fame is silenced, and the poem ends:

> In measure and in time they danced about,
> Each in their turn the Muses nine took out,

In numbers smooth did run their nimble feet,
Whilst music played, and songs were sun most sweet.
At last the bride, and bridegroom went to bed,
And there did Homer get Fame's maidenhead.

("PURCHASE", LL. 129-34)

The final lines of the poem move from the metaphorical bodies of poetry, dancing in "measure" and "numbers", to real gendered bodies of Homer and Fame as Homer's victory is one of sordid transaction and sexual conquest. In this abrupt and jarring final line, we see classical authors not as austere or inspiring, but as competitive and rapacious: "there did Homer get Fame's maidenhead". Competition for poetic originality becomes one over land (Helicon) and then one over the female body (Fame's maidenhead).

Lara Dodds has interpreted Cavendish's attitude to her literary influences through Sianne Ngai's framework of ugly feelings, especially envy and resentment, which (in Ngai's formulation) can be politically constructive as well as damaging.[54] I have shown that in "The Purchase of Poets" Cavendish projects these ugly feelings onto Homer, Ovid and Virgil. Instead of a lineage of great writers, we see a squabbling marketplace of male egos. But alongside this narrative excluding women, Cavendish also appropriates one particular poet for a feminine tradition: Ovid. As each poet chooses a fictional or historical character to speak on their behalf, Pythagoras advocates for Ovid:

Pythagoras for Ovid thought it meet
To speak, whose numbers smooth, and words were sweet.
Ladies, said he, are for varieties,
And change as oft, as he makes beasts, birds, and trees:
As many several shapes, and forms they take,
Some goddesses, and some do devils make.
Then let fair Fame sweet Ovid's lady be,
Since change doth please that sex, none's fit but he.

("PURCHASE", LL. 51-58)

Cavendish draws on Pythagoras's speech about transformation in Book XV of *Metamorphoses*, including eternal flux, spontaneous generation (frogs born from mud, for instance), the moon's waning and waxing, the flowing of rivers and time. She characterizes Ovid as a poet of change. Cavendish then makes an unusual critical move: she reads his poetics as intrinsically feminine. Ovid's Pythagoras draws on both male and female examples of changeability in his extraordinary speech. Cavendish adapts this into a semi-ironic celebration of feminine changeability. When Pythagoras says "Since change doth please that sex", Cavendish is putting in his mouth a standard misogynistic connection between women and changeability. This often manifested in accusations of fickleness and sexual betrayal, as Shakespeare also invokes in Sonnet 20 "A woman's gentle heart, but not acquainted / With shifting change as is false women's fashion".

Cavendish co-opts misogynistic charges of female malleability and redescribes these as an Ovidian poetics of change; at the same time, she redescribes Ovid as feminine: "Since change doth please that sex, none's fit but he". Cavendish uses similar techniques of paradiastole (rhetorical redescription) elsewhere in her arguments for female creativity. In one of the prefaces to her first work, *Poems and Fancies*, addressed "To all Noble, and Worthy Ladies", she argued that

> Poetry, which is built upon fancy, women may claim, as a work belonging most properly to themselves: for I have observed, that their brains work usually in a fantastical motion: as in their several, and various dresses, in their many and singular choices of clothes, and ribbons, and the like; in their curious shadowing, and mixing of colours, in their wrought works, and divers sorts of stitches they employ their needle, and many curious things they make, as flowers, boxes, baskets with beads, shells, silk, straw or anything else.
>
> (SIG. A3R)

Cavendish embraces the charges of women as vain and fanciful, transforming these into a logical argument for a women's poetics: one of imagination and craft. Elsewhere, she adopts the common analogy of textiles and texts, defending poetry as a female art because it is "spinning with the brain" with the image of Arachne behind it (sig. A2r). Here Cavendish twists images of domesticity and exclusion, and turns them into an argument for the opposite: women are distinctively suited to works of creation and craft including poetry. Similarly in "The Purchase of Poets", she co-opts misogynistic accusations of women's changeability and fickleness, and makes these into an Ovidian metamorphic poetics.

Cavendish's portrayal of Ovid points to a central principle of her poetics: creative changeability. The female figure of Nature who presides over her poems is defined by her power of change. As Debapriya Sarkar argues, "Cavendish refuses to accept the commonplace that women's propensity to change is a liability. Instead, she perceives it as the vital ingredient that makes possible female writers' organic connection to Nature's infinite variety".[55] In Cavendish's collection *The Worlds Olio*, an essay is devoted to "Change in Nature". This in turn is connected to the human brain: "Nature hath not only made bodies changeable, but minds; so to have a constant mind, is to be unnatural".[56] Cavendish's principle of change in nature is often harnessed to rebut excessive learning. Nature's power to change and create is an alternative image of poetry to imitation of the classics, and one which Cavendish calls upon as feminine. Here we can see Cavendish's developing idea of originality, not as a fixed pattern or exemplar (she eschews catalogues of exemplary women, positioning only herself as an "Original") but in terms of natural, changing, self-generating newness.

Cavendish characterizes herself as a "child of Nature", a phrase she also uses elsewhere to describe "wit".[57] As a self-description, this comes in a remarkable passage, veering between self-assertion and doubt, as she overemphatically claims that she is a "Legitimate Poetical Child of Nature". She adds "although but a brownet". "Brownet" is an earlier form of the French borrowing "brunette", and it is characteristic of Cavendish's claims not to know other languages that she adopts the word but Anglicizes it.[58] Her implication here that dark hair might compromise her lineage from Nature adds a potentially racialized image to her claim for legitimacy, or at least one bound up with fairness as both an aesthetic ideal and a superior form of "naturalness".[59] As Jessie Hock argues in her brilliant reading of women and Lucretian poetics, Cavendish uses such self-representations to stress her own singularity and also "establish her as part of a class of natural poets". The ultimate predecessor of this class of poets is Ovid, who she calls "Nature's favourite".[60] She extends this category to Shakespeare, whose natural poetics she pits against Jonson's erudition, describing Shakespeare as "a natural orator, as well as a natural poet".[61] Here Cavendish is an early precursor to the view that developed in the eighteenth century of Shakespeare's superiority to Jonson, as articulated by Edward Young a hundred years later: "Jonson, in the serious drama, is as much an Imitator, as Shakespeare is an Original".[62] Cavendish also—in "the first critical essay ever to be published on Shakespeare"—depicts Shakespeare as a shape-shifter, like Ovid, and indeed a gender-shifter.[63] Shakespeare, she says, can be seemingly "Metamorphosed from a Man to a Woman". Ovid, we recall, in "The Purchase of Poets",

[...] makes beasts, birds, and trees:
As many several shapes, and forms they take,
Some goddesses, and some do devils make.

("PURCHASE", LL. 54–56)

Cavendish was ahead of her time in theorizing Ovid in this way.[64] Dryden admires Ovid's ability to depict "Nature in disorder",[65] Abraham Cowley evokes Ovid in some really complex gendered ways, through a profound interest in female biology and medicine, including women's physical transformative processes including menstruation, childbirth, and breastmilk.[66] But over a decade earlier, Cavendish was pioneering in her characterization of Ovid as a gendered poet of change, or even a poet of gendered change.[67] She is a precursor to twenty-first century understandings of Ovid as a poet for whom "the female body; indeed, its very porousness and permeability, its capacity for mutation and multiplication, make it stand for the very principle of transformation itself."[68]

Ovid is a crucial element of Cavendish's formulation of female creativity. Characterizing his as a poetics of change, nature, and femininity, she claims his legacy for women poets. She reclaims gendered fickleness or malleability as a poetics of metamorphosis. Moreover, Cavendish's reading of Ovid is itself a rich and important act of literary criticism; she was writing a decade before Cowley drew attention to Ovid's feminine poetics of change, and Dryden's depiction of Ovid as the poet of "Nature in disorder". For Cavendish, imitating Ovid is in fact a potent claim of originality and a profoundly gendered one.

Divine Originality: Lucy Hutchinson

"Original" was one of Lucy Hutchinson's favorite words. She uses it 24 times in her authoritative translation of Lucretius's *De rerum natura*.[69] Her editors David Norbrook and Reid Barbour comment that as well as choosing it to render Lucretius's *primordia rerum*, it is "elsewhere a favourite term"; and that, it recurs "throughout her later writings with a wide range of meanings beyond the atomic".[70] Do these usages have anything to do with literary originality? It might seem not: Hutchinson uses "original" as a noun, in keeping with most seventeenth-century usage. She uses it to refer to original texts (that are then translated or copied) and, most of all, the origins of the world. In this sense, it is for her an existential word: she uses it to define her writing identity and women's desire for access to knowledge. It is also, I argue, central to a developing sense of literary originality. Hutchinson's frequent and multivalent usages suggest that women claimed proximity to the divine as a form of intellectual, moral, and poetic originality in this period.

In the mid- to late- seventeenth century, Hutchinson wrote two finely crafted statements of her intent as a poet, and of the purpose and responsibility of poetry far more broadly. These were the preface to her Genesis poem, *Order and Disorder*, and the dedication to her translation of Lucretius's *De rerum natura*. These poetic works span different periods of Hutchinson's life, which was turbulent in political and personal terms. She probably translated Lucretius in the 1650s, but returned to it in the 1670s, claiming in the dedication to Arthur Annesley, Lord Anglesey, that she had realized a copy of her "wanton dalliance" with the godless Lucretius was circulating and that she wanted to distance herself from it. Several critics have commented on the multivalent effect of disowning a radical text by circulating a presentation copy of that text. Jake Arthur has even argued that Hutchinson actively intended this copy for publication.[71] In between her translating and apparently disowning Lucretius, Hutchinson composed several political, theological, and lyrical works, including *Order and Disorder*, which combines all these modes. Written in the 1660s, and partially printed in 1679, this long Genesis poem also spans different points in Hutchinson's career. Part of it was repurposed as one of Hutchinson's elegies on the death of her husband, a republican and regicide who died in prison after the Restoration. As this repurposing suggests, *Order and Disorder* (like Milton's biblical epic) opens itself to political as well as theological interpretation. Despite their obvious differences, critics have also revealed the connections between these two apparently opposed works, in imagery, politics, and materialist philosophy.[72]

The language in which Hutchinson connected these two major poetic works was one of origins: she describes *Order and Disorder* and *De rerum natura* as competing accounts of "the original of things".[73] In the dedication to her Lucretius translation, claiming her regret at the translation circulating, she describes Lucretius as "this lunatic, who not able to dive into the true original and cause of beings and accidents, admires them who devised this casual, irrational dance of atoms".[74] Atomism is an alternative account to the "true original" of the Bible. In the preface to the published part of *Order and Disorder* (1679), Hutchinson explains:

> These meditations were not at first designed for public view, but fixed upon to reclaim a busy roving thought from wandering in the pernicious and

perplexed maze of human inventions; whereinto the vain curiosity of youth had drawn me to consider and translate the account some old poets and philosophers give of the original of things: which though I found it blasphemously against God, and brutishly below the reason of a man, set forth by some erroneously, imperfectly and uncertainly by the best; yet had it filled my brain with such foolish fancies, that I found it necessary to have recourse to the fountain of Truth, to wash out all ugly wild impressions, and fortify my mind with a strong antidote against all the poison of human wit and wisdom that I had been dabbling withal.[75]

In this origin story, Hutchinson represents herself as drawn by curiosity to translate Lucretius's account of "the original of things", and then drawn by piety to "wash out" this poison with the "fountain of Truth", Genesis. In highly-wrought prose, she pits two sources against each other, each with a liquid metaphor: the poison of Lucretius and the fountain of the Bible. As we have seen, springs and fountains were prominent metaphors for literary origins, and as sources of poetic originality. And Hutchinson goes on to make explicit her connection between sacred and profane (water) sources:

> Lest that arrive by misadventure, which never shall by my consent, that any of the puddled water my wanton youth drew from the profane Helicon of ancient poets should be sprinkled about the world, I have for prevention sent forth this essay; with a profession that I disclaim all doctrines of God and his works, but what I learnt out of his own word, and have experienced it to be a very unsafe and unprofitable thing for those that are young, before their faith be fixed, to exercise themselves in the study of vain, foolish, atheistical poesy. (p. 296)

Hutchinson imagines Lucretian poetry as water from Helicon, in contrast to the fountain of Truth. In her dedication to the Lucretius translation, in which Hutchinson claims to distance herself from this work, she criticizes tutors and poets who praise pagan poetry, saying that "they puddle all the streams of Truth, that flow down to them from divine Grace, with this Pagan mud".[76] In suggesting that the fountain of truth is dirtied with the mud of paganism, Hutchinson castigates herself, as a translator of pagan philosophy, but she also has other Lucretian poets in her sights. Further, Hutchinson wishes to "warn incautious travellers", like a "seamark", that "the Muses' groves, are enchanted thickets". She uses the verb "tipple at", meaning to drink alcohol and also to squander, to characterize how writers fill themselves with poison, "drowning their spirits in those puddled waters, and neglecting that healing spring of Truth".⁷⁷ Again, reiterating the message and the metaphors of her preface to *Order and Disorder*, Hutchinson imagines these two accounts of origins as water sources: Helicon v. the spring of Truth.

With the evocative "tipple at their celebrated Helicon", Hutchinson imagines contemporary poets drinking intoxicating liquor from Helicon, while also squandering their talents. Like Margaret Cavendish in "The Purchase of Poets", Hutchinson is also critical of poets who claim Heliconian inspiration. Both women, for very different reasons, hold to account contemporary poets who emulate ancient models. For Hutchinson, this is because modern poets should be better equipped with Christian resistance to paganism or atheism than Lucretius; for Cavendish this is because of contemporary male poets' competitive, territorial, and predatory attitude to poetry and their poetic inheritance. Hutchinson has masculine hubris in her sights, too: her opening line takes aim at John Evelyn (without naming him), as "a masculine Wit [who] hath thought it worth printing his head in a laurel crown for the version of one of these books" (p. 5), while she herself translated all six. In fact, despite their very different attitudes to biblical verse and authority, Hutchinson and Cavendish claim access to the source in some surprisingly similar language. Cavendish writes that in difficult times in her writing career "I strove to turn the stream, yet shunning the muddy, and foul ways of vice, I went to the well of Helicon, and by the well's side, I have sat and wrote this work" (*The Worlds Olio*, sig. A7r–v). While Cavendish rejects vice in favor of Helicon, and Hutchinson rejects Helicon in favor of the divine "fountain of Truth", both claim moral and poetic authority from their access to the original or source. Reflecting on her own experience (however artfully), Hutchinson regrets that

> It is a misery I cannot but bewail, that when we are young, whereas the lovely characters of Truth should be impressed upon the tender mind and memory, they are so filled up with ridiculous lies, that 'tis the greatest business of our lives, as soon as ever we come to be serious, to cleanse out all the rubbish our grave tutors laid in when they taught us to study and admire their inspired poets and divine philosophers. (p. 297)

In Hutchinson's powerful phrase, "the rubbish our grave tutors laid in", the verb "laid in" could be transitive or intransitive: the tutors lie in rubbish (wallowing in it); they also lay rubbish in the minds of their pupils (like textiles in a chest). This striking rejection recalls Cavendish on learned men's brains as "lumber stuffed with old commodities" (*The Worlds Olio*, p. 5).

explicitly refuses the possibility that she will have any kind of successors or tradition to follow her:

> you are the first great lady, that ever wrote so much and so much of your own: and, for ought we can divine, you will also be the last. (*Letters and Poems*, pp. 117–8)

This is a trope which Charleton returns to again and again, elaborately repeating the idea that Cavendish was an innovator, but also inimitable, a dead end: "You have indeed, given the world an illustrious example; but you have given what it cannot take, the Example being of that height, that it is hardly attainable" (116–7). And, as we saw earlier, when he writes this "as you have made your self an original, so are you likewise secure from being copied", he seems to borrow from Mary Evelyn's acerbic insult: "[I hope that as she] is an original, she may never have a copy".[81] The proximity of Charleton's apparent flattery to Mary Evelyn's directly insulting use of this formulation shows up the double edge of his praise.

This chapter started with Jeff Dolven's paradoxical formulation of style, as something both unique and imitable. Colin Burrow sees something similar in Ben Jonson, whose knowledge of the history of imitation "enabled him to imitate not just poems but styles, and to make in the process a style which was itself imitable".[82] Originality in its modern sense works rather like this too: once a writer is original, their style can be copied; or perhaps, once their style has been copied, we can see what is original about them. And it is the futurity, the lineage, the openness to imitation, that writers like Charleton were so keen to prevent in women writers. While this is most obvious in responses to Cavendish (they tell her, you "may never have a copy"; "you will also be the *last*"), indeed many women writers were seen as exceptional in the senses both of without precedent *and* without successor: matchless, peerless, anomalous. To be both original and influential has been a privilege accorded largely to early modern men. But women writers themselves appropriated this language into one of originality, and the ideas of Cavendish, Bradstreet, Southwell and other seventeenth-century women poets changed the course of literary history.

The seventeenth century saw the word "original" transform from being literal (a source, more often a noun) to stylistic (an original poetic style, more often an adjective): from origin to original. Women were at the forefront of this development; propelled into the vocabulary of originality through double-edged praise of their anomalousness, they embraced the concept and forged influential aspects of literary originality. Colin Burrow sees Milton as a midpoint in his history of imitation; David Quint sees Milton more as an endpoint in his of originality.[83] This chapter has suggested a different "seamark" (Lucy Hutchinson's term) to Milton, that of women poets including Southwell, Bradstreet, Cavendish, and Hutchinson. Cavendish's focus on nature as the source of inspiration has both Renaissance precursors and Romantic successors; her use of nature as a particularly female source of originality, in distinction to male brains "stuffed with old commodities", is her own intervention in mid-century poetics. She brings Ovid to this debate in what is itself a very original literary critical interpretation, seeing him as a feminine poet of change and transformation. The poem in which she articulates this view, "The Purchase of Poets", is itself an original and wittily acerbic takedown of male literary claims to originality from the classical spring of Helicon.

For Lucy Hutchinson, the term "original" has a very different sense: she uses it repeatedly to discuss the beginnings of the world, theological debate and rival accounts, especially those within her own oeuvre, between her Lucretius translation and her Genesis poem. For her too, though, the concept of originality is a gendered issue: she wishes to learn from God's "own words" and to "to understand"—and herself write about—things she had "heard so much discourse of at second hand". Originality is connected to a desire for unmediated access: to the Bible, to Latin philosophy, to literary history and the classical past. Formulations of the term and concept of originality by women have implications for our sense of the development of literary criticism and of periodization, pre-empting many eighteenth-century concepts of originality which are later tied by men to both naturalness and ownership (through copyright). To return to Kunjummen's argument with which I opened: "Male authors have been read as agents of historical change more regularly than their female counterparts". Or, to put it another way, women were original before men were.

4

Irregular

It will be seen that the 18th line has only eight syllables. This frequently occurs throughout the poem. Perhaps her children happened at such times to be making a noise and so caused her to miscount "the threads of the canvas" and consequently "the syllables of her translation."

—HUGH MUNRO, ON LUCY HUTCHINSON'S
LUCRETIUS TRANSLATION (1858)[1]

I am sick of hearing of the sublimity of Milton

—MARY WOLLSTONECRAFT,
THOUGHTS ON THE EDUCATION OF DAUGHTERS (1797)[2]

[...] she had the happiness, in her composures, to avoid the two extremes, either of uncorrect looseness in her style, or starched affectation.

—ANONYMOUS, PREFACE TO KATHERINE PHILIPS, POEMS (1667)

IRREGULARITY IS ELUSIVE. None of these epigraphs use the term itself, but they all suggest something about the meaning of poetic irregularity in early modern England, and far beyond. In the preface to her version of Lucretius's *De rerum natura*, Lucy Hutchinson evoked a domestic scene for her radical work of translation. In a finely balanced humility topos, she claimed that she had "turned it into English in a room where my children practised the several qualities they were taught, with their tutors, and I numbered the syllables of my translation by the threads of the canvas I wrought in".[3] Some two hundred years later, Hugh Munro (who elsewhere praises Hutchinson for her integrity, skill, and concision) noticed prosodic irregularities in her translation, commenting that lines "frequently" do not conform to iambic pentameter's ten syllables.[4] For explanation, rather than seeking answers in her style or subject matter, he looked to her life, and specifically the domestic scene that she had evoked in the preface to her translation. He suggested, possibly wryly, that "Perhaps her children happened at such times to be making a noise and so caused her to miscount 'the threads of the canvas' and consequently 'the syllables of her translation'". Munro takes at face value the gesture of sprezzatura in which she claimed to have translated this difficult and radical Latin poem while not only supervising her children's education but also working on a piece of needlework. Mary Wollstonecraft's exclamation responds to an entirely opposite way of reading: that of many readers who have identified in Milton's poetry not loose threads and the distractions of childcare, but sublimity. Wollstonecraft is exasperated with hearing of Milton's sublime poetics. I simplify here, of course: Milton's verse is, by various seventeenth- and eighteenth-century definitions, sublime, and it is not only any perceived irregularity which makes it so. Prosody is fundamental to David Norbrook's conception of Milton's republican sublime, but we cannot be sure whether Wollstonecraft was thinking of his prosody, or imagery, or other senses of the sublime.[5] We might note, though, that Wollstonecraft's peer Edmund Burke aligned his famously gendered concept of sublimity with irregularity—not necessarily of poetic form, but an important yoking of these terms: "Sublime objects are vast in their dimensions, beautiful ones comparatively small; beauty should be smooth, and polished; the great, rugged and negligent".[6] So while we cannot be absolutely sure what kind of sublimity Wollstonecraft has had enough of, her exasperation speaks to the assumptions that underlie gendered habits of reading: that men are more likely to be sublime while women are "loose", whether through distraction, incompetence, or immorality. And so, in the third epigraph here, the preface to the posthumous edition of Katherine Philips's poems situates her as the ideal mean between aesthetic extremes of "uncorrect looseness" or "starched affectation". The terms here suggest a certain gendered charge, through the connections of "looseness" to morality and propriety (always more charged for women), and the laundry connotations of "starch". But what exactly are these extremes, who defines them, and according to which standards of writing or behaviour?

How irregular was a female poet permitted to be? This chapter will explore both early modern writing *about* women's irregularity, and women writers' actual use of irregularity in their poems. The rich history of women poets' use of formal irregularity ranges from local moments of metrical disruption to wider patterns of usage, and genres such as the "irregular ode". It is also a history of reception and definition or, rather, a history of reading. How have readers perceived male and female poets' irregular forms, both in the early modern period and the contemporary? Do critics read male and female poets' meter differently? The history of the term irregularity and its practice spans both aesthetics and ideology, and it is only by exploring the interaction of these ways of reading that we can understand this complex term and its enduring role in defining which—and whose—poems are valued.

"Irregular", "uneven", and "loose" were all used to describe poetic style in the early modern period. They were also all used for morality and behaviour, specifically, moral disorder, as in Mary Chudleigh's description of "irregular passions".[7] And, indeed, these usages of the words often overlapped, irregular forms of literacy or style were connected to moral value or behaviour. William Davenant characterized English drama as "a regular species" that he wished to emulate, and described the experience of having both "friends" and "books" "regulate" his imagination, and "make them more correct, easie, and apparent".[8] Turning to the negative, John Harington describes as *"loose"* an "unattentive" reader, one who is not closely enough tied to the text to follow it well.[9] Aphra Behn writes of "loose and gross Imagination", specifically that of her critics who create fault in her works if they find none.[10]

Irregular was used in grammatical and formal senses, for shapes and architecture as well as for language and poetic style. The medieval period saw discussions of transgressive sex and sexual identity being compared to irregular grammar.[11] By the eighteenth century—and possibly earlier—"regular" was being used to describe bodily regularity such as bowel movement and menstruation (OED 4c and d). The seventeenth century saw a shift from referring to menstruation as "flowers" (derived from a horticultural maxim about flowers coming before fruit) to terms which defined menstruation by its regularity: courses, terms, period, "menstruation".[12] To be regular in the seventeenth century could also mean to be ruled by someone else. In *An English Expositor* (1616), John Bullokar glossed regular as "under rule, or living according to a set rule". Irregularity and regularity, then, and their many overlapping terms, have meanings which move easily between the aesthetic, linguistic, moral, and corporeal: regular meter; well-regulated behaviour; regular bodily functions. And the regulations being enforced or deviated from are often explicitly or implicitly gendered.

The characterization of certain aspects of form as externally imposed restrictions is, though, one which has indisputably endured into modern sensibilities.[13] Some fifty years ago, Rosalie Colie expressed the widespread assumption that literary forms were "brands of an unimaginative establishmentarianism, or (at their worst) self-made prisons in which we acquiesce".[14] Simultaneously, critics have drawn attention to the way poets have found "that not only the adoption of formal constraints but the presentation of psychological constraints has been peculiarly and continuously empowering for poets".[15] Andrea Brady has cautioned critics against accepting such statements without considering their ethical stakes. When many suffer the realities of actual enslavement and constraint: "being able to take a category as metaphor (often for poetic productivity)—whether it is gender, race or bondage itself—is often an outcome of particular forms of privilege".[16] Brady argues powerfully that metaphors of bondage are complicit in literal bondage: by using bondage and constraint as metaphors, writers risk erasing the suffering of those who are literally bonded and constrained. By relishing the paradoxical metaphor of constraint as possibility and bondage as freedom, poets from Thomas Wyatt to John Milton to Emily Dickinson have effaced actual exploitation and oppression. Milton's note "On the Verse", added to the 1668 edition of *Paradise Lost*, has long been central to these debates, as it established the connection between form and politics in explicit terms. Specifically associating regular rhyme with political constraint, Milton famously eschewed the "modern bondage" of rhyme.

The poetic-critical texts on rhyme and constraint around Milton's *Paradise Lost* also reveals aspects of rhyme and regularity that were bound up with gender in the period. In *Paradise Lost*, when Raphael tells Adam about the Son of God, Milton uses the term "irregular" in a very striking sense

> That day, as other solemn days, they spent
> In song and dance about the sacred hill,
> Mystical dance, which yonder starry sphere
> Of planets and of fixed in all her wheels
> Resembles nearest, mazes intricate,
> Eccentric, intervolved, yet regular
> Then most, when most irregular they seem:
> And in their motions harmony divine
> So smooths her charming tones, that God's own ear
> Listens delighted.[17]

Milton is using "eccentric", "charming", and "fixed" to represent surprising planetary orbits and the music of the spheres but these can also be read as analogues of his prosody, refusing the obvious patterning of rhyme. This gorgeous passage imagines that the divine workings of the universe are like a maze or a dance. These movements of the planets and stars might seem "Eccentric, intervolved" from nearby, but with a cosmic viewpoint they have a clear pattern. The verb "intervolve" is rare; Milton either coined it or was a rare user of it (the next usage in OED is 150 years later). And here the elements that are intervolved are regularity and irregularity: one enfolded within the other. Milton's divine harmony is a nest of unimaginable mazes which are "regular [. . .] most when most irregular they seem". And Milton presents this regular irregularity as feminine. It is "harmony divine" who "smooths *her* charming tones." The iambic regularity here of "So smooths her charming tones, that God's own ear" breaks into the metrically irregular yet semantically pleasing conclusion of the sentence with "Listens delighted".

A decade later, Nathaniel Lee wrote a poem to accompany Dryden's *The State of Innocence and Fall of Man,* his rhymed, dramatic adaptation of *Paradise Lost*. Lee praises Dryden's reworking of Milton's raw materials: "For Milton did the Wealthy Mine disclose / And rudely cast what you could well dispose". He then turns to a different set of metaphors, from extraction to a different kind of cultivation, that of feminine style:

> Forgive me, awful poet, if a muse,
> Whom artless nature did for plainness choose,
> In loose attire presents her humble thought,
> Of this best poem, that you ever wrought.[18]

Milton's prosody is represented here as "loose attire", with loose an adjective often used for poetic irregularity, as well as clothing. It is also a term, as we have seen, used for morality, and for (lack of) regulation in social and emotional terms, and therefore one that can have a gendered charge. And indeed Lee imagines Milton's "loose attire" clothing a female body:

> He first beheld the beauteous rustic maid,
> And to a place of strength the prize conveyed;
> You took her thence: to court this virgin brought
> Dressed her with gems, new weaved her hard-spun thought
> And softest language, sweetest manners taught.
>
> ("TO MR. DRYDEN", LL. 18–22)

Lee uses a series of gendered figures to imagine Milton's poem and Dryden's dressing of it: rustic maid, courtly lady. Here Lee uses female figures to represent the styles of both Milton and Lee, evoking other characteristics to distinguish them, particularly class. Milton's irregular poem, in its "loose attire" is a "rustic maid", beautiful but with "hard-spun thought". In his rewriting of *Paradise Lost*, Dryden transforms her through a process of softening, cultivation ("sweetest manners", "taught"), ornamentation ("dressed with gems"). This is a transformation that leans towards eighteenth-century ideals of gendered and poetic decorum, and which Rowan Ricardo Phillips characterises as "frill and code", both ornamental and connoting a strict underlying order.[19]

For Lee, Milton's poem is a "prize" to be carried away to a secure "place of strength" and reformed. The violence underlying this narrative of cultivation suggests that the stakes of irregular or "loose" prosody are those of society and politics as much as aesthetics. (As Chapter 5: Smooth will show, soft and sweet were used to praise and diminish styles perceived as feminine.) Lee's depiction of Dryden cultivating and regulating *Paradise Lost* suggests the interrelation of aesthetic and social regularity: regulating with rhymed couplets is like regulating a woman's "hard spun thoughts" into bejewelled softness, recalling Bullokar's definition of regularity as living "under rule", here that of a male cultivator. Here we might recall the meanings of the term "regular" that are associated with ideas of biological sex explicitly, and the regulation of women's bodies to fulfil expectations that they be "regular" in their biological functions, as well as their moral and social identity.

Milton's and Lee's feminine embodiments of irregularity and poetic form make clear the ubiquity and significance of gender in discussions of poetic regularity. However widespread these feminized emblems of poetic regularity or irregularity, though, there remains a gap in understanding what women themselves thought about them, and how they themselves manipulated and theorized prosody more broadly. Their deployment of strategic irregularity has often been erased or "corrected". Through attending to women's aesthetic effects of irregularity we will explore an implicit theory of irregularity, one that has been masked by critical and editorial judgements of what a women's style should be. I will focus on women poets writing in two very different forms: heroic couplets and irregular odes. The first is defined by its regularity, the other by its irregularity. These very labels show how prosodic or formal labels are often weighted with ideological implications: irregular/regular; closed/open; and heroic. Yet their relation to gender has not so far been explored, and especially not how women writers intervened in debates over regularity.

Lucy Hutchinson's Couplets

In her twinned works of Biblical and philosophical enquiry, *Order and Disorder* and *De rerum natura*, Hutchinson developed strategic irregularity. Her readers not only observed this irregularity, but emended or commented on it in ways which reveals early modern readers' attitudes to female-authored irregularity. The pentameter couplet was a common choice in the seventeenth century for long poetry but not yet the default form. Moreover, scholars have shown the very different styles of couplet writing, from conversational to argumentative, satirical to harmonious.[20] The history of the couplet is bound up with the history of regularity, and both feed into—and are driven by—social and ideological values as well as prosodic ones. When we call a couplet "regular", "heroic", "open", "closed", or "balanced", we draw on a long history of inflecting this flexible form with political, social, and gendered meanings.[21] In the hands of Hutchinson, we can add theological and philosophical inflections. Hutchinson's corpus, rediscovered and illuminated in the last two decades, demonstrates the range and depth of Restoration women writers' use of the long pentameter couplet poem.[22] Yet, I will argue, it also reveals a hidden history of how women's couplets have been read and misread, in the seventeenth century and today.

Hutchinson's major Genesis poem was partially published with the title *Order and Disorder* in 1679, and Hutchinson both practises and theorizes the poem's title terms, order and disorder. It does so through prosody as well as theology. God's ordering of living creation into couples is strikingly emphasized in this couplet poem. God orders the animal kingdom, including man, into pairs and this is represented emphatically as the ordering of "like" elements:

> 'Tis only like desires like things unite:
> In union likeness only feeds delight,

(ORDER AND DISORDER 3., LL. 263–64)

Here Hutchinson uses the couplet structure to reinforce the importance of likeness: sounds and semantic units are echoed across the two lines of the couplet ("only [...] only", "like [...] like [...] likeness", "unite [...] union", "desires [...] delight"), and the colon itself acts as a hinge, uniting the two lines as the latter reiterates and emphasizes the former.

> For the whole world nor order had, nor grace,
> Till severed elements each their own place

> Assignèd were, and while in them they keep
> Heaven still smiles above, th'untroubled deep
> With kind salutes embraces the dry land,
> Firm doth the Earth on its foundation stand,
> A cheerful light streams from the ethereal fire
> And all in universal joy conspire.
> But if with their unlike they attempt to mix,
> Their rude congressions everything unfix;
> Darkness again invades the troubled skies,
> Earth trembling under angry heaven lies;
> The sea, swollen high with rage, comes to the shore
> And swallows that which it but kissed before;
> Th'unbounded fire breaks forth with dreadful light
> And horrid cracks which dying nature fright,
> Till that high Power which all powers regulates
> The disagreeing natures separates,
> The like to like rejoining as before,
> So the world's peace, joy, safety doth restore.
>
> (ORDER AND DISORDER, 3, LL. 265–88)

We see a combination of aural effects here. Hutchinson deploys a bold enjambment in one line ("Till severed elements each their own place / Assignèd were"), running the line on not within the couplet but between non-rhyming lines to dramatic effect. The line which opens the disorder—"But if with their unlike they attempt to mix"—is itself slightly irregular. But when the elements are assigned their place, Hutchinson's couplets are largely end-stopped by punctuation as well as rhythm. Combined with verbs like "rejoin", "assign", "regulate", and "unite", rhyme is used positively to convey the divine nature of God-given order. As God's creation is ordered by providing each creature with a mate, so the poem is ordered by providing each line end with its rhyming pair. And as Julie Crawford has argued, the focus on similarity here can be interpreted in ways beyond the narrative's overt focus on heterosexual mates: "The 'likeness' that queer scholars have noted in *Paradise Lost* certainly animates Hutchinson's account of creation as well".²³ Here Hutchinson's more closed couplets reinforce the sense of union and order in the couples it describes. She does not entirely forego the endstopped couplet for her depiction of disorder, it is true, and I will return to the rhythmic ambiguities of lines such as "A cheerful light streams from the ethereal fire". Though the poem's overall scheme is the regular pentameter couplet, this passage suggests that

Hutchinson's language draws attention to the relationship between her form and her subject matter as she moves between order and disorder. Here we can see that when Hutchinson writes about man's need for a mate before the creation of Eve, the movement from single elements to a conjunction of two is presented as a move from disorder into order.

Order and Disorder is structured according to vacillations between the order and disorder of its title. Hutchinson interprets Genesis as a cyclical narrative of God's goodness followed by man's sinfulness, redeemed by God's goodness, and so forth. As Jonathan Goldberg describes it, the poem's narrative is "the story over and again of the chosen seed, the holy seed, and how it regenerates itself, how these seeds of light separate from the seeds of darkness"[24]. This movement between binaries—held forcefully in tension—drives the narrative rhythm of the poem, and it can be seen to inform the rhythm of individual passages and even lines as well. Hutchinson uses the idea of order very clearly to connote divine control and creation. At the fall, with God seemingly absent, it is His *order* that is dramatically missing:

> And while he seemed withdrawn whose grace upheld
> The order of all things, confusion filled
> The universe. The air became impure,
> And frequent dreadful conflicts did endure
> With every other angry element;
>
> (ORDER AND DISORDER 6., LL. 321–25)

Without the order brought by God's grace, the world is all confusion, impurity and conflict. These lines are metrically regular, yet use the resources of the line to convey the push and pull of order and disorder. The first two lines here, one expressing order, the other disorder, are enjambed in the same way, with the line run on after the verbs: "upheld, "filled". God's grace upholds order against the tide of confusion filling the universe, in an entropic image conveying the ineluctable drive towards disorder. The first use of "disorder", the poem's second title word, happens at the fall, as Hutchinson describes Adam and Eve's changed perception of the world around them; they see it now as "disordered" (*Order and Disorder*, 4, l. 237). Here we can read Hutchinson's practice as theory: her use of terms that signify not only theological but also poetic beliefs signals to readers her strategic manipulation of form for semantic and even devotional purposes. It also, I argue, suggests that we read together her poetic terminology and poetic practice as a form of theory. She reflects on the uses, strengths, and dangers of poetic form in ways which engage contemporary debates around rhyme, constraint, and politics, just as Margaret Cavendish's focus on the concepts of exemplarity and exemption is an intervention in contemporary debates around originality.

Hutchinson's other long poem in iambic pentameter couplets, her translation of Lucretius's *De rerum natura*, has often been seen as *Order and Disorder*'s opposite and also its double (see Chapter 3: Original). This is the impression given by Hutchinson herself, who describes writing *Order and Disorder* as an "antidote" to the pagan impiety of Lucretius, which she refers to as "poison of human wit and wisdom that I had been dabbling withal".[25] It may also show her deploying a distinctively different use of the couplet. Hutchinson's translation of Lucretius is characteristically metrically irregular with one in a hundred lines having either more or fewer than ten syllables.[26] As we saw at the opening to this chapter, the Victorian scholar Hugh Munro was troubled by the frequency of these eight- or twelve-syllable lines, attributing them to Hutchinson's distraction by her children or needlework. Hutchinson had famously claimed of her Luretius translation that she "turned it into English in a room where my children practised the several qualities they were taught, with their tutors, and I numbered the syllables of my translation by the threads of the canvas I wrought in".[27] Early modern women frequently brought together the symbols of needle and pen, whether to contrast or align these creative works, and here Hutchinson deftly diffuses the radicalism of her translation through domesticity.[28] The modesty of her homely scene must also be read as sprezzatura, of a domestic rather than machismo kind. Hutchinson takes the conventional analogy and makes it much more specific and technical: the analogy is not only between pen and needle but between threads and syllables, the particular tools of each artwork which she crafts simultaneously. Yet as we saw in the epigraph to this chapter, Munro picked up Hutchinson's domestic scene and conjectured, seemingly acerbically "Perhaps her children happened at such times to be making a noise and so caused her to miscount 'the threds of the canvas' and consequently 'the sillables of her translation'".[29]

These short and long lines can, though, be read as aesthetically meaningful. The first short line in the whole translation (and one that Munro points out) invites a mimetic argument:

> He by evincing arguments o'erthrows
> Proves that no bounds the world enclose
> That bodies and vacuities confine
> Each other only [...]

(LUCRETIUS, ARGUMENT OF THE FIRST BOOK, LL. 17–20)

The short second line here might reflect ideas of enclosure. A more ingenious—arguably more tenuous—reading might see Hutchinson deploying a short, thus *more* bound, more enclosed, line to articulate Lucretius's rejection of boundaries. Critical debate continues over Hutchinson's relationship to her Latin original. Certainly her later preface, in which she distances herself from the poem while also circulating it, captures her complex attitude to this poem. Critics have argued that she changed her mind about the poem between translating it and writing the dedication; that her distancing dedication was pure feint; that she admired Lucretius's position as a challenge to superstition rather than to religion; that she was drawn to his anti-war position. Most recently, Jessie Hock has argued that Hutchinson was influenced even—or especially—by the lines from Lucretius which she did not include in her translation: "Lucretius's scandalous description of sexual desire (the lines from Book 4 of *De rerum natura* that Hutchinson refuses to translate) is an implicit touchstone for *Order and Disorder*'s account of fallen psychology".[30]

We might see Hutchinson's prosodic irregularity as part of this ambivalent relationship. Is the translator wittily distancing herself from her material, or even undermining Lucretian assertions through her formal choices? As the Oxford edition points out, this line (l. 18 "Proves that no bounds [...]") is in Hutchinson's own hand, so it cannot be put down to the scribal error which may account for some of the long and short lines in the manuscript. Hutchinson elsewhere corrects some lines of irregular length. While this may seem a distinct and even opposite phenomena to her deployment of irregularity, I would suggest that we read the coexistence in her work of irregular lines which she corrects metrically and irregular lines which she lets stand as mutually-reinforcing evidence of the same phenomenon: this is a writing style which is attentive to the effects of prosodic regularity, and which deploys irregularity strategically and artfully. Book 6 of *De rerum natura*, which is transcribed by Hutchinson herself, also includes more of these lines than the other scribal books, again suggesting that Hutchinson herself intended to write these irregular lines, and to keep them in this presentation manuscript. It is possible that she was influenced by John Denham who "consistently imitated" Virgil's incomplete lines in the *Aeneid*, in a translation which we know Hutchinson read (she transcribed it into her notebook) or Cowley's *Davideis*.[31] De Quehen and Norbrook have also argued that Hutchinson's irregularity of line length across the whole work is a stylistic feature which emulates Lucretius's famous roughness and density.[32] Hutchinson's irregularity has been understood differently through the contexts of politics and of shifting taste as she writes against certain kinds of Restoration Augustanism.[33]

Reading these couplets alongside those of *Order and Disorder* also raises the further possibility that Hutchinson was using metrical irregularity to represent a disordered universe. The increased irregularity of the last book might suggest Hutchinson's own increasing anxiety about the poem and desire to distance herself from a worldview which she had come to find "blasphemously against God, and brutishly below the reason of a man".[34] So could the increased irregularity towards the end of the poem suggest the disorder which can only increase in such an ungodly universe? This would be a sort of poetic version of entropy, the law of Physics which dictates that unless there is input of energy, the natural progression of the universe is towards disorder. Reading *De rerum natura* before breakfast one day, Gore Vidal mused that Lucretius "anticipates the second law of thermodynamics, not to mention giddy entropy" in his view of ongoing decay.[35] Neither Lucretius nor Lucy Hutchinson wrote with the benefit of modern Physics, but Hutchinson did come to see *De rerum natura* as the representation of a world in decay. This is also how the world of *Order and Disorder* would be without the Christian God at its centre: God is the force of unity which the ordered couplets of *Order and Disorder* represent. Lucretius's universe lacks that Christian order, representing (in Hutchinson's view) a world of disordered passions. Hutchinson crafts an aesthetics of irregularity to represent Lucretius's "casual, irrational dance of atoms" as opposed to divine fixity portrayed by terms such as "regiment", "design", "upholding ordering and governing", "seamark", "most wise and fixed purpose".[36]

In her preface, as we have seen, Hutchinson casts *Order and Disorder* as a pious "antidote" to her translation of Lucretius.[37] Characterizing *De rerum natura* as the dark double of *Order and Disorder*, she inevitably yokes them together as a pair, and the materialist vocabulary of Lucretius echoes in the Scriptural world of *Order and Disorder*.[38] Critics including Jonathan Goldberg and David Norbrook have shown the connections between *Order and Disorder* and *De rerum natura* as well as their differences.[39] Hutchinson shares Lucretius's hatred of superstition, and borrows some of his materialism for her Genesis poem, as Milton did for his.[40] And, indeed, parallels can be found in her manipulation of the couplet in the two works as well. David Norbrook has argued that Hutchinson "aims at poetic sublimity not through Milton's expansive blank verse but through fluid, open pentameter couplets, the syntax of which is often hard to confine within the boundaries of modern punctuation conventions".[41] We saw this openness in the lines from canto 6 which explore how God upholds order against moral disorder, in which the lines were enjambed not within but between couplets. Hutchinson's couplets in *Order and*

Disorder are not only open but also metrically irregular in a similar way to those of her Lucretius translation. And my investigation of the manuscript and print versions of *Order and Disorder* suggests the possibility of a higher level of irregularity in the poem as Hutchinson composed it.

The manuscript of *Order and Disorder*, now at Yale's Beinecke Library, reveals evidence that Hutchinson's own prosody might originally have been much more irregular than the print and even the manuscript version we now have. The manuscript includes fifteen more cantos than the version of *Order and Disorder* printed in 1679. It is in a notebook which belonged to Anne Wilmot, Countess of Rochester, Lucy Hutchinson's cousin and the mother of John Wilmot, Earl of Rochester. *Order and Disorder* (here simply titled "Genesis") is in two scribal hands and three different hands of readers marking the text can also tentatively be identified. Each of the probably distinct hands on the manuscript correct Hutchinson's meter. Anne Rochester, owner of the manuscript, mostly corrects the poem to be closer to the print version. But this is not the whole story. This hand—probably Anne Rochester—continues correcting the manuscript poem beyond the first five cantos which were printed in 1679, so not all the changes can be explained as an attempt to align the reader's MS with the print edition. What can we deduce about the motivations, or at least effects, of these changes? Some of these changes seem to be metrical corrections, such as this change from "fiery" to "fierce":

In her wild brest, Jacob with a fier~~y~~^ce crie[42]

There are approximately twenty-five revisions which make previously irregular lines into iambic pentameter. Many of these changes involve simply adding or removing single-syllable words or syllables, but some readerly emendations go further by adding or removing a whole foot in order to "correct" what could formerly be read as tetrameters or alexandrines, as in the following example:

As hounds layd on ~~on~~ ^and traind by a fresh sent
The whole troope with unanimous ardour went
~~Glorying~~^Boasting in their great zeale so to exact"

(20. 93–95)

Here a later seventeenth-century reader (perhaps the book's owner Anne Rochester, or perhaps another member of the household) emends two lines. The corrector's agenda seems partly at least to be prosodic regularity, emending "laid on on" to "and trained by" and "glorying" to "boasting". One reader's

> Each man puts on his armes, mounts his swift steed
> And follow's Jacobs track with furious speed,
> As hounds layd on, ~~and~~ and trained by a fresh sent
> The whole troope with unanimous ardor went
> ~~Glorying~~ Boasting in their great zeale so to exact
> A vengeance for the sacrilegious fact

FIGURE 1. Manuscript of Lucy Hutchinson, *Order and Disorder*, Osborn MS fb 100, James Marshall and Marie-Louise Osborn Collection, Beinecke Rare Book and Manuscript Library, Yale University], fol. [320]; lines 20. 93–95

attention to prosody seems to move beyond metrical length to metrical stress, replacing "devout" with "pious" to make a line more iambically regular:

> There Israe-lls ~~devout~~ pious congregations joyn'd
>
> (15. 179)

This reader of the manuscript seems to have seen "pious" as creating a more clearly iambic rhythm. It is possible that the reader preferred "pious" for semantic reasons, but its usage was close enough to "devout" that it seems likely the consideration here was pronunciation and prosody. In the passage on man's need for a mate, we can see Lucretian influence in the terminology, and perhaps also in the form of these lines:

> But if with their unlike they a'ttempt to mix,
> Their rude congressions everything unfix;
>
> (3. 277–278)

Hutchinson is unusual in her use of the term "congressions", here and also several times in her Lucretius translation.[43] In *De rerum natura*, Hutchinson sometimes uses it to translate Lucretius's "congressa" (5. 192). Sometimes she also adds this term to convey the lack of design in the Lucretian universe. For instance in one of her own marginal notes, she glosses Lucretius's account "That the world sprung from the casuall congression of attoms". The word "casual" alongside "congressions" indicates her wariness of Lucretian disorder:

"casual" is an adjective she would deploy distastefully, twice, in the dedication to *Lucretius*.[44] Here in *Order and Disorder* the Lucretian idea of "congressions" is played out in the irregularity of the poem, but only in the manuscript version. The first line here was hypermetric, but its meter is corrected (through elision) by a reader of the Yale manuscript into more regular iambic pentameter:

> But if with their unlike they a̶ttempt to mix,

Order and Disorder refutes the content of *De rerum natura* as its Christian account of the world refutes Lucretius's proto-atheistic view. This theological correction to a disordered universe might be embodied in prosody. In this reading, Hutchinson uses irregularity to embody the unnaturalness, the disordered world view that she sees in Lucretius's atheistic poem. If so, then we might read Hutchinson's irregularity in *Order and Disorder* as vaunting poetic faults as a sign of humility before God.

Indeed, Hutchinson uses irregular prosody to generate an irregular poetics throughout her career. In the early 1650s, Hutchinson harnessed irregular poetics to the service of political and poetic satire. In her close imitation and parody of Waller's panegyric to Cromwell (discussed further in Chapter 5: Smooth) Hutchinson satirizes Cromwell's increasingly monarchical conduct. She does so through intimately inhabiting and exposing the poetic form used by Cromwell's panegyrist, Edmund Waller. Hutchinson's anti panegyric exists in one fair scribal copy belonging to Henry Hyde, Earl of Clarendon and now held in the British Library. Criticizing Cromwell for emulating monarchical vices, and Edmund Waller for praising Cromwell, she demands:

> Let the unbridled muses, then painting the shame
> Of such unworthy bondage reinflame
> True English hearts, and make their country see
> How glorious 'tis to rescue liberty.[45]

This bold rebuke responds to Waller with close attention to his images and form:

> Then let the muses with such notes as these
> Instruct us what belongs unto our peace;
> Your battles they hereafter shall indite,
> And draw the image of our Mars in fight:[46]

The first line of Hutchinson's retort here is hypermetric. We might see Hutchinson's own numbers becoming unbridled as she calls for "unbridled muses" rather than Waller's servile ones. The effect is heightened by the emphatic enjambment over each line end, in distinct contrast to Waller's end-stopping. Hutchinson encodes poetic irregularity as political protest here in a way that is more familiar to us from the note on the verse to *Paradise Lost* and the connections Milton made between rhyme and "bondage". There are differences of course: Milton rejects rhyme not metrical regularity, and debate over the meaning of the note on the verse, Milton's prosody, and their connections to political principles remains vigorous.[47] While Milton's poem is prefaced by a statement which explicitly connects his style to an historical precedent and a political message (however fraught with multiple interpretations this statement may be), Hutchinson's poem went into the world anonymously and without such commentary. This puts more pressure on readers' interpretation of the poem's form, both in the seventeenth century and today. Do men and women use these metaphors, and formal regularity and irregularity, differently? What might we gain and risk by reading Hutchinson's prosody in the politically encoded way Milton instructs us to read his?

There are risks in taking a single manuscript as evidence of authors' or readers' intentions. Yet when we read Wyatt, Donne or Milton (or even Waller or Crashaw or Cowley) we usually start from the assumption that everything they do with rhyme and meter is for aesthetic effect and probably our readings are the richer for this premise. Many contemporary critics have investigated the history of Thomas Wyatt's intriguing prosody in the various manuscript and print versions of his poems. Instead of reading him as "floundering about for a foothold on stresses" (as a 1929 reviewer did), critics now interpret his destabilizing rhythms as signs of a poet "acting outside the constraints of meter", or as creating a distinctive kind of "compact beauty".[48] Today's critics find not error but apt acoustic effects in the perceived irregularities of Wyatt's and Milton's lines. The premise in both cases is intentionality. Jason Powell and John Leonard speak for many when they argue that we should start from the assumption that Wyatt and Milton *meant* these lines to sound as they do, in some ways, irregular.[49] Surely we should read women in this way too?

The study of both women's writing and of manuscripts brings questions of intentionality to the fore. Arguing that an effect is accidental is certainly just as methodologically problematic as to argue that it is artful.[50] When we face a history of very partial survival of manuscript texts, we have to read for what these manuscripts represent, not the greater number of examples on which we would ideally wish to base arguments.[51] Moreover, however partial and messy the evidence of manuscripts might be, it also reveals how writers were read. This is not always clear-cut: a reader who elides a vowel in Hutchinson's poem might be seeing her prosody as faulty, or making explicit in this manuscript a pronunciation Hutchinson expected readers to deduce anyway. These changes could be aimed at assisting other readers, perhaps women or younger pupils in the Rochester household who might need guidance in such matters. All of these hypotheses tell a story about expectations of women writers and women readers. Jason Powell sees at play in Wyatt's manuscripts a "lively community of poets", and in Osborn fb100 we can at least see a community of readers, some of whom changed Hutchinson's verse.[52]

Male poets have also had their meter corrected by contemporary readers, editors and publishers for a variety of reasons.[53] But one of her acquaintances does call direct attention to Hutchinson's status as a woman poet, and its impact on her poetic style. While Hutchinson was working on her translation of *De rerum natura* in the 1650s, Alexander Brome was also working on his own translation. Their mutual acquaintance Aston Cokain wrote these lines to Brome:

> I know a lady that hath been about
> The same design, but she must needs give out:
> Your poet strikes too boldly home sometimes,
> In genial things, t'appear in women's rhymes,
> The task is masculine, and he that can
> Translate Lucretius, is an able man.
> And such are you; whose rich poetic vein,
> And general learning perfectly can plane,
> And smooth your author's roughness, and give
> Him such a robe of English as will live,
> Out-wear, and all such works exceed, and prove
> This nation's wonder, and this nation's love.
> Therefore proceed, (my friend) and soon erect
> This pyramid of our best dialect.[54]

The "Lady" is likely to be Lucy Hutchinson.[55] Cokain flatters his friend, Alexander Brome, that he is a more able and appropriate translator of Lucretius than Hutchinson. Lucretius may be problematic in his atheism and sexual frankness, yet Cokain's poem suggests that by appropriately remaking the poem into English, he could be coopted into an acceptable and even colonializing project: he calls on Brome to "erect / This pyramid of our best dialect." With the phrase "*Your* poet" he establishes Brome's ownership of Lucretius, and a sense of male community rallying against the female interloper. And his reason is clearly both gender and style. Cokain writes that Lucretius's subject is "genial things" where genial bears its now obsolete sense of relating to procreation (OED 1.). Cokain suggests that the Roman poet's frank discussion of sexual desire and reproduction are inappropriate for a woman. But the poem then suggests that it is actually Lucretius's language and style which might be the barrier to a woman translator. *De rerum natura* requires "an able man" to translate, writes Cokain, and this is not mankind but specifically man here, as the contrast to "women's rhymes" makes clear. Though "rhymes" was not always derogatory, in the context of Cokain's poem the phrase "women's rhymes" suggests a scornful dismissal, a sense of women's poems as mere versification. A woman poet would not be able to "plane", "smooth", and dress Lucretius's roughness in smooth English robes. In the seventeenth-century printing of this poem, "plane" is spelt "plain", and while this was a common spelling for the verb "plane" it seems here to work as a punning reference to both smoothing Lucretius's style and making it more plain. The next chapter will further explore the complex gendering of poetic smoothness. Smoothness could be both an attribute of female bodies, and of male poetics, that is, the smoothness achieved by craft, education, mastery, as with Cokain's belief that Brome is more capable of smoothing Lucretius than Lucy Hutchinson.

Cokain's poem makes clear that the stakes of poetic style go far beyond the aesthetic into the social and political. We do not know whether Hutchinson saw this poem. But whether she had read it or not, she may have had such slights in mind when she wrote her playful and defiant preface in which she placed her masterful Lucretius translation into the wrily domestic context of a children's schoolroom, in which their mother embroidered while translating poetry which was sexually explicit, religiously radical, and linguistically difficult. Furthermore, this poem suggests a counter-narrative about the style of Hutchinson's Lucretius, with its irregular lines. While Cokain praises the male poet who might fit Lucretius's rough Latin into a smooth "robe of English", how might we characterize the unspoken alternative? A translation which retains—or creates a new version of—the "author's roughness"? Hutchinson's translation, as we have seen, was significantly irregular, in ways which might reflect the aesthetic of her original rather than the inadequacy of her own "women's rhymes".

Katherine Philips's Odes

The couplet has often been seen as an icon of regularity, especially in its mid-seventeenth century incarnation through the use of Edmund Waller (whose famous smoothness will be discussed in the next chapter), though we have seen how it was used in flexible and sometimes "irregular" ways, by poets including Lucy Hutchinson. We turn now to a poetic form which was coded as the opposite to regularity: the so-called "irregular ode".

Abraham Cowley was prominent in claiming Pindar as a model for irregularity: he wrote extensively both in the Pindaric ode form and, crucially, about it. In the notes and preface to his "Pindarique Odes" and his editor Thomas Sprat's later preface, the specific structure of Pindar's original form was subordinated to a broader emphasis on irregularity, as well as difficulty and digression. Cowley frequently codes poetic irregularity as a form of liberty (even though, as we will see, his odes are often irregular in quite regular ways). His ode "Upon Liberty" formulates the poem's theme through its "numbers":

> Mine the Pindaric way I'll make,
> The matter shall be grave, the numbers loose and free.
> It shall not keep one settled pace of time,
> In the same tune it shall not always chime,
> Nor shall each day just to his neighbour rhyme.[56]

The poet-speaker describes both his desired position in the world and his prosody as "free", with the multivalent adjective "loose" bringing together freedom and irregularity. We saw earlier that "loose" was often used in a gendered sense, often referring to clothing or morals (as in Nathaniel Lee's praise of Dryden for amending Milton's loose-dressed maid, *Paradise Lost*), and we will return to this term in the next chapter, in the hands of Aphra Behn. But here, we can see how these terms are further drawn out in Cowley's preface to his *Works* of 1656 in which he claims:

> the numbers are various and irregular, and sometimes (especially some of the long ones) uncouth, if the just measures and cadencies be not observed in the pronunciation [...] And though the liberty of them may incline a man to believe them easy to be composed, yet the undertaker will find it otherwise.[57]

As we will see in the conclusion, Cowley's emphasis on the difficulty of crafting his apparently free odes is complex and in part gendered. For the present discussion, let us attend to the parallels here between the terms he uses to describe irregular prosody and freedom of thought. The poem's "numbers" (or prosody), are "various and irregular" and "loose and free". Cowley's theorization of his prosody in the *Pindarique Odes* was just as influential as his practice. The legacy of his odes, and his theory of irregularity and liberty, was ambivalent. Later scholar-poets would counter Cowley's version of Pindaric form. In the early eighteenth century, William Congreve drew attention to the regularity of Pindar's own odes, which he characterized as a "secret connection" between the elements that might not be immediately apparent). He criticized the contemporary fashion for intepreting Pindaric regularity as irregularity: "a bundle of rambling incoherent thoughts, expressed in a like parcel of irregular stanzas, which also consist of such another complication disproportioned, uncertain and perplexed verses and rhymes".[58] These complaints were echoed by Samuel Johnson who wrote of Cowley's influence: "this lax and lawless versification so much concealed the deficiencies of the barren, and flattered the laziness of the idle, that it immediately overspread our books of poetry".[59] Where Cowley saw irregularity as "loose and free", Johnson perceives it as "lax and lawless". Milton's famous "Note on the Verse" of course, with its far more influential theorization of rhyme as modern bondage, comes in the middle of this debate. Cowley's odes, too, have been the subject of much political interpretation, with critics arguing that they are either royalist, or purposefully ambivalent, or aspiring to political withdrawal or distraction.[60]

Beyond the specific connotations of the Pindaric, the ode more broadly has been a crucial form for critical poetics. As Susan Stewart writes, "odes give birth to poets". Looking at Pindaric odes and beyond, Stewart argues,

> Yet in hymns and odes, the poetic speaker expends praise as a gift or implicit sacrifice offered by an individual out of a position of authority, license, or supplication. The odist's expenditure will be rewarded by forms of grace or blessedness, or by a more concrete payment: from Simonides and Pindar forward, odists are, more often than not, paid for their work or thanked for their gift. What is this work, this reporting of knowledge expressed in poetic form that is offered up as a product of skill? How is it that value is placed on a residual, ongoing potentiality of the poet rather than inferred only from the existence of finished works?[61]

This dynamic is even more complex when men write odes to women, and vice versa. In the early 1660s, Katherine Philips and Abraham Cowley wrote odes to each other. Cowley's two odes to Philips, one published in 1663 before her death and one after her death, in 1667, tread a delicate line between praise and bathos (a similarly uneasy combination of tones familiar to us from praise poems to Margaret Cavendish discussed in Chapter 3). When Philips wrote her own ode to Abraham Cowley she also incorporated strands of resistance or critique as well as praise and affiliation, as I have shown elsewhere.[62] This is Philips's only poem labelled as an "ode" and it engages directly with Cowley's Pindaric odes. Here she also develops her own distinctive manifestation of the form: one that is as much about her own identity as a poet of retirement as it is in praise of Cowley. I have argued elsewhere that while Philips clearly wrote in ode form in part as a compliment to Cowley, who had written influential odes, her own ode in turn influenced his odes and his prose writing on retreat and poetics. Philips's ode to Cowley is especially significant in her corpus because her other poems are characteristically regular in prosody. Across the various stanzaic forms Philips uses we can see a coherent poetic vision: in Rebecca Rush's terms, "[v]erse, for Philips, is designed to reinforce and even enforce divine order".[63] Containing fervent emotion and bold argument within closed couplets and finely balanced stanzas, Philips is "remarkably adept at pouring passion into iambic regularity" (in Rush's words).[64] And indeed Philips herself theorized such formal containment. In her letters to Charles Cotterell (explored in Chapter 2: Feminine), she discusses the translation of Pierre Corneille's *La Mort de Pompée* by Waller and his collaborators (which she was also translating as her play *Pompey*). Criticizing their use of verse form, she comments "the sense ought always to be confined to the couplet, otherwise the lines must be spiritless, and dull."[65] For Philips to write an ode, then, in its late seventeenth-century incarnation as an intrinsically irregular and unconfined form, is a conscious intervention in poetic debates.

In her irregular ode, Philips adopts fairly frequent rhymes and a significant number of rhyming couplets, but different line lengths. She embraces the ode form's associations with digression, as a poem addressed to another poet becomes one focused on solitude and self-mastery:

> In my remote and humble seat
>   Now I'm again possessed
>   Of that late fugitive, my breast;
> From all thy tumults and from all thy heat
> I'll find a quiet and a cool retreat;
>   And on the fetters I have worn
> Look with experienced and revengeful scorn
>   In this my sovereign privacy.
>   'Tis true I cannot govern thee,
>   But yet myself I may subdue,
> And that's the nobler empire of the two.
>   If ev'ry passion had got leave
>   Its satisfaction to receive,
> Yet I would it a higher pleasure call
> To conquer one, than to indulge them all.[66]

Unusually, for this poem we also have evidence of how a seventeenth-century person read it, and specifically its ode form. The Bodleian Library now holds a verse miscellany including poems by Cowley, Quarles, Rochester, psalm paraphrases, and other seventeenth-century material. It is entitled "A Collection of Verse Fancyes and Poems, Morrall and Devine", and was probably compiled in the late seventeenth or early eighteenth century.[67] In this manuscript, the verse structure of Philips's retirement ode has been changed. This poem has various titles in the different manuscript and print witnesses, but what all of the different titles for this poem do agree upon is that this is an ode, and its print title is "Ode upon retirement". In the Bodleian manuscript miscellany, however, the poem is simply titled "Retirement", its generic designation as an ode removed. Furthermore, the compiler seems to be tussling with the ode form in the poem itself. Here we can see some lines from the ode first as they appear in the printed edition of 1667, and then in the Bodleian MS:

Go, get some other fool,
Whom thou mayst next cajole:
On me thy frowns thou dost in vain bestow;
For I know how
To be as coy and as reserved as thou.

In my remote and humble seat
Now I'm again possessed
Of that late fugitive, my breast
From all thy tumults and from all thy heat
I'll find a quiet and a cool retreat;

(PHILIPS, POEMS, 1667, PP. 122–3)

Go, get some other fool,
Whom thou mayst next cajole:
On me thy frowns thou dost in vain bestow,
For I know how to be as coy and as reserved as thou:

In my remote and humble seat now I'm again possessed:
Of that late fugitive, my breast,
From all thy tumults and from all thy heat
I'll find a quiet and a cool retreat;

(BOD MS RAWL 90, FOL. 5V)

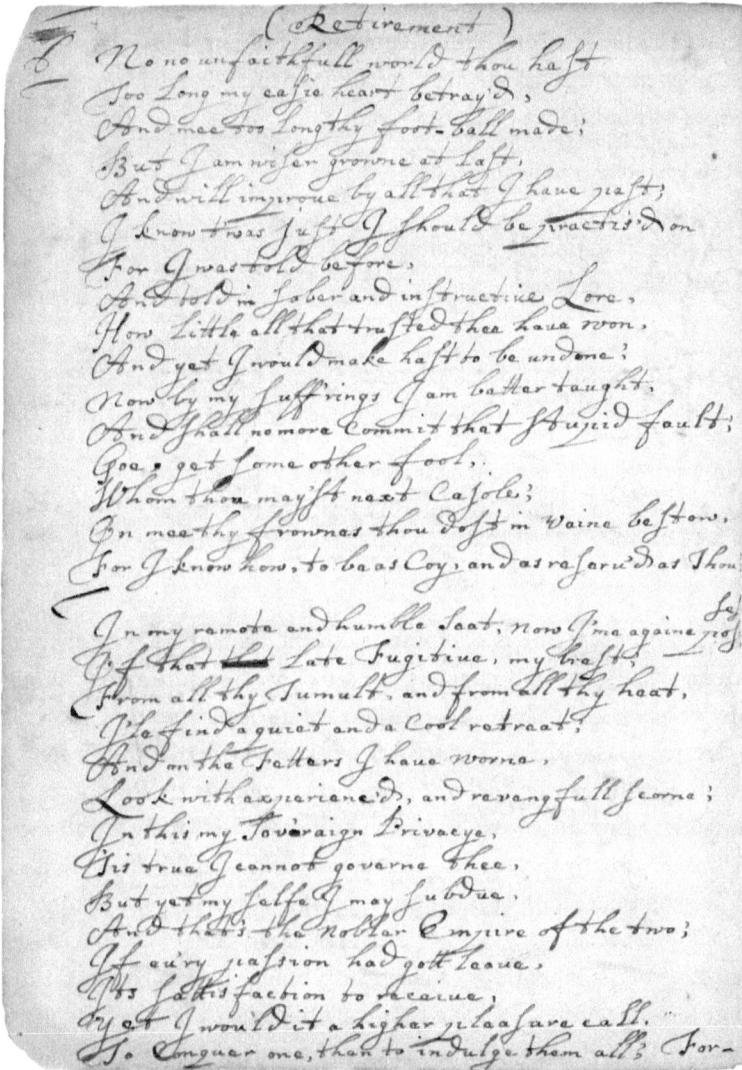

FIGURE 2. Copy of Katherine Philips, "Retirement", The Bodleian Libraries, University of Oxford, MS Rawl Poet 90, fol. 5v. Reproduced according to the Creative Commons licence CC-BY-NC 4.0

The reader has removed several line breaks so as to collapse two shorter lines into longer ones, retaining rhymes and creating longer lines overall. Changes have been made to other poems, too. Some other poems by Philips are retitled in ways which were quite common in seventeenth-century miscellany culture.[68] So for instance, "A Country Life", becomes "In Praise of a Country Life". This poem, like the Retirement ode, is changed formally too. The print witnesses from Philips's lifetime represent it as a tetrameter and trimeter poem with alternate rhymes (common meter, but laid out in continuous lines without stanza breaks):

> How sacred and how innocent
> A country life appears
> How free from tumult, discontent,
> From flattery or fears!

(PHILIPS, POEMS, 1667, P. 88)

The Bodleian MS reader transforms this stanzaic poem into one of couplets:

> How sacred, and how innocent a country life appears
> How free from tumult, discontent, from flattery or fears,

(BOD MS RAWL 90, FOL. 3R)

Each tetrameter line is combined with the following trimeter to make fourteen-syllable rhyming couplets. We can only conjecture as to whether the reader's aim was to reshape the retirement ode into something more like a couplet poem, as with "A Country Life", or indeed whether they were trying to accentuate the Cowleyan style of the poem through ever-longer lines. What is certainly significant, though, is that this process of reshaping lineation is not enacted consistently through the manuscript; the reshaping of poems is selective. The compiler's desire to change the poem's form is focused on the Philips poems.[69] Most strikingly, Cowley's own ode "Upon Liberty", with its assertive connection of the Pindaric ode's irregularity to liberty, is transcribed without changing its lineation.[70] While it is difficult to deduce the exact intentions of any reader, then, it does seem to indicate someone reading widely in the period's poetry and deciding that it was Philips' works which required formal reshaping. Furthermore, Philips's identity was well-known so it is likely that the compiler and readers knew her name and gender. The ode form is also one which places peculiar weight on the identity of the poet (and addressee) for its value; we recall Stewart's questioning formulation "How is it that value is placed on a residual, ongoing potentiality of the poet rather than inferred only from the existence of finished works?". And claiming the ode's formal authority, its "ongoing potentiality", as a female poet was especially charged, as we can see in a poem from 1683. This is the second poem in a collection which opens with a defiantly proto-feminist preface and then an ode by an

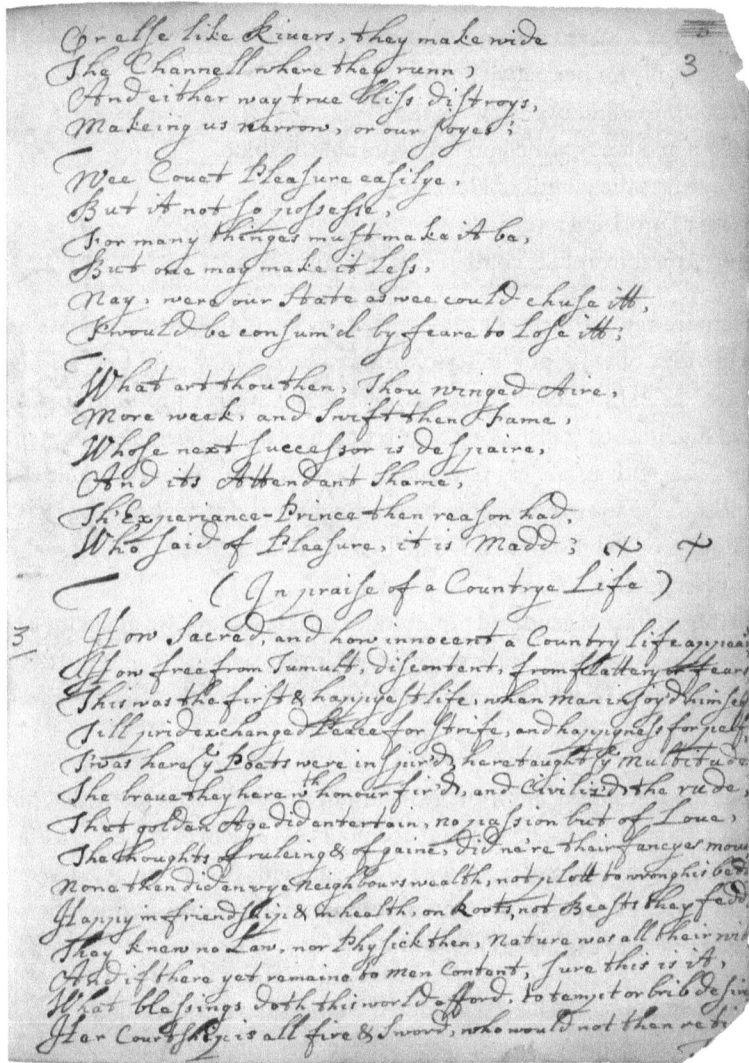

FIGURE 3. Copy of Katherine Philips, "In praise of a Countrye Life", The Bodleian Libraries, University of Oxford, MS Rawl Poet 90, fol. 3r. Reproduced according to the Creative Commons licence CC-BY-NC 4.0

anonymous woman, claiming women's right to poetry. The ode that follows, by a man, challenges not only women's claimed right to write, but to write pindarics especially:

> What daring female is't who thus complains,
> In masculine Pindaric strains,

> Of great Apollo's Salic Law;
> Both breaks it, and pretends that she
> Pleads only for her native liberty.
> Whilst in a rapid over-flowing tide
> Of wit and fancy, which no banks are able to abide,
> She strikes the guards of Helicon
> With a surprising awe,
> And Amazonian-like, compels 'em to withdraw [. . .][71]

Here we can see further evidence that seventeenth-century readers had a specific idea of what poetic style women could and should use: "women's rhymes", as Aston Cokain put it. And as with Cokain's prohibition against Lucy Hutchinson's translation of Lucretius, here again the issue is women appropriating both an ancient Greek model and irregular meter, a double poetic ambition. The anonymous poet here articulates the view that women poets like Philips or Behn should not dare to write Pindaric odes, though seems to acknowledge their success: "a surprising awe".

In this context of gendered prohibitions on ode writing, we might look back to how Cowley and his editor theorized his irregular odes. And it is strikingly gendered. Sprat knew that some readers would criticize Cowley's *Pindarique Odes*, and pre-emptively commented:

> But these admirers of gentleness without sinews, should know that different arguments must have different colours of speech: that there is a kind of variety of sexes in poetry as well as in mankind: that as the peculiar excellence of the feminine kind, is smoothness and beauty: so strength is the chief praise of the masculine.[72]

Thomas Sprat's model here is gendered but not, as we might expect, in claiming poetic innovation for men. Sprat's defence of Abraham Cowley's irregular odes championed irregularity as strength and by so doing connected irregularity to masculine style. Yet it also argued that Cowley, a male poet, could—and indeed should—adopt both masculine and feminine styles. While many other writers used terms such as variety, unevenness or roughness, Sprat uses the term "irregular": "If the irregularity of the number disgust them, they may observe that this very thing makes that kind of poesy fit for all manner of subjects" (*Works*, sig. b1v). Sprat theorizes irregularity here as flexibility, and we can see that irregularity has long been a poetic feature malleable enough to be shaped to any subject, coded in political protest, or freedom of conscience, or solitude, or philosophical scepticism. In this strikingly modern understanding of form, we can see the multivalent importance of irregularity and therefore the stakes of identifying women poets' use of it.

Cowley and Milton have long been seen to provide models of experimental prosody that influenced later poets. Their importance has been recognized not only because their poetry has been influential, but because they explicitly theorized their rejection of regularity, or rhyme. These theorizations were specific to particular poems. Milton's note "On the Verse" to *Paradise Lost* rejects rhyme endings in this poem, not across his works, and similarly Cowley's preface is specific to his Pindaric odes, yet these statements have developed an independent life. These allegories of form by which two poets writing from very different political positions argue for the ideological, political and even gendered charge of formal decisions have been crucial guides for later interpreters. Can we read Lucy Hutchinson and Katherine Philips into this history of form, freedom and irregularity? For writers who do not publish explicit theories of style to accompany their poems, we need to work harder to understand the charge of their formal decisions. With manuscript poetry, often unattributed in its own time and circulation, we need to work even harder. Are we reading innovations rather than inconsistencies of style or quirks of a particular material text? Should we follow contemporary readers who seem to have assumed error, such as Hutchinson's early readers? The complex evidence of these manuscripts might be illuminated by the wider literary culture of the period, and also vice versa, as readers' marks on these manuscripts tell us how they treated the poems they were reading. This chapter has traced evidence of two movements which suggest their neglected part in this history of poetics. First, we have seen that both Hutchinson and Philips were using certain kinds of irregularity, whether the ode or the regularly irregular couplet, strategically in their poems of the 1650s and 1660s. Secondly, we have seen that the evidence of manuscripts in the Beinecke and Bodleian Libraries suggests that contemporary readers of Hutchinson and Philips were not only noticing their poetic irregularity but correcting it.

Does this matter? It matters if it contributes to a wider erasure of women from important traditions, and especially those connected with radicalism, rule-breaking, and even modernity. We can see the stakes of reading women's poetic irregularity as strategic and aesthetic by looking at a longer narrative of poetic development. And this is exactly the kind of narrative into which the irregular ode has been written. In *A History of Free Verse*, Chris Beyers writes of the early modern period:

A poetry driven by the notion that faithful translation of poetic inspiration necessitates the poet to supersede the normal conventions of verse; one that insists that form must represent, not just be appropriate for, its subject; that maintains that its lack of symmetry is evidence of greater, more organic poetry; that demands more of its reader while promising greater transport; and that uses contextual prosody: [. . .] The irregular ode *was* the standard-bearer of the tradition that led to free verse.[73]

Beyers's comments on the early modern period reveal the importance of identifying strategic irregularity not only in understanding the development of the irregular ode alongside and after Cowley, but in plotting far longer histories of poetic form.

If seventeenth-century readers thought Philips and Hutchinson were making mistakes, rather than pioneering irregular prosody, they have written them out of the history of poetry—and so have we. The reader of Bodleian Rawl Poet 90 may not have single-handedly changed literary history in making Philips' ode into couplets. Nor perhaps the anonymous readers of Hutchinson's poetry who corrected her hypo- and hypermetric lines, nor Hugh Munro in his dismissal of Hutchinson's irregular lines as evidence of the distractions of domestic duty. But cumulatively, these cases reveal a pattern of reading women poets that starts from the assumption that they have made errors, rather than that they are breaking the rules. Moreover, while for Philips and Hutchinson we can reconstruct possible histories of irregularity either through print copies or the evidence of manuscript alteration, how many other women poets might have had their experimental poetics regularized entirely out of literary history? We know that Hutchinson translated *De rerum natura* despite Aston Cokain's scorn for a woman's ability to translate Lucretian boldness, and that Philips and Behn wrote odes despite the anonymous poet who forbade women from writing "masculine Pindaric strains", but how many others might not have dared, or might have had their work corrected, censured, and even destroyed?

Some years later, Aphra Behn took up the baton, addressing women's exclusion from certain kinds of poetry even more explicitly than Hutchinson or Philips. She did so in a poem about Lucretius, which is itself an irregular ode. Behn was writing in praise of Thomas Creech, the first full translator of Lucretius after Hutchinson (and she probably didn't know about Hutchinson's translation). We will return to this poem's defence of women's access to poetry further in subsequent chapters. For now, we will focus on one of her

5
Smooth/Soft

Morbidezza: softness, wantonness, effeminacy, lasciviousness, ease [...]. Also smoothness. Also fruitfulness, or rankness.

—QUEEN ANNA'S NEW WORLD OF WORDS, JOHN FLORIO (1611)[1]

Some of Mrs. Behn's songs are very tender, but she is so abominably vile a woman[.]

—LETTER FROM GILBERT BURNET TO ANNE WHARTON, ABOUT APHRA BEHN (1682)[2]

IN HIS ENGLISH-ITALIAN DICTIONARY, dedicated to Queen Anne of Denmark, John Florio defines the term "morbidezza", a word apparently introduced from Italian to describe a technique for painting flesh and skin.[3] Florio glosses it as "softness, wantonness, effeminacy, lasciviousness, ease, world at will. Also smoothness. Also fruitfulness, or rankness". This chapter will explore several of this series of terms. These words, especially smooth and soft, become highly charged and gendered descriptors of poetic style in the seventeenth century. Florio's definition here demonstrates a process traced throughout this poem, whereby an aesthetic term—here, morbidezza—carries moral, bodily, social and sexual implications (wantonness, effeminacy, lasciviousness, ease), and continues to imply these when it is used to characterize style. Florio's book was dedicated to and named for a woman, as were many dictionaries and books of hard words. The address of these books to a female audience is not a simple matter, and likely as much a marketing ploy as a desire to increase female literacy.[4] It shows that women were both subjects and objects in the process of defining early modern language use. After exploring uses of "smooth" and "soft" by male poets and critics, this chapter looks at women not only as the audience and object of such terms, but also shows how they used and defined them to their own critical ends. In the second epigraph, over half a century later, we see Gilbert Burnet using the charged adjective "tender" to describe Aphra Behn's poetry, implying a sensuality that is both admirable and troublesome. We will see how Behn herself, and her poetic correspondent Anne Wharton, redefined the term tender, as well as soft, claiming it as a defining characteristic of a superior feminine poetics.

Like "irregular", and even "original", and more so even than these terms, "smooth" was used in the seventeenth century to characterize styles and bodies, both of which were often gendered. "Smooth" could be a term of aesthetic, moral or bodily praise. It could also, as we will see, be a term of critique. It could suggest that something (or someone) was ideal, natural, crafted, diplomatic, or that they were oleaginous, deceptive, and sensual. In his *Model of Poesy*, probably written in 1599, William Scott creates a taxonomy of poetic styles. These include "perspicuity", "purity", "fullness or completeness", "plentifulness", and "softness or smoothness".[5] The combined characteristic of "softness or smoothness" is a valued style alongside masculine "sinewy strength". But the terms for strength, "sinewy" and "brawn[y]", suggest the gendering of these styles, and their connection to gendered bodies. We have seen how Roman and early modern writers used metaphors of virility, manliness, and muscularity to define style. These writers also shored up masculine style against its opposites: feminine or, more specifically, effeminate styles. The idea of effeminacy yoked together misogyny and homophobia to represent the soft, passive, often copious alternative to the muscular, active, virile masculine style. More recently, critics have articulated other alternatives to poetic virility which formed in a lineage from classical through early modern European poetics: Jenny C. Mann has defined Marlowe's Ovidian poetics as "soft style", showing how he reformed his "slack" or flaccid muse from a symbol of impotence to one of creativity. Jessie Hock has defined as "voluptuous style" a Lucretian mode transmitted through Montaigne.[6] Yet none of these revelatory readings has focused on the intervention of women poets themselves in debates around softness, smoothness, masculinity, femininity, and style.

It is not hard to see why. Even as they theorized gendered style, early modern poets were often notably elusive when it came to discussing how women themselves wrote. Ben Jonson's *Timber, or Discoveries*, is a work both deeply indebted to classical writing and profoundly modern, as we saw in Chapter 3: Original. Here Jonson discusses "Women's poets":

Others there are that have no composition at all, but a kind of tuning and rhyming fall in what they write. It runs and slides, and only makes a sound. "Women's poets", they are called, as you have "women's tailors".

> They write a verse, as smooth, as soft, as cream;
> In which there is no torrent, nor scarce stream.
> You may sound these wits, and find the depth of them, with your middle finger. They are cream-bowl- or but puddle-deep.[7]

This passage tells us much about women *and* style—but not about women's own style. The critique of women and poetry here is of men who write for women, not women writers themselves: "'Women's poets' [...] as you have 'women's tailors'". Taste here is equally bodily and evaluative: different readers prefer different styles and this style is written for women. It is doubtless committed to shoring up poetry as a masculine realm, but not against women poets, more against women as consumers or arbiters of taste, and also against effeminacy, one of the antonyms against which masculine style is defined. Hutson has shown that Jonson's gendered images of style are underpinned by Roman homophobia as well as early modern misogyny. These critiques of style are profoundly connected to gender and sex, then, but in complex ways that combine homophobia, misogyny, and cultural stigmas around effeminacy.

Jonson combines metaphors of sound, taste, and touch in his definition of smooth style. The "tuning and rhyming fall" may be a reference to "feminine rhyme" which is musical yet lacking meaning: it "only makes a sound" (as we saw in Chapter 2: Feminine). And here smoothness is not a marker of craft, such as the smoothness of a polished stone, an image that George Puttenham had used for the "glorious lustre" of a polished style. In explaining the technique of amplification called "exargasia" or "expolitio", Puttenham says of the latter, Latin name, that it is "a term transferred from these polishers of marble or porphirite, who after it is rough hewn and reduced to that fashion they will, do set upon it a goodly glass so smooth and clear as ye may see your face in it".[8] By contrast, Jonson's gendered smoothness is a soft, malleable smoothness, that of a viscous liquid: "as smooth, as soft, as cream". The combined metaphors of women's bodies, and the implicit sexuality of smoothness, liquids, and fingers, evoke a corporeal experience of poetry: one focused on taste, consumption, sexuality. Although Jonson also critiques excessively rough, artificially masculine style, his characterization of gendered smoothness remains importantly negative. Smooth is usually a surface attribute, it is tactile but can be hard (like polished marble) or soft (like skin or fabric), but Jonson's feminization of it here defines it as both soft and shallow: a distinctly gendered and devalued smoothness.

Poetic smoothness, then, was often an embodied style, associated with women as readers and women's bodies; its exact nature and value were complex and subject to debate and redefinition. Later in the seventeenth century, Thomas Sprat praised Abraham Cowley for having a smooth *and* strong style. As we saw in the previous chapter, he defends Cowley's Pindaric odes, specifically, against those who might actually prefer smoothness and criticize "strength" (elsewhere defined as roughness and irregularity). Sprat does so in explicitly gendered terms:

> But these admirers of gentleness without sinews, should know that different arguments must have different colours of speech: that there is a kind of variety of sexes in poetry as well as in mankind: that as the peculiar excellence of the feminine kind, is smoothness and beauty: so strength is the chief praise of the masculine.
>
> (SIG. B1V)

Like William Scott, half a century earlier, Sprat argues that smoothness and strength are both necessary. He also correlates them with feminine and masculine. But this is a sex of style and not person: a poet like Cowley can write *both* masculine and feminine poetry. Though there is often a hierarchy between masculine and *effeminate* style (as in Jonson), masculine and feminine can be seen as valuable opposites. And Henry Vaughan had praised Katherine Philips's poetry in similar terms,

> The poem smooth, and in each line
> Soft as yourself, yet masculine [...]⁹

At first read, the gendering here is clear: "yet" establishes "soft" and "masculine" as opposites, softness as usually feminine. But Philips is seen as a unique blend of male and female. Where does smoothness fit? Should we read smooth and soft as yoked together, or does smoothness stand in a different category, able to be both masculine (the smoothness of craft, perhaps, of Puttenham's rhetorical trope as a hard polished stone; or even a strong sinew) and feminine (the feminine smoothness of Jonson's "cream-bowl")?

Katherine Philips's poetry, and critical poems about her, reveal the mixed characterization of smoothness as feminine and as masculine. More widely, poems about Katherine Philips are a nexus of discussion of gendered style. As

Paula Loscocco has shown, poems about Philips from the 1660s (especially after her death in 1667) praise her poetry as both masculine and feminine in style, in a neoclassical model that valued both.[10] Cowley writes:

> I must admire to see thy well-knit sense,
> Thy numbers gentle, and thy fancies high,
> Those as thy forehead smooth, these sparkling as thine eye.
> 'Tis solid, and 'tis manly all,
> Or rather 'tis angelical,
> For as in angels, we
> Do in thy verses see
> Both improved sexes eminently meet,
> They are than man more strong, and more than woman sweet.[11]

Cowley praises Philips's style through analogies with her body ("as thy forehead smooth, these sparkling as thine eye") in a move that we have seen again and again in this book. Smoothness signifies the poet's youthful complexion as well as her poetic style (she died at the age of 32). But Cowley also praises Philips in a way that sees a stylistic ideal in the mixing of male and female: an "angelical" meeting of sexes which improves both, making masculine style more strong and feminine style more sweet than those sexes themselves. A poet under the pseudonym Philo-Philippa ("admirer of Philips") also wrote extensively in praise of Philips's style. Debate continues as to the likely identity and gender of Philo-Philippa. If Philo-Philippa was a woman, as the pseudonym implies, this is a rare example of an extended critical appraisal by one woman of another; if a man, it is a fascinating ventriloquism of praise by a woman.[12] Philo-Philippa defines Philips's verse as "smooth" and "soft" with an array of gendered and ungendered metaphors:

> A gliding sea of crystal doth best show
> How smooth, clear, full, and rich your verse doth flow:
> Your words are chosen, culled, not by chance writ,
> To make the sense, as anagrams do hit.
> Your rich becoming words on the sense wait,
> As maids of honour on a queen of state.
> 'Tis not white satin makes a verse more white,
> Or soft; iron is both, write you on it.
> Your poems come forth cast, no file you need,
> At one brave heat both shaped and polished.[13]

Both smooth and soft are here aspirational styles. While the image of maids of honor and queen may be gendered, the subsequent image of the forge seems powerfully to disrupt such femininity and courtliness. Philips becomes an emblem of a style which is both feminine and masculine. Leah DeVun and others have shown how certain, often biblical, figures of the androgyne or hermaphrodite have moved between idealization and monstrosity in medieval and early modern culture.[14] Yet while Philips's physical body (her face) is often aligned with the beauty of her poetry, these repeated descriptions of her poetry as hermaphroditic seem focused on her style. She is represented as indubitably feminine in character, while her poetry can be simultaneously both feminine and masculine, like Cowley's. The metaphoric landscape of this poem yields further complexity, as Philo-Philippa asserts that instead of white satin, she should write on iron in a forge, white-hot and more indelibly imprinted. The poem's promotion of whiteness as a condition of legibility may also be inflected with racialized ideals.[15] The idea of softness as malleability—here in the image of heat-softened iron—will become crucial to this chapter's later exploration of softness as a gendered, creative principle.

Later in the century, smoothness is increasingly valued, and roughness or strength have to be defended. Alexander Pope's *Essay on Criticism*, praises "the easy vigour of a line / Where Denham's strength and Waller's sweetness join" (ll. 360–1)[16]. Pope sees English poetry maturing in the seventeenth century to appreciate the value of softness and smoothness. In his later poem, a version of Horace's Epistle to Augustus, he represents progression towards smoothness:

> Britain to soft refinements less a foe,
> Wit grew polite and numbers learned to flow
> Waller was smooth; but Dryden taught to join
> The varying verse, the full resounding line,
> The long majestic march and energy divine.[17]

In Pope's retrospective literary history, Dryden combines the refined softness and smoothness of Waller with majesty and divinity. Pope's association of Waller with smoothness is characteristic of many depictions of Waller's style, in his lifetime and afterwards, and criticism continues to wrangle with the exact nature of Waller's prosody, and indeed the whole narrative of Augustan smoothness and refinement.[18] Waller's career spans much of the chronological scope of this chapter, from the 1640s to 1680s. He was both a famed poet of smoothness, and a poet who regularly wrote to and was addressed by women poets. These aspects of his identity are connected in complex ways:

his renowned smoothness and even feminine style may have made him an obvious point of identification for women poets, while it also pressed his male peers to go out of their way to assert the masculinity of his smooth poetry against that of women poets.

Later writers co-opt Waller's smoothness to their own narratives of literary history. Pope had imagined Dryden adding gravity to Waller's smoothness. Aubrey sees Waller's writing as a program of reform saying: "When he was a brisk young spark, and first studied poetry, me thought, said he, I never saw a good copy of English verses; they want smoothness; then I began to essay".[19] Aubrey casts Waller as critic and literary historian as well as poet, promulgating smoothness in theory and practice. But by the nineteenth century smoothness—specifically, Waller's smoothness—had fallen out of favor. Waller's Victorian biographer despaired of his "honied monotony", saying that he "worshipped smoothness, and sought it at every hazard", turning to biblical narratives to see him foolishly preferring "the Jacob of a soft flowing commonplace to the rough hairy Esau of a strong originality, cumbered with its own weight and richness".[20] Here honor and roughness are contrasted with self-serving smoothness.

What happened between these points, from the ascendancy of smoothness through the seventeenth century to its depreciation by the nineteenth? In a persuasive account, Paula Loscocco suggests that there was a shift in the value of poetic smoothness and its relation to strength and softness. Smoothness became more closely associated with strength and masculinity, while softness was devalued and feminized. Moreover, by focusing on the afterlife of Katherine Philips's poems, she argues that gender was a factor in this shift. Loscocco reads the poems quoted above about Philips, by Cowley and Philo-Philippa, as evidence for a chronological change in the status of smoothness, softness, masculine, and feminine styles:

> By explicitly gendering "strength" as masculine and "sweetness" (or "softness") as feminine, Cowley used neoclassical terms in ways common to the authors of his era. And by positing an ideal balance between these terms, Cowley joined other writers in assigning equal value to contemporary concepts of literary masculinity and femininity. [...] Mid-seventeenth-century writers, as I have shown, linked the terms "strong" and "sweet" to contemporary concepts of masculinity and femininity. By the end of the century, however, these terms had acquired an entirely different set of gender-associations: "strong" and "sweet" had come to be attached only to masculinity.[21]

Loscocco's account is compelling, characterizing Philips's changing reception and its place in a wider cultural development which reified sex and style. By the end of the seventeenth century, women's poetry could only be "soft" while men's verse could be both "smooth" and "strong". The blend of masculine and feminine styles which Sprat had praised in Cowley, and Cowley in Philips, was no longer possible: smoothness now belonged to the realm of masculine poetry. This chapter builds on that work, and also argues that Loscocco's trajectory is not quite the whole story. It asks how women poets themselves—not just the male poets writing about them—participated in this shift.

How were "smooth" and "soft" used *by* women poets? I will answer these questions through two clusters of poems. We will see women writing poetry that is profoundly critical of mainstream uses of smooth and soft. And "critical" here consciously evokes both senses of the term, as we saw in Chapter 1. In the ideologically freighted terms explored throughout this book, women's literary criticism (in the sense of theory) often emerged as they responded to criticism (in the sense of negative judgment) of their own work, or as they criticized their male peers. First, I explore how two women poets in the early and mid-seventeenth century claimed to be the opposite of smooth. Anne Southwell and Lucy Hutchinson developed a distinctive poetics of roughness, ruggedness and a satirical critique of smooth style. Secondly, I will argue that a series of poems from the 1680s–90s by Aphra Behn and Anne Wharton show women as important *theorists* of Restoration smoothness and softness, not just the objects of such description. Anne Wharton and Aphra Behn defined themselves by adapting the associations of smoothness with femininity to their own ends. Moreover, they adopt softness as a peculiarly female quality. As Loscocco argued, "literary femininity—frequently but not always signaled by the term "softness"—had in fact become a potent tool of critical dispraise".[22] But by examining critical poems by women themselves, many of which remain unpublished, we can see a strong counter current of criticism: instead of identifying women's softness with malleability and fickleness, they developed softness as a valued critical principle of emotional receptivity. For Wharton and Behn, women's softness made them better poets.

Smoothing Up and Rugged Verse:
Anne Southwell, Lucy Hutchinson, Edmund Waller

What is smooth style? Is it gendered in writings by women and by men? Chapter 4 showed how irregularity in women poets' works has sometimes been read as error, when in male poets it is more likely to be read as strategic. This chapter shows that women not only deployed roughness or irregularity, they also theorized it. Poems by Anne Southwell and Lucy Hutchinson suggest that women poets embraced accusations of roughness, or rather, they rejected the conventional feminization of smooth style and theorized roughness in entirely new ways.

Anne Southwell, whose virtuosic use of feminine rhyme we saw in Chapter 2, left two complex manuscript collections, now in the British Library and Folger Shakespeare Library, containing poetry from different phases of her life but with a core from the 1620s. A poem about the fourth commandment may seem an unexpected place to find literary criticism but Southwell's "Precept 4" is a dense work of poetic theory-in-practice, as we saw in Chapter 1 with her pioneering use of the verb "criticize". Here she writes a scathing characterization of contemporary poets:

> To lay fair colours on a wrinkled hide
> Or smooth up vice with eloquent discourse
> Who writes for pence, be he so turpified
> And let those nine chimeras be his nurse.
>> To teach him crawl the Heliconian hill
>> And in Parnassus dip his ivory quill.
>
> For me, I write but to my self and me
> What God's good grace doth in my soul imprint
> I bought it not for pelf, none buys of thee
> Nor will I let it at so base a rent
>> As wealth or fame, which is but dross and vapor
>> And scarce deserves the blotting of a paper.[23]

Southwell defines two distinct *styles*, her own as ruggedly frank, other poets' as smoothly allusive. Here smoothing is an action of concealment or erasure, smoothing "up", covering something rather than polishing it. And here it is also connected to a duplicitous, and probably female body, as the smoothing is a cosmetic process, concealing the wrinkles of ageing skin conveyed with the disparaging "hide" and making it falsely "fair". Fair here suggests beauty, of course, and youth (in contrast to "wrinkled" age) and also a conventionally idealized whiteness.[24] Southwell imagines the male poet, aspiring to Helicon, and using an ivory quill to write with the water of Parnassus (we might recall here Cavendish's satirical portrait of male poets competing over access to Helicon in "A Purchase of Poets", in Chapter 3: Original). While she may be imagining a quill made of actual ivory, the poem also suggests that it is the pen (the deceptive pen) that makes women ivory-skinned, and young, and beautiful. The ivory quill, like cosmetics, is a tool used to "smooth up" what is really there, to lay "fair colours" on it.[25]

While Southwell evokes the conventional beauty, youth, and racialized fairness of the poetic lady, she rejects these as a poet: she herself embraces the side of roughness, wrinkles, plainness, and a selfhood which has not been made falsely "fair". Southwell plays out the two styles in her own diction: the first stanza here uses classical images of poetry (Helicon, Parnassus, Chimera); recondite vocabulary (the rare Latinate "turpify"); and rhetorical terms including "discourse" and "colors". The second stanza instead adopts frank monosyllables: "I bought it not for pelf, none buys of thee". The rhythm of this poem itself is metrically and rhetorically smooth, though the feminine rhyme of "paper" and "vapor" adds a hypermetric syllable, calling attention to its own "blotting" (as Chapter 2 showed, feminine rhyme was often seen either as error or excess). Southwell's assertion of privacy and plainness—"I write but to my self and me"—is not a simple claim of modesty: instead it is a claim for a plain, rough, *superior* style. By coding plainness as Christian and erudition as classical, she clears the male inheritance out of the way and asserts her own, religious style as superior. Plainness here is a texture that does not need smoothing.

Southwell turns misogynistic gendering of style back on to male authors. She forcefully rejects smooth, cosmetically—and rhetorically—enhanced styles: those styles often damningly characterized as feminine by late sixteenth-century rhetoricians.[26] Instead, Southwell defines a smooth style which is divine:

> Who wrote the gravest, smoothest, highest style
> Or who dives deepest in the sea of nature,
> If clouds of error do not truth beguile
> Our reason quickly will resolve this matter
>   Why those, whose eyes did never see the light,
>   Should want the skill to hit the mark aright[27]

This is not a style which has been smoothed up or over, but one which is innately smooth, available only to God. Man and womankind, because fallen, cannot attain such perfect smoothness; Southwell removes gender from smoothness, creating a distinction between human and divine rather than male and female. And instead of aspiring to divine smoothness, Southwell describes her own poetry as "rugged".[28] And here she suggests that the ruggedness of her verse, pitted against an artificial smoothness, derives from her love of God:

> Tis love hath wove this rugged twine of mine
> Quickening my heart with such a sprightly flame
> That frozen death can never make it pine
> Nor sad affliction hath the power to lame.
>   For love and fire each other best resemble
>   Both hot and bright, both vigilant and nimble.[29]

Modesty is at play here ("this rugged twine of mine") but, in a rhetorical twist often deployed by women writers, Southwell invokes modesty as a proof of God's love. Moreover, she claims her own voice as authentic, not smoothed up or over. In many of her poems and letters, Southwell reflects on the use of poetry for erotic love. Here she defines her own poetics as one also of love, but love of Christ. She evokes the terms of erotic poetry ("quickening my heart") and of Petrarchism (fire and ice) in order to reject them. And the textile image of her poem as "rugged twine" may even allude to the work of her distant relative the famous Jesuit poet Robert Southwell, who portrayed his own devotional poetry as a "few coarse threads".[30]

Southwell also takes up the often misogynistic trope of women as soft. In the early modern period, a false etymology was thought to connect "mulier" (woman) with "mollis" (tender, soft).[31] As we saw in Chapter 1, in his influential *Queer Philologies*, Jeffrey Masten called for a philology which "analytically doubles back and studies itself, highlighting philology's own normalizing categories and oversights".[32] The example of mulier and mollis reveals how perniciously etymology and philology were once co-opted to defend gendered stereotypes, representing women as inherently malleable.[33] Though women's softness could be a source of praise, this was usually double-edged. In James Shirley's poem "Would you know what's soft?", the speaker holds up the female beloved as the epitome of softness. Yet the women's innate softness is used to depict an object of erotic attraction who is ideal partly because she is silent, as the subsequent problematic metaphors of taste, class and race suggest: Shirley's ideal is soft, sweet-tasting, white-skinned.[34] It could also be used to condemn women as fickle, disloyal and inconstant, as we saw in Chapter 3: Original. Shakespeare's Sonnet 20 plays with a long-established association of fickleness as female when he associates women with "shifting change". This connection was sometimes put in the mouths of women, such as Mary Stuart's casket sonnet vii "[you] think my heart is weak as wax".[35] In the case of the casket sonnets, likely forged by those wishing to incriminate Mary for sexual and political crimes, we can see the dangerous connection of women with moral as well as corporeal softness. And one of literary history's "oversights" (in Masten's terms) is how women themselves reacted to such philological premises for prejudice.

Anne Southwell adapts and resists such ideals of women's softness. Performing her own act of queer philology through poetics, Southwell reimagines female softness as a position of critique. Here she addresses women, first seeming to articulate the misogynistic trope of women's malleability:

> And since your strength is snow against the sun,
> Or wax that yields to every slight impression
> Know here your joy or sorrow is begun;
> Your foul deformity or rare perfection
> Tis to be matched to one that upright
> For your chameleon hue turns as your sight[36]

Southwell turns this trope into a challenge: she critiques marriage by arguing that women are malleable to their husbands. Marriage, then, can be a source of joy or sorrow because of women's malleability or responsiveness to their husbands. In the previous chapter, we saw that Margaret Cavendish embraced the connection between women and malleability, replacing its misogynistic connotations with an Ovidian model of creative transformation. And Philo-Philippa's image of Philips writing on iron is specifically not an image of engraving, but of the forge: iron as soft. Philo-Philippa's emblem of writing is one of craft and permanence, but associated with softness of white-hot iron, rather than filing of a rough substance into smoothness. These poets embrace gendered softness and reshape it into a potent image of poetic creativity. Southwell takes a different approach, though one which also challenges stereotypical associations of women with passive or suspicious softness. Southwell is, in Gillian Wright's phrase "visibly female only when she wants to be", and in these manuscript poems we see a complex interplay between ventriloquizing misogynistic tropes and challenging these.[37] Southwell adopts a rough poetics which works against the association of smoothness and softness with femininity: instead she creates a texture and vocabulary of sharpness and ruggedness. This is semantic and also aesthetic, through her many feminine rhymes, startling technical diction, satirical tone, and wit. When she does articulate feminized softness, she reformulates it as a strength. As Cassandra Gorman has eloquently argued: "her reference to the chameleon departs from the vulnerability of yielding wax and gestures instead at the skills and advantages of adaptability, resilience, and physical sensitivity".[38]

Two decades after Southwell's death, Lucy Hutchinson embarked on her own sharply satirical critique of smoothness. We saw in Chapter 4 how Hutchinson used prosodic irregularity to strategic aesthetic effect in her paired long poems: *Order and Disorder* and *De rerum natura*. In an earlier poem addressed to Edmund Waller, we can see her as a theorist of smooth style. The poem is attributed on the manuscript, now in the British Library: "Mrs Hutchinson's Answer to Mr Waller's Panegirique to Cromwell".[39] Her poem is a parodic response to Waller's panegyric to Cromwell, a lavishly praising poem about Cromwell as providential and heroic leader. Waller's poem remains much debated: critics have argued that it is a poem of success or failure, of conscious ambivalence, of Augustanism, or Machiavellianism, of nationalism or empire building. It is probably in some ways all of these. But to Lucy Hutchinson, writing out of her republican disillusionment, it was a poem which duplicitously celebrated Cromwell for betraying the radical principles of earlier years of the revolution. Coming, as it did, in between his panegyric to Charles 1 and that to Charles II, Waller unsurprisingly was the target of attacks from all political directions. Lucy Hutchinson's response to Waller's poem was one of at least four satires on the poem after its publication in May 1655, most of them royalist.[40] The royalist responses tended to threaten the return of the true monarch but Lucy Hutchinson's "To Mr Waller" instead focuses on exposing the false praise of the Protector, and thereby satirizing the poet as well as subject. It is, as Timothy Raylor describes it, a "line for line demolition" of Waller's poem.[41] And it also shows Hutchinson as a theorist of political style.

Waller had used a vocabulary of strength and gentleness to characterize Cromwell, in his own poem:

> Whilst with a strong, and yet a gentle hand
> You bridle faction, and our hearts command,
> Protect us from ourselves, and from the foe,
> Make us unite, and make us conquer too.[42]

Hutchinson picks up Waller's praise of Cromwell's gentle strength and turns it into a condemnation of Waller's servile smoothness:

> Whilst with a smooth but yet a servile tongue
> You court all factions, and have sweetly sung
> The triumphs of your country's overthrow,
> Raising the glory of her treacherous foe.[43]

Here Waller's style is just as culpable as Cromwell's tyranny—indeed, the poem opens by criticizing the panegyrist rather than the politician. Both use their "servile tongue" to court factions. While Waller became famous for his smooth style, as we saw earlier in comments by Pope and Aubrey, Hutchinson is prescient here in defining his poetics in this way. And in condemning it, she goes against the tide of mid-century poetics. Smooth here comes closer to its sense of insinuating, flattering (OED 6b), even oleaginous. William Cavendish would also claim that Margaret Cavendish's orations surpass the "perfumed and oily tongues" of classical orators.[44] In both cases, women have a position slightly outside, or aslant to, the spheres of rhetoric and public poetry, enabling them to critique the flattering smoothness of panegyrists and orators. Hutchinson herself claims a kind of truth-telling roughness against Waller's smooth-tongued flattery. We saw how Southwell condemned smooth and rugged styles and played out in her own poem the contrast between recondite classical vocabulary and plain-speaking monosyllables. So also here Hutchinson uses line-by-line parody to expose Waller's smoothness not as perfection but as servility. This is smoothness as concealment and redescription: smoothing over, smoothing up.

Waller praises Cromwell as the country's healer:

Your never-failing sword made war to cease,
And now you heal us with the acts of peace:
Our minds with bounty, and with awe engage,
Invite affection, and restrain our rage.

(WALLER, "A PANEGYRICK TO MY LORD PROTECTOR", LL. 109–112)

In her retort, Hutchinson introduces the idea of softness:

Our soft remorse made civil wars to cease
And we are healed now with the axe of peace,
Which doth our quiet spirits disengage,
Turns our affections and revives our rage.

(HUTCHINSON, "TO MR WALLER", LL. 109–112)

Hutchinson redescribes "Acts of Peace" as "Axe of Peace" which is, as David Norbrook observes, "a brilliantly compressed rendition of a whole tradition of Roman republican thought which sees monarchical peace as a specious façade for the threat of violence".[45] She also adds the phrase "soft remorse", instead of Waller characterizing Cromwell's "never-failing sword". Here softness is disingenuous, even morally dubious. Like Anne Southwell, Hutchinson is aware of the whole gendered history of softness through the connections which were argued as etymological (mulier/mollis) and biological, but actually social and cultural.

How is Hutchinson drawing on this tradition when she uses softness to depict Waller's political fickleness? "Soft remorse" certainly conveys the ambivalence of this cycle of political disengagement and reengagement: while the cessation of civil war may be welcome, no kind of meaningful consensus can be reached only through an "axe of peace". Hutchinson argues that Waller uses his "smooth [...] tongue"—his metrical regularity and rhetorically balanced lines—to smooth over his political deceit (or "smooth up", in Southwell's formulation). Throughout her parody, Hutchinson adopts terms that Waller uses for Cromwell, and redirects them against Waller himself, in a satirical act of paradiastole (or rhetorical redescription). By doing so, she shows up what she perceives as Waller's initial act of paradiastole: forcibly reimagining defeat as victory, acquiescence as consensus, disappointment as peace. And the terms she uses to do so are those of smoothness and softness. Here these are entirely negative.

Restoration Praise Poems and the Politics of Smoothness: Anne Wharton, Aphra Behn, Edmund Waller, Gilbert Burnet

Edmund Waller's tongue continued to attract comment. Francis Atterbury's influential claims for Waller as a prosodic reformer focused on his smoothness, in an oddly uncomfortable metonymy: "The tongue came into his hands, like a rough diamond; he polished it first".[46] Smoothness here is not innate but achieved: Atterbury praises Waller's "workmanship". It is a process of crafting, polishing, and of refining raw or "rough" materials". And yet the diamond metaphor is unsettled by the not fully metaphorical "tongue": there is a momentary painful image of Waller polishing a tongue. This section will explore such slippages between descriptions of styles and those of bodies.

Waller was notoriously smooth as a poet. He also engaged in correspondence-in-verse with several women poets. In different ways, both these features make him a useful locus for exploring the idea of poetic smoothness and its gendered connotations as it developed in the Restoration.

A cluster of poems from the 1680s provides evidence of two women poets defining their own poetics—in part a poetics of smoothness and softness—in distinction to their male peers. Waller wrote a poem in praise of Anne Wharton; she wrote one to him; she also wrote one to Aphra Behn, and vice versa; both also wrote in praise of John Wilmot, Earl of Rochester. The history of women as theorists is a matter of reinterpretation—looking again at familiar descriptions of gendered style—and also one of new evidence. There are still discoveries to be made, and the poetry of Anne Wharton is a crucial case. Several of Wharton's poems from a manuscript in Yale's Beinecke Library remain unpublished. Some of the poems analysed in this chapter exist in different print and manuscript versions which reveal both Behn and Wharton under pressure from their male peers to change their poems. Wharton's correspondence with Gilbert Burnet provides crucial evidence of her literary critical views, and those of the culture in which she and Behn wrote. Drawing together little-known manuscript materials with more familiar statements on style demonstrates an archive of theory by and about women poets in the 1680s.

Anne Wharton, whose life remains largely a mystery, has a dual reputation as both pious biblical poet and (by her brother-in-law's seemingly malicious account) a woman "debauched" as a young girl at court.[47] These identities combine, somewhat implausibly, in her identity as adoring niece of the period's most dissolute poet, John Wilmot, Earl of Rochester. His deathbed conversion allowed him to be seen in drastically divergent ways: as a figure of piety as well as one of debauchery. Both Wharton and Behn drew on these apparently contradictory aspects of his reputation, as they forged their own. Crucial elements of Wharton's financial, medical, and personal life remain unknown, which has led to inaccurate biographical accounts.[48] Her maternal grandfather had been a regicide, Henry Danvers, with connections to several women poets: Elizabeth Cary, Lucy Hutchinson, Katherine Philips. Her mother Anne Danvers died when she was only days old; her father Henry Lee had died before she was even born. Anne Wharton and her sister were brought up largely by their grandmother, the Countess of Rochester, whose other son (from a different marriage) was John Wilmot, Earl of Rochester and who was herself the cousin of Lucy Hutchinson. Anne Wharton's marriage was not happy. She suffered chronic illness while her husband trained horses, was unfaithful to her, and pulled off various public pranks. After her death, Thomas Wharton went on to use Anne's money to support his own political aims.[49]

Wharton writes lavishly in praise of her uncle Rochester, and has been both saved and condemned by her connection to this famous man.[50] Even in modern attempts to recover the details and importance of Wharton's life and career, she has been defined by men: Germaine Greer's article on her is called "Rochester's Niece". But this chapter seeks to show that Wharton herself used dialogue with male writers to define her own identity and poetics, and that Aphra Behn did so, too. Together, they define a poetics of softness which is about style, not bodies, and an important development of earlier principles of smoothness. They do so through praise and an often satirical wit in writing to, with and against Waller, Rochester and Gilbert Burnet. These little-studied materials show women defining a "soft poetics" which is both gendered *and* highly-valued.[51]

The cluster of poems between Wharton and Behn provides different evidence with which to develop the analyses of "virile style" and "soft poetics" (by Parker, Hutson, Mann and others) which have so far focused on male writers. In order to do so, we will take what might seem a deviation through Wharton's critical praise poems, their material, social and reception history, before investigating their redefinition of softness in tandem with Aphra Behn.

Wharton exchanged poems with the famously smooth Edmund Waller, and their poetry was published together. Her reputation in her lifetime and afterwards was partly built on a collection of poems between her and Waller. Their poems appear together both in print and also in manuscript. Edmund Waller published a poem in praise of Anne Wharton's paraphrase of Isaiah 53.[52] Wharton responded in her poem "To Mr Waller". Here she defines Waller as an influential precedent for smooth style:

> All who before you came, as hoarsely sung,
> As if by Mars, Apollo's harp was strung,
> And tuned to drums' loud echoes and alarms;
> But you have taught us soft and lasting charms [...]
> [...] His sprightly wit revives with every dawn,
> For ever active, and for ever young,
> His numbers smooth, his sense for ever strong.[53]

Soft charms, smooth numbers, strong sense: Wharton uses similar vocabulary here to Lucy Hutchinson's own poem, also called "To Mr Waller", but while Hutchinson satirized, Wharton praises. Wharton's praise of Waller is, though, complex. The poem opens with lines which seem conventionally humble:

> Now I shall live indeed, not by my skill
> But wisely you your prophesy fulfil

("TO MR WALLER", LL. 1–2)

We might expect this to turn into a familiar modesty topos ("I cannot create a reputation through my poetic skill") but Wharton immediately deviates:

> And, kindly careful of my growing fame,
> Have twisted it with your immortal name.
>
> ("TO MR WALLER", LL. 3–4)

Instead of denying her skill, she reminds the reader that Waller has already praised her, joining hers with his own "immortal name". It becomes a kind of self-commendatory poem. Moreover, here she adapts an image from Waller's poem in praise of her, when he described her poem on Isaiah 53 as binding herself to Isaiah. He had written:

> As ivy thrives, which on the oak takes hold,
> So with the prophets may her lines grow old [...]⁵⁴

It is hard to tell whether a contemporary reader might have detected a note of critique in the image of Wharton as parasitic ivy feeding on biblical oak, or if this would have seemed an image of harmonious symbiosis. Either way, Wharton diplomatically nods to this image in her own metaphor, saying that "you":

> Have twisted it [my name] with your immortal name
>
> (WHARTON, "TO MR WALLER", L. 4)

Like the oak and the ivy, the allusion suggests, Wharton's and Waller's names are bound symbiotically together. And there may be another resonance in the image of "twisting": that of needlework and textile production. Yarns could be combined, or twisted, and this process would also have been one of smoothing as well as strengthening: binding two threads into one smooth one.⁵⁵ Wharton's voice in this poem is bold. She pre-empts and defies critics who might denigrate her work:

> What brainless critic dares his envy raise
> To blast a style which you incline to praise?
>
> ("TO MR WALLER", LL. 5–6)

She asserts that she has been "raised by you to immortality", a powerful claim for herself as well as for Waller's cultural capital: "Once mentioned in your verse I cannot die". The poem constantly promotes Wharton's own poetics before pulling itself back to the stated task of praising Waller. This movement is enacted by the line break in the following lines:

> I'm both inclined by swift poetic rage,
> And gratitude, to give due praise to you:
>
> ("TO MR WALLER", LL. 33–34)

Wharton is propelled and inspired by "poetic rage" (echoing her description of Waller's own "poetic fire") until she calls back her muse to the appropriate stance of "gratitude" and "due praise" of Waller. The gesture of calling back her aspiring muse recurs in this poem, as she rebukes it saying "Down haughty muse" and "Cease haughty muse", articulating both her sense of the necessary modesty of poetic decorum and her desire to climb beyond it. In this poem, Wharton predicted that her name would be "twisted" with Waller's "immortal fame". In fact we can see that *his* fame was written in *her* words. She apostrophizes Waller as "parent of English poesy alone" and this term was taken up by Francis Atterbury, in the influential portrayal of Waller with which this section started: "parent of English verse". Atterbury follows Wharton in the less common "parent" rather than "father" of poetry, and his use of the phrase (borrowed from Wharton) provides part of Waller's legacy in the period.

Yet this poem has further secrets to reveal about Wharton's career, and the pressure she was put under by male correspondents to change her own poetry. Published in 1685, in a miscellany collected by Nahum Tate, Wharton's poem exists in several other print and manuscript sources. And in at least two of these, there is an extra passage which further develops Wharton's literary critical depiction of Waller, and it does so in ways he may not have found fully flattering. Wharton's poems continued to be published for a century after her death, focusing on her piety as a biblical poet. A version of Wharton's poem "To Mr Waller" was published in *The Gentleman's Magazine* in 1815. Tracing the changes to this poem helps us to understand Wharton's delicate and strategic praise of Waller as a poet of smoothness and of smoothing over. And although Wharton's poem is explicitly one of praise, I suggest there is a strand of critique visible especially in the omitted lines. The 1815 magazine version has extra lines:

> If you were not as you are, ever just,
> Yet to your judgment we might safely trust:
> You could not wrong us, for all envy's lost

In those whose fame is raised too high to boast.
Worth cannot lose its due when you are by,
The lordly lion scorns t'oppress a fly.
This 'tis that makes good judgments still commend,
Or who amongst the bad would seek a friend?
If more were such, but such are hardly found,
Then censures would be few, which now abound.[56]

Published nearly a hundred and fifty years later, it might be tempting to assume these were a later interpolation. But another version, from nearer

FIGURE 4. Anne Wharton, "Answer to Mr Waller", *Poems by several hands, and on several occasions collected by N. Tate* (London: 1685), 222–23 and 224–25, from The Burke Library at Union Theological Seminary, Columbia University in the City of New York. Image published with permission of ProQuest LLC. Further reproduction is prohibited without permission. Image produced by ProQuest LLC as part of ProQuest® Early English Books Online (EEBO), www.proquest.com

Wharton's own lifetime, also includes these lines. Yale's Beinecke Library owns a manuscript collection of 24 poems by Wharton, many of them unpublished. The version of "To Mr Waller" here also includes these lines. And there is also evidence of why it was changed, in the form of a letter. This is part of a correspondence between Wharton and Bishop Gilbert Burnet. Burnet had tended to Rochester in his final months, and Wharton may have written to him seeking similar spiritual counsel or relief. But if this is the case, Burnet went far beyond this brief. In a tone of "unctuous superiority", he feels the need to comment on many other aspects of Wharton's life.[57] His letters are by turns flattering and upbraiding. In January 1682/3, Burnet wrote to Wharton about a poem she had sent him:

> About the middle of that for Mr Waller there are six lines from *worth cannot lose*, that I think were as well left out; they are good, but the rest are wonderful, and they do not equal them [...].[58]

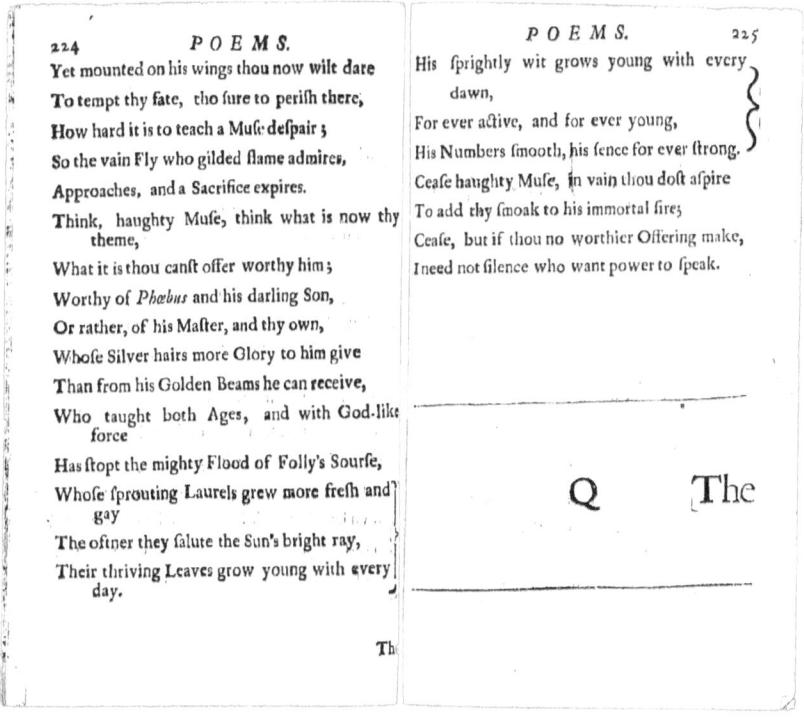

FIGURE 4. (*continued*)

nesse that he was in an honest place: And also that every master and fellow shall come to th' Assemble, and it be within fifty myles about him, if he have any writeinge. And if yee have trespassed against the science, for to abide the award of masters and fellowes, and to make them accorded if they may, and, if they may not accord them, to goe to the Common lawe: And also that noe maister ne fellowe make noe molde nor squyar nor rule to noe layer, nor set noe layer within the lodge nor without to hew noe molde stones. And also that every Mason receive and cherish strange fellowes when they come over the countryes, and set them a worke and they will as the manner is, (that is to say) yf he have noe mould stones in his place, he shall refresh him with money into the next lodge. And also that every Mason shall truly serve the lord for his paie, and every master truly make an end of his worke be it taske or jorney, if yee have your covenants and all that yee ought for to have. These charges that wee now rehearsed to you and to all other that belongeth to Masons, yee shall keepe, soe helpe you God, and your holydome, and by this booke, unto your power. Amen."

Letters from Dr. G. BURNET to the Marchioness of WHARTON *.

LETTER III.

I HOPE, after you have been so many days in the country, it is not too soon to ask you, noble Madam, if you have read any thing of

---

* The following are the Verses by the Marchioness referred to in p. 397.

"To Mr. WALLER.

"NOW I shall live indeed, not by my skill,
But wisely you your prophesies fulfill,
And, kindly carefull of my growing fame,
Have twisted it with your immortal name.
What brainless critic dares his envy raise
To blast a stile which you incline to praise?
Envy I long have scorn'd, but now defie,
Since raised by you to immortality:
Once mention'd in your verse, I cannot die.
You, with the flame of your poetick fire,
Purge off the dross, and leave the sense entire.
You praise what's worthy praise, the rest omit, [forget;
And teach th' ill-natur'd world how to strike [like.
The world, whose peevish memories still
At what is worst, omitting what they
If you were not as you are, ever just,
Yet to your judgment we might safely trust:
You would not wrong us, for all envy's lost [boast.
In those whose fame is rais'd too high to
Worth cannot lose its due when you are by,
The lordly lion scorns t' oppress a fly.
This 'tis that makes good judgments still commend, [friend?
Or who amongst the bad would seek a
If more were such, but such are hardly found, [abound;
Then censures would be few, which now
Parent of English Poesie, alone,
To you we owe the art we call our own;
All who before you came, as hoarsely sung, [strung,
As if by Mars Apollo's harp was
And tun'd to drums, loud echoes, and alarms; [charms.
But you have taught us soft and lasting
Pride of the past, life of the present age,
I'm both inclin'd, by swift poetick rage
And gratitude, to give due praise to you:
But I'm too weak to pay the debt I owe.
Down, haughty Muse; canst thou behold the sun? [ger shun:
Ah! no, withdraw; thy threatening danHe, like an eagle us'd to face the light,
Ere he adopts thee, tries thy tender sight;
Yet, mounted on his wings, thou now wilt dare [there,
To tempt thy fate, tho' sure to perish
(How hard it is to teach a Muse despair!)
So the vain flie the gilded flame admires,
Aproaches, and a sacrifice expires.
Think, haughty Muse, think what is now thy theme,
What is it thou canst offer worthy him:
Worthy of Phœbus and his darling son,
Or rather of his master, and thy own:
Whose silver hairs more glory to him give, [receive;
Than from his golden beams he can
Who taught both ages, and with godlike force [source.
Has stopt the mighty flood of Folly's
Whose springing laurels grow more fresh and gay, [ray;
The oft'ner they salute the sun's bright
Their thriving leaves grow young with every morn; [dawn,
His sprightly witt revives with every
For ever active and for ever young,
His numbers smooth, his sense for ever strong.
Cease, haughty Muse, in vain thou dost aspire
To add thy smoak to his immortal fire;
Cease—but if thou no worthier off'rings make,
I need not silence who wants power to speak."

Burnet seems to have taken against Wharton's counter-factual: "If more were such, but such are hardly found, / Then censures would be few, which now abound". Wharton suggests that if more people were as noble as Waller there would be no need for "censure" of anyone, but the lines leave open the possibility that the censures which "now abound" are of Waller. Wharton undercuts her praise with suggestive omissions: "If you were not as you are, ever just". This a technique familiar from poems like Ben Jonson's to his patrons, for instance, which we are very used to reading as ambivalent. Gaps and silences, indeed, run throughout Wharton's poem, as she points out Waller's own carefully selective technique. Here we can see Wharton portraying Waller's not as the "poetry of limitation" (Warren Chernaik's characterization), but as the poetry of omission. She writes "You praise what's worth praise, the rest omit" and argues that he "[...] teach[es] the ill-natured world how to forget".[59]

Wharton does praise Waller but she introduces ambivalence with the idea of wilful omission and erasure, of smoothing over, or smoothing *up* (in Southwell's formulation). And this ambivalence is accentuated in the manuscript version now in the Beinecke library. In this version of the poem the theme of gaps and silences is taken even further, as the poem ends with a joke embedded in its material form:

> Cease: but if thou no worthyer offring make
> I need not silence, who wants power to spe

This is probably a scribe's hand, but presumably copying a version by the author. It is certainly is not a mistake: the ornamental line below shows that the poem has been carefully completed with this witty gap, an aposiopesis (a deliberately incomplete ending). So even the material form of her poem accentuates a counter-current of critique. It foregrounds Wharton's own mastery of form even as she denies articulacy. Gilbert Burnet's criticism may have caused Wharton to censor some lines of her poem, yet teasing out the material and critical history of this poem allows us to write Wharton's critique back into literary history, and specifically into the ambivalence of Waller's legacy for poetic style.

FIGURE 5. Anne Wharton, "To Mr Waller", *The Gentleman's Magazine*, Vol. 85, pt. i (June 1815), 493. (Image published with permission of ProQuest LLC. Further reproduction is prohibited without permission. Image produced by ProQuest LLC as part of ProQuest® British Periodicals Series, www.proquest.com)

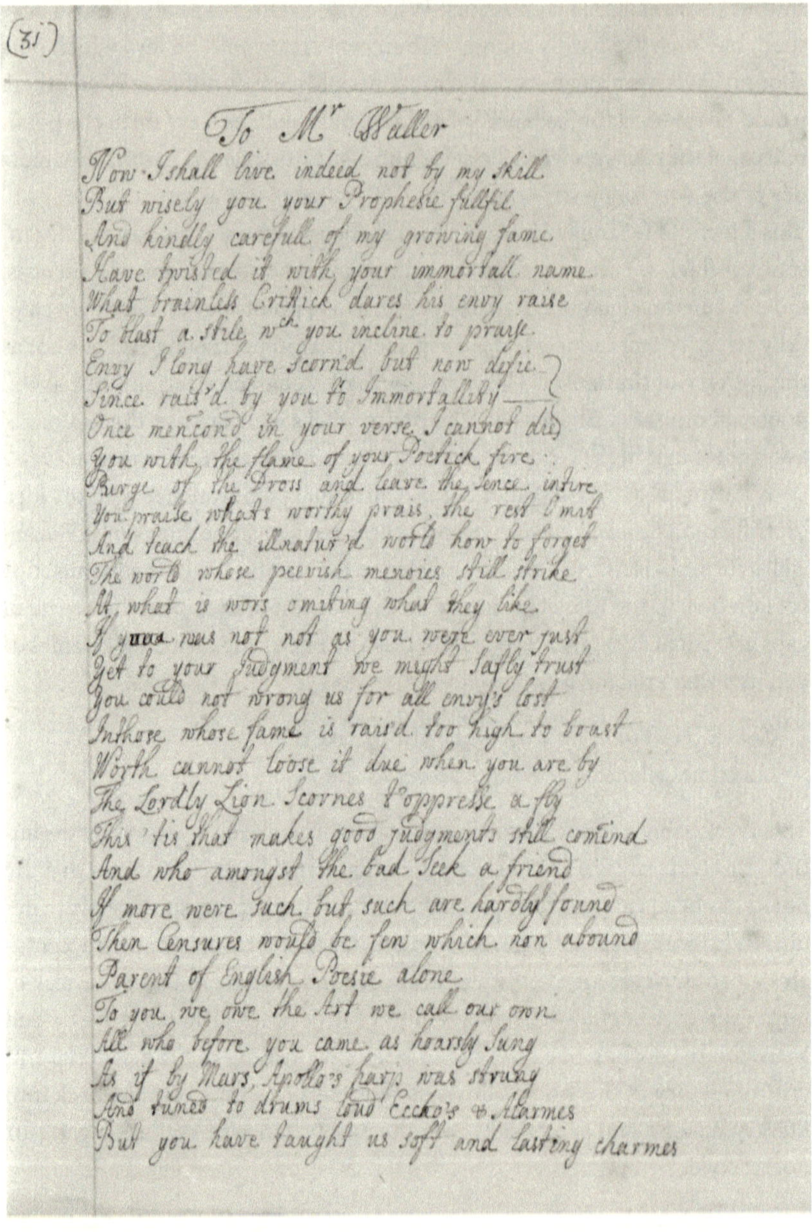

(31)

To Mr Waller

Now I shall live, indeed not by my skill
But wisely you your Prophesie fullfill
And kindely carefull of my growing fame
Have twisted it with your immortall name
What brainless Critick dares his envy raise
To blast a stile w[ch] you incline to praise
Envy I long have scorn'd but now defie
Since rais'd by you to Immortallity
Once men͂con'd in your verse I cannot die
You with the flame of your Poetick fire
Purge of the Dross and leave the sence intire
You praise what's worthy prais, the rest o'mit
And teach the illnatur'd world how to forget
The world whose peevish memories still strike
At what is wors omiting what they like
If yours was not not as you were ever just
Yet to your Judgment we might safly trust
You could not wrong us for all envy's lost
In those whose fame is rais'd too high to boast
Worth cannot loose it due when you are by
The Lordly Lion scornes t'oppresse a fly
This 'tis that makes good judgments still comend
And who amongst the bad seek a friend
If more were such, but such are hardly fonnd
Then Censures would be few which now abound
Parent of English Poesie alone
To you we owe the Art we call our own
All who before you came as hoarsly sung
As if by Mars, Apollo's harp was strung
And tuned to drums loud eccho's & Alarmes
But you have taught us soft and lasting charmes

FIGURE 6. Anne Wharton, "To Mr Waller", Osborn MS b408, James Marshall and Marie-Louise Osborn Collection, Beinecke Rare Book and Manuscript Library, Yale University, fol. 32

(32)

Pride of the past, life of the present age
I'm both inclin'd by swift poetick rage
And gratitude to give due praise to you
But I'm to weake to pay the debt I owe
Downe haughty muse canst thou behold the Sun
Ah! noe, withdraw thy threatening danger shunn
He like an Eagle us'd to face the light
Ere he adopts thee trys thy tender sight
Yet mounted on his wings thou now will dare
To tempt thy fate though sure to perish there
(How hard it is teach a Muse dispair)
So the vaine fly who guilded flames admires
Approaches and a Sacrifice expires
Think haughty muse think what is now thy theme
What is it thou canst ofer worthy him
Worthy of Phebus & his darling Son
Or rather of his Master and thy own
Whose Silver haires more glory to him give
Then from his golden beams he car receive
Who taught both ages, and with Godlike force
Hath stop'd their mighty floud of folly's Source
Whose sprouting lawrells grow more fresh and gay
The oftner they Salute the Suns bright Ray
There thriving Leaves grow young with ev'ry day
His sprightly wit revives with ev'ry dawne
For ever Active and for ever young
His number smooth, his sence for ever strong
Cease haughty muse, in vaine thou dost aspire
To add thy smoke to his immortal fire
Cease: but if thou no worthyer ofring make
I need not silence, who wants power to spe

Wharton to Behn, Behn to Wharton

Wharton also wrote a praise poem to Aphra Behn, and Behn to Wharton, in the early 1680s. These were triangulated through the praise of another male poet, one who had recently died: John Wilmot, Earl of Rochester, Wharton's uncle. In this poetic dialogue, Wharton and Behn engage further in defining the shifting connections between smoothness and softness, and their relationship to poets' sex and gender.

Behn's poem on Rochester's death had praised him for "freely" bestowing the gifts of "poetry, and love".[60] Wharton responded in a poem "To Mrs. A. Behn, On what she Writ of the Earl of Rochester" which, like her poem to Waller, is also explicitly about poetic style, history and value. Again, her poem opens by unsettling the reader's expectations:

> In pleasing transport rapt, my thoughts aspire
> With humble verse to praise what you admire:[61]

A poem addressed to Behn turns out to be in praise both of Behn and the object of her own praise in turn, Rochester.

> Few living poets may the laurel claim,
> Most pass through death, to reach at living fame.
> Fame, phoenix-like, still rises from a tomb;
> But bravely you this custom have o'ercome.
> You force an homage from each generous heart,
> Such as you always pay to just desert.
> You praised him living, whom you dead bemoan,
> And now your tears afresh his laurel crown.

("TO MRS. A. BEHN", LL. 3–10)

This is a praise poem about a praise poem: it is also a critique of the genre of elegy itself. She praises Behn for her consistency: "You praised him living, whom you dead bemoan". Wharton here suggests Behn's moral integrity and critical prescience in praising Rochester in life. She suggests that most elegists write hyperbolically about those figures after death who in life they might have criticized or ignored: elegy, like the ode as we saw in the previous chapter, was a form used to gain social capital. Perhaps elegy, like panegyric, could also be seen as a mode in which poets smoothed over inconvenient truths (like their unfriendly relationship to the deceased in life) in order to promote themselves.

Yet Behn, Wharton writes, is coherent in her praise of Rochester in life and in death. The poem then shifts from Rochester to Behn herself:

> It is this flight of yours excites my art,
> Weak as it is, to take your muse's part,
> And pay loud thanks back from my bleeding heart.
> May you in every pleasing grace excel,
> May bright Apollo in your bosom dwell;
> May yours excel the matchless Sappho's name;
> May you have all her wit, without her shame:
> Tho' she to honor gave a fatal wound,
> Employ your hand to raise it from the ground.
>
> ("TO MRS. A. BEHN", LL. 11–19)

Wharton represents herself and Behn as reciprocally inspiring: Behn's poem inspires Wharton who writes back in turn to Behn, wishing her further "wit". And it is a poem about both women as artists, as Behn's "muse" excites Wharton's "art". The poem only moves to consider their female identities when Wharton turns to Behn's reputation. She is acutely aware of how women poets' reputations are built on their bodies not their poems. Here she draws on the archetypal figure of a woman poet with vexed reputation: Sappho.

Wharton's lines here are charged with the connotations of Sappho's identity and her poetics: "May yours excel the matchless Sappho's Name; / May you have all her wit, without her shame". Of the damage caused by Sappho to "Honour", Wharton encourages Behn to

> Right its wronged cause with your enticing strain,
> Its ruined temples try to build again.
> Scorn meaner themes, declining low desire,
> And bid your muse maintain a vestal fire.
> If you do this, what glory will ensue,
> To all our sex, to poesy, and you?
> Write on, and may your numbers ever flow,
> Soft as the wishes that I make for you.
>
> ("TO MRS. A. BEHN", LL. 20–27)

Wharton sees Behn as the worthy heir to "matchless" Sappho but also superior; Behn is able to redeem "honour" and bring glory to women and poetry.

Wharton's mention of Sappho does have an overt sense of judgement: she warns Behn not to be dishonorable like Sappho. And there are precedents for this connection, within Wharton's circle: Edmund Waller had praised Wharton for not being a Sappho, when he admired her for writing "Such pious lines! When wanton Sapphos live" ("Of Divine Poesy"). Yet I would argue that Wharton's evocation of Sappho here is more complex. Alongside warning of the dangers of Sappho's reputation, she also suggests a lineage which connects herself to Behn, and does so *through* Sappho. Aphra Behn had compared herself to Sappho. Behn was one of a group of writers brought together to translate Abraham Cowley's *Sylva*. In her Book 6 of his *Plantarum*, she says to the Laurel / bay tree "Let me with Sappho and Orinda be / Oh ever sacred nymph, adorned by thee; and give my verses immortality."[62] In much of this poem Behn is distanced twofold from the speaking voice, as she writes both a translation and a prosopopeia (making an inanimate thing speak). But here she steps out of both, and signals explicitly that she speaks for herself: "The Translatress in her own person speaks". While both Edmund Waller and Gilbert Burnet were praising Wharton for being, respectively, *not* like Sappho and *not* like Behn, Wharton was herself actively pursuing these associations. She was writing her poem in praise of Behn and one based on a Sappho lyric.[63] Wharton's poem "Sapho to Phaon Englished out of Boileau" appeared anonymously in 1685.[64] It engages closely with Boileau's translation of Sappho's lyric (from Longinus), and exists in an intriguingly different version in the unpublished Osborn collection manuscript, at Yale's Beinecke Library.[65] And in this poem, Wharton associates her own voice with Sappho's. Not only does she adopt Sappho's first-person voice, she also uses terms which she also used to define her own, Behn's and Rochester's style: "soft languishments", where she chooses "soft" to translate the French "douce" which could mean both soft and sweet.

Far from distancing herself from Sappho, then, Wharton's Sapphic poem was not only published, but published with a collection of Behn's works.[66] Gillian Manning has even suggested that Behn might have been responsible for some of the changes made to the poem for its publication.[67] These connections suggest a different interpretation of Wharton's reference to Sappho's "shame". Wharton is here describing not her own assessment of Sappho's morality, but the imputations against her. She might be telling readers (like Burnet and Waller) not to impute shame to Behn, rather than warning Behn herself of the dangers of libertine poetry and behaviour; the danger is not to women themselves but their reputations amongst men.

Critical attention to this poem has focused on Behn either ignoring Wharton's recommendation that she avoid Sappho's model (Todd) or responding with a model of male influence (Chernaik; Spencer). But we can see Wharton instead suggesting a transhistorical lineage for passionate female poets whose poetics was defined by softness—by emotional susceptibility and responsiveness. The final couplet develops softness as a critical and moral principle: "Write on, and may your numbers ever flow, / Soft as the wishes that I make for you." In this almost zeugma, soft is both a stylistic category (referring to Behn's "numbers") and a moral one (referring to Wharton's "wishes" for her peer). Through the metaphor of "flow", soft becomes not the quality of a malleable solid, but of a liquid. As we saw earlier, the latter seventeenth century sees a move away from a model of style in which manly strength and feminine smoothness could be combined by poets of either sex. By the later Restoration, smoothness has been coopted as a term of praise used for male poets. Loscocco argues that women are left with the far lower-valued "soft".[68] Despite (or perhaps because of) its far higher numbers of women poets in print, the later Restoration sees a reification of gendered categories of style, attaching them to male or female authors. And Wharton indeed praises Waller for his smoothness: as Atterbury writes, Waller polishes the English tongue. But these poems by Wharton, many of them unpublished, and her poetic conversation with Aphra Behn, reveal a different counter-narrative. Far from being devalued, Wharton claims "soft" as a central principle of her critical poetics.

Softness is also central to Behn's poetics. She replies to Wharton with her poem "To Mrs. W. On her Excellent Verses (Writ in Praise of some I had made on the Earl of *Rochester*) Written in a Fit of Sickness".[69] The poem is a feverish reverie in which the unwell Behn is visited by the ghost of Rochester, prompted by Wharton's poem. Janet Todd describes the poem's central figure as a "vision of the coalesced Rochester-Wharton".[70] Behn describes the apparition, saying:

> In every part there did appear,
> The great, the God-like Rochester,
> His softness all, his sweetness everywhere.
>
> It did advance, and with a generous look,
> To me addressed, to worthless me it spoke:
> With the same wonted grace my muse it praised,
> With the same goodness did my faults correct:
> And careful of the fame himself first raised,

> Obligingly it schooled my loose neglect.
> The soft, the moving accents soon I knew
> The gentle voice made up of harmony;
> Through the known paths of my glad soul it flew;
> I knew it straight, it could no others be,
> 'Twas not allied but very very he.
>
> (LL. 30–43)

Here Behn portrays softness and sweetness as fundamentally characteristic of Rochester's style, and, by extension (through the poem's title and addressee) to Wharton's. Behn's poem reveals the complex ways in which stylistic features are applied to bodies. "Soft" here is connected to pleasing harmony but may also evoke the morally troubling malleability which was often attributed to women, and to libertine principles and behaviors. We saw in Chapters 3 and 4 that feminine rhyme and irregular prosody were often sites of slippage between poetics and personhood. And in Behn's poem to Wharton and about Rochester we can see a close relationship between her subjects (these two poets themselves) and their style. "Soft" is prosodic as well as erotic (like "loose" and "tender", as we will see). As Ros Ballaster has argued, Behn crafts a posthumous Rochester who is "a softly commanding stimulus to female creativity", in contrast to the male sexual violence implied in some of his writings and life.[71]

Behn combines praise of Rochester with implicit response to Wharton. This is another poem of self-definition through praise, triangulated through a male poet. The poem's title makes clear its interest in poetry itself: it is a poem by Behn to Wharton about her poem written in response to Behn's poem about Rochester (and his poetry). In another context, Ros Ballaster has written about Behn's "deployment of Rochester as pretext for the image of her own art".[72] In these poems we see Rochester as a pretext for both Behn and Wharton to explore their own art in contradistinction to each other's, and to Rochester's, and to write against their detractors. Rochester's identity at this moment brought together two apparent contraries: extreme libertinism and extreme piety. These identities were consecutive: an apparently pious death followed his life of dissolution and law-breaking. His biographers, including Wharton's correspondent Gilbert Burnet, stressed his deathbed conversion, while others focused on his depravity. As well as being Wharton's uncle, Rochester was a public figure with whom both Wharton and Behn could associate themselves for his unusually divergent reputation as both pious and libertine. In Behn's poem, the "phantom" of Rochester appears to Behn when she is ill and looking back over her life. It opens dramatically: "Enough kind Heaven! To purpose have I lived, / And all my sighs and languishments have shed". Rochester's ghost appears to her, shaking her out of her melancholy:

> With the same goodness did my faults correct:
> And careful of the fame himself first raised,
> Obligingly it schooled my loose neglect.[73]

The sense of "schooled my loose neglect" is complex. It may suggest that the ghost of Rochester was kindly scolding Behn for neglecting herself: she describes herself as depleted by illness and mourning for Rochester, "Sad as the grave", "pensive", "melancholy" and he "schools" her into taking care of herself. But might the "faults" also be poetic? The phrase "loose neglect" opens up a prosodic and poetic sense as well as an emotional one. In this reading, Behn pre-empts criticism of her own verse, and responds specifically to Wharton. Behn is making clear that she realizes she was being warned by Wharton's poem about the risks of Sapphic "shame". As with almost all the many praise poems of the seventeenth century, Wharton's poem to Behn had trodden the line between praise and blame, and Behn knows it: Wharton's poem implicitly tried to "school" Behn and correct her "faults", warning or protecting her from the criticism of men like Burnet. Behn mitigates this criticism through referring to Rochester's support of her. Wharton had asserted that Edmund Waller's support had "raised [her] to immortality" and Behn similarly claims that Rochester was "careful of her fame" having "first raised" it. Behn allies both Wharton and herself closely with Rochester, so that any criticism of her Sapphic, sensual verse has to be directed also at the dead, idolized poet, Rochester. Wharton has often been defined in relation to men but this cluster of poems between Wharton, Waller, Behn and Rochester suggests an alternative. In what has been seen by one critic as a homoerotic collaboration between Wharton and Behn, the body of the male poet—here ventriloquized after death—allowed women poets to construct a female lineage and dialogue.[74]

Aphra Behn's Tenderness

These slippages between styles and bodies become a topic for debate in Wharton's correspondence as well as her poems. As we saw earlier, the correspondence between Gilbert Burnet and Wharton reveals extensive discussion of poetry. Despite the survival of only Burnet's letters, we can conjecture at some of Wharton's views from the gaps and responses in the correspondence. Burnet's letters reveal his profoundly gendered theory of sexuality and style, which Wharton disputes. Burnet wrote to Wharton in December 1682:

> Some of Mrs. Behn's songs are very tender, but she is so abominably vile a woman and rallies not only all religion, but all virtue in so odious and obscene a manner, that I am as heartily sorry she has writ anything in your commendation, as I am glad, (I had almost said proud) that you have honoured me as you have done.[75]

Here Burnet weighs up the value of two praise poems, and two women poets: Behn's praise of Wharton risks devaluing Wharton's praise of him. He also describes the value of Behn's poetry immediately in terms of her character—vile, odious, obscene—while her poems are "tender". And indeed, these terms may be connected. When Burnet grudgingly praises Behn's poems as "tender", he is still envisaging her poetry through her body and character. The emotional sense of "tender" was both active and passive, as it could mean both expressing gentle emotions, and susceptibility to these.[76] And this emotional sense of "tender" derived from its more physical one, which itself also implied a narrative of interaction: responsiveness to touch, even taste. Its meanings could be descriptive, often for food or plants, suggesting something fragile, easily yielding to touch, and (if edible) succulent, which would develop in the subsequent century into the verb of softening by violence: "tenderize".[77] When the term was used figuratively, it accumulated troubled and gendered meanings, including effeminacy.[78] In *Cymbeline*, Shakespeare evokes the false etymological connection between women and softness, specifically translating "mollis" as "tender":

> The piece of tender air, thy virtuous daughter,
> Which we call *mollis aer*; and *mollis aer*
> We term it *mulier*.[79]

Florio's glossing of "morbidezza", a term for the painterly rendering of flesh, had also included "tender": the term is aesthetic and also bodily, even potentially erotic or obscene, as in Burnet's slighting usage for Behn.

Burnet warns Wharton, then, of the risks of associating herself with Behn. But within a week, it seems, Wharton had sent her own poem in praise of Behn to Burnet. As we have seen, her poem acknowledges accusations of Behn's Sapphic shame, and reshapes these into praise: she claims for Behn the power to raise honour from shame. We can read her poem as a response to his letter, and his belligerent censure of Behn's vileness. This poem treads a delicate line, both engaging with criticism of Behn yet also defending herself, Wharton, and Behn, from the censure of her male coterie. If Behn can "scorn meaner themes", Wharton claims, then she will bring "glory" to women and poetry, as well as to herself. She also boldly, given Burnet's strong censure, binds herself to Behn: "Write on, and may your numbers ever flow, / Soft as the wishes that I make for you". And from his letter in response, we can see that Gilbert Burnet is clearly very cross. He reiterates his censure of Behn, again moving the grounds from poetry to morality:

> I am very much pleased with your verses to Mrs. Behn; but there are some errors in women, that are never to be forgiven to that degree, as to allow those of a severe virtue to hold any correspondence with them. (p. 353)

His letter shifts the grounds of argument from poem to person, from verses to women. He then goes on to complain that all Wharton wants to discuss is poetry: "But how comes it, that write what I will to you on other subjects, I can get no answers but concerning poesy?". This sounds like a complaint that Wharton is refusing to discuss Behn's character with him. We can see this tension also in his previous letter where his admission of Behn's poetry as "tender" moves into censure of her as so "vile a woman". Burnet may wish to focus on Behn's identity and not her poetry; Wharton insisted that their conversations focused on the latter. And Gilbert Burnet indeed complains that Wharton will only write about, and *in*, verse: "Are your thoughts so engaged unto numbers, that you cannot write loose and in plain English prose? To tell you truth, I am much delighted with wit, especially when it is so fine and soft as yours is [. . .]". The terms in which he praises Wharton—"soft", "fine"—uncomfortably recall his grudging praise of Behn's "tender" poems (in the context of her vile person).

William Atwood's poems after Anne Wharton's death also assert her distance from Behn, describing Behn as a "counterfeit Astrea" who has "debauch[ed] the too effem'nate Age" with "lustful rage".[80] And even though he praises her, Atwood's praise for Wharton suggests its own unsettlingly physical, even sexual, subtext as he describes Wharton encouraging him and Waller to write:

> When that soft hand whence Waller has his dues,
> Strokes, and encourages my backward muse;
> Feeds it with praise, and teaches it to fly:[81]

Of course "hand" can often be a metonymy for "writing" and (as we have seen) "soft" can be stylistic too. But the combination here in "soft hand" is somehow inescapably corporeal. And while "dues" means that she gives Waller the praise due to him, it also has an edge of threat or sexuality—or both.

For Wharton this was all highly charged. While praise poems during her short lifetime and afterwards are suffused with praise for her piety (in contrast to Behn's debauchery), other accounts of her life were salacious. Most prominently, her brother-in-law Goodwin Wharton let it be known that she had been "debauched" at court as a young girl and that in adulthood she had tried to seduce him (which he claimed, of course, to have resisted).[82] Even in twentieth-century discourse she was often portrayed in this light: Greer conjectures that the illness that blighted her life and killed her at the age of 26 may have been sexually transmitted. Pulling in an opposite direction, yet equally damaging, was the rumor that her husband had refused to have sex with her. While my own aim is not to draw Wharton's poetry into gossip about her life, I do want to show up the hypersexualized undertone in the apparently lavish poems praising her virtue. Through their poems to each other, and through the figure of the dead Rochester, Behn and Wharton create a shared poetics of softness and tenderness. In their formulation, softness connotes both highly emotional responsiveness and a quality of literary criticism. It is critical in the sense that Wharton and Behn define a certain kind of feminized poetics out of the terms which were also being used to diminish women's poetry in the Restoration. And their relationship continued through publication, as Behn printed her poem to Wharton in her first poetry collection (1684) and, later, Wharton's poem "Despair" in her own *Miscellany*.[83] Yet she did not publish Wharton's poem to her, about Rochester, in which Wharton advises her to continue to write soft lyrics, though without Sappho's shame. Janet Todd conjectures that this publication was obstructed either by Wharton's family or Burnet. If this is the case, then we can see that Wharton's and Behn's creation of a female poetic lineage and community was perceived as a threat to the pious reputation that figures like Burnet wanted for Wharton, even if she did not seek this image herself. Wharton's poem to Behn recuperates Behn and even Sappho (who is "matchless"), showing that piety and "tenderness" are not mutually exclusive.

We have seen that the word "tender" provided a pivot around which Burnet could characterize both poem and woman as softly yielding. Behn herself was also using this term, but to satirize exactly such criticisms as Burnet's. She deploys the terms "tender" and "soft" in her virtuosic ode on Thomas Creech's translation of Lucretius:

> But I of feebler seeds designed,
> While the slow-moving atoms strove
> With careless heed to form my mind,
> Composed it all of softer love:
> In gentle numbers all my songs are dressed;
> And when I would thy glories sing,
> What in strong manly verse should be expressed
> Turns all to womanish tenderness within [...][84]

Here Behn rather playfully interpolates a Lucretian basis for sexual difference: different atoms create different sexes.[85] There is something sardonic in Behn's characterization of herself as designed of feebler seeds and therefore her style as "tender". With "Strong Manly Verse", Behn here is critically astute in gesturing to the view of Lucretius's style as distinctively masculine. There was a precedent in defining Lucretius' style through bodily metaphors. Richard Fanshawe had described John Evelyn's translation as smoothing Lucretius's hairiness: "though it retain neither his voice, nor yet his hairiness [...] it hath both his soul, and his lineaments".[86] Fanshawe praises Evelyn here for retaining some of Lucretius's masculinity while taming others. We saw in Chapter 4 that this view was weaponized against women, with Aston Cokain's prohibition on women (probably specifically Lucy Hutchinson) translating Lucretius. In this usage, it is not just Lucretius's Latinity which excludes women, but some innate masculinity in his subject and even style. Wittily embracing the misogyny of this view, then, Behn adopts a pose of coyly extreme modesty with her contrast between "strong manly verse" and "womanish tenderness". In this context, it is also striking that Behn writes an ode, a form widely used by this point, which had been influentially portrayed by Abraham Cowley as irregular, bold, and masculine (as explored in the previous chapter). This essentialist poetics (and Behn's playful adoption of it) helps us interpret Burnet's comments on Behn in his letter to Wharton: "Some of Mrs. Behn's songs are very *tender*, but she is so abominably vile a woman." Multiple times in his letters to Wharton, Burnet moves in one sentence from Behn's poetry to her identity as a woman. In this context, even when "tender" might mean delicate or fine in a positive sense, it is also profoundly connected to meanings of malleability, changeableness, and consumption. Even when Burnet refers to Behn's songs positively as "tender", he is still defining her poetic style according to her sex.

Wharton, we remember, ended her poem to Behn: "Write on, and may your numbers ever flow, / Soft as the wishes that I make for you". Wharton suggests that Behn should eschew some elements of the Sapphic, possibly a concession to the views of her censorious correspondent Burnet. But Wharton then actually encourages Behn to continue to write sensual poetry ("enticing"). She rejects the sexist connotations of softness. Rather than shying away from Behn's reputation for "tenderness", Wharton defiantly claims softness as an ideal for women poets. This was also, as we saw, an adjective she herself had chosen in her own Sappho poem.

Wharton and the Soft Poetics of Complaint

Anne Wharton would go on to investigate the critical principles of softness in one particular poetic mode: complaint. In three little-known poems, two of which remain unpublished, she explores the mode of complaint specifically in terms of gendered softness. While critics have long perceived complaint as a mode preoccupied with gender, this has almost always been in men's uses of the form to ventriloquize female voices, from Ovid's *Heroides* to Shakespeare's *A Lover's Complaint*. But recent work by Sarah C.E. Ross, Rosalind Smith and others has revealed a rich corpus of female-authored complaint.[87] Wharton's little-known poems can help us define the key contributions of this newly revealed body of work. In Wharton's poems "Unchangeable", "The Inconstancy of Woman Kind", and "Melpomene against Complaint" she writes what I define as critical poetics. Through this cluster of poems she both embodies and critiques the complaint mode, exploring its gendered usages. Wharton also (most pertinently for this chapter) defiantly reclaims the feminized attribute of softness as an advantage.

Wharton's poem, "The Inconstancy of Woman Kind", has at its heart a short lament by Aminta, framed by commentary from a first-person narrator. In the frame parts of the poem, Wharton comments on the nature of complaint and of women, undermining both the lament and the woman at its centre. The poem has never been published before; here it is in full:

"The Inconstancy of Woman Kind"

Whilst on the shore Aminta lay
I saw the yielding sand give way
To the much softer fair, who pressed

The car[e]less billow with her breast.
Rude sighs broke fiercely from her heart,
And seemed to fly love's piercing dart,
Which complained was entered there,
And drove forth peace to let in care;
Thus on her bed her fingers wrought:
"Love thou bright object of my thought,
Rather than change I'll yield my breath
And crown with constancy my death
Thus to thy name I'll altars raise
And deck it with immortal praise".
These were her words, but who can trust
Word spoke by women, wrote in dust?
The inconstant tide of women's love
Will soon those monuments remove;
The streams have washed away the sand
And her false heart directs her hand[88]

In this fascinating complaint poem, a female author ventriloquizes both an implicitly male, misogynistic narrator and a lamenting woman.[89] The narrator watching Aminta immediately associates her with softness: she lies on "yielding sand", against which her own body is even "softer". These associations with malleability are turned against Aminta. After she has written her lament in the sand, the narrator observes sharply that her words are both morally and materially changeable, transient, soft. This is exactly the misogyny that Aminta has rejected, asserting her firm resolve and "constancy" against "change" even in the face of death ("I'll yield my breath"). But her words are written "in dust", removed by the ebbing "tide" of both literal waves and women's inconstant emotions. In this polyvocal poem, Wharton ventriloquizes the stereotype of female changeability and softness. Yet does she also challenge this view? From the opening, the narrator blurs the woman's body and the narrator's own perception: it is the sand which yields to Aminta's body, yet her own morals are perceived as yielding. Moreover, Aminta's act of ephemeral writing evokes a famous sixteenth-century precursor: the sonnet tradition broadly, and Spenser's *Amoretti* 75 in particular. In this sonnet, Spenser's speaker moves between admission of the transience of his writing,

One day I wrote her name upon the strand,
But came the waves and washed it away [. . .]

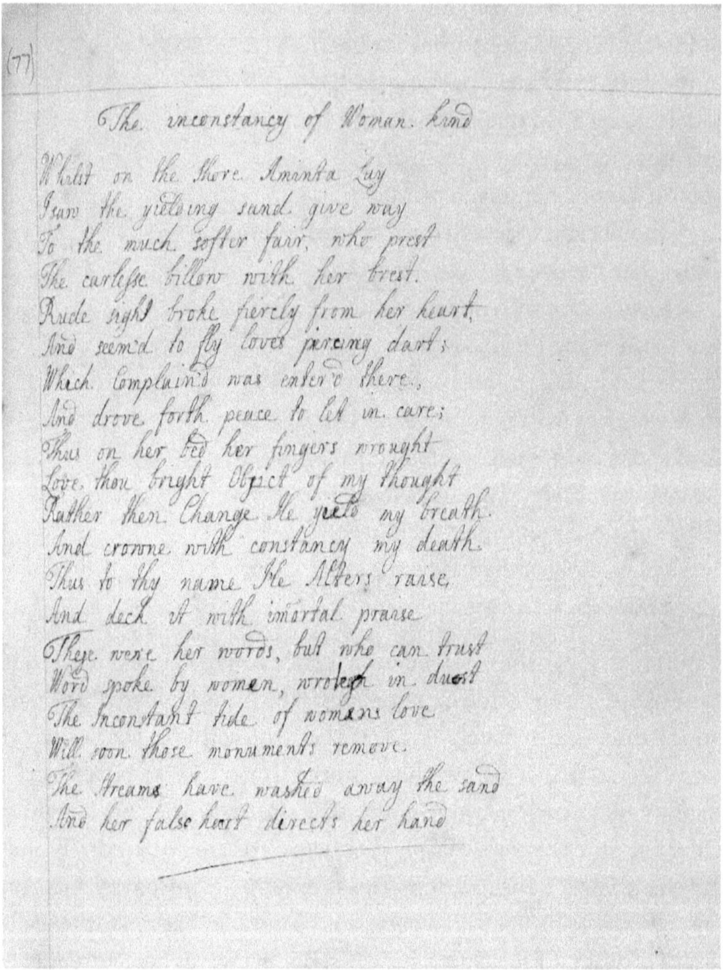

> (77)
>
> 6 The inconstancy of Woman. kind
>
> Whilst on the Shore Aminta Lay
> I saw the yielding sand give way
> To the much softer fair, who prest
> The carlesse billow with her brest.
> Rude sighs broke fiercely from her heart,
> And seem'd to fly loves piercing dart;
> Which Complain'd was enter'd there,
> And drove forth peace to let in care;
> Thus on her bed her fingers wrought
> Love, thou bright Object of my thought
> Rather then Change He yeild my breath
> And crowne with constancy my death.
> Thus to thy name He Alters raise,
> And deck it with imortal praise
> 6 These were her words, but who can trust
> Word spoke by woman, wrote in dust
> The Inconstant tide of womans love
> Will soon those monuments remove.
> The Streams have washed away the sand
> And her false heart directs her hand

FIGURE 7. Anne Wharton, "The inconstancy of Woman Kind", Osborn MS b408, fol. 77, James Marshall and Marie-Louise Osborn Collection, Beinecke Rare Book and Manuscript Library, Yale University

and assertions of its permanence:

> [...] My verse your virtues rare shall eternize,
> And in the heavens write your glorious name [...][90]

While Spenser's poem uses the metaphor of writing on sand to reinforce his defiant claim for the permanence of his writing, Wharton's speaker uses it to articulate the proverbial misogyny of women's inconstancy. And with its title

"The Inconstancy of Woman Kind", her poem may even be a reply to the witty misogyny of another famous sixteenth-century poem, John Donne's "Women's Constancy". The title of Donne's poem proves bitterly ironic as his lover can only claim to have loved him for "one whole day". Women, like sand, are soft and changing. Wharton's little-studied, and in this case still unpublished, poems show that women themselves were profoundly engaged in this debate.

"The Inconstancy of Woman Kind" is not Wharton's final word on women's softness. In fact, her poems in manuscript Osborn b408 represent a sustained critique of the idea of women as both soft and changeable. Wharton's short poem "Unchangeable" also muses on the complex cultural and romantic associations of change. The gender of neither the speaker nor the lover is specified. We could interpret the lover as male because he is referred to metaphorically as "My Proteus" and therefore the speaker as female, but the poem leaves both only implicit. Here is the poem; again, as far as I know, it has been unpublished until now:

"Unchangeable"

Priests preach, and poets teach us, that all harms
Are shunned by constancy's defensive arms.
Achylis's sire by constancy at last
Forced Proteus to a stand and held him fast;
My toil hath as unwearied been and great,
But all in vain my Proteus changes yet.
I ask no more of heaven to make him stay
Now every shape of his I'd drive away.[91]

The poem opens by recalling how authority figures preach constancy as the cure to all harm. But the poem challenges this advice of constancy above all. While it is hard to say whether "great / yet" would have functioned as a full rhyme, to a contemporary reader it feels like a shift into uncertainty at this moment of the poem: the rhyme scheme becoming more malleable as her Proteus changes. Moreover, Wharton uses the poem's mythical underpinning to unsettle the priests' and poets' imperative of constancy. First, the speaker challenges ideas of female changeability by invoking Proteus, a male figure of change, to characterize her lover: "my Proteus". Her emblematic figure of constancy is Peleus, father of Achilles, who was able to stop Proteus transforming. Secondly, as an emblem of constancy this is not one of Christian endurance but of mythical violence. Peleus did not negotiate with but

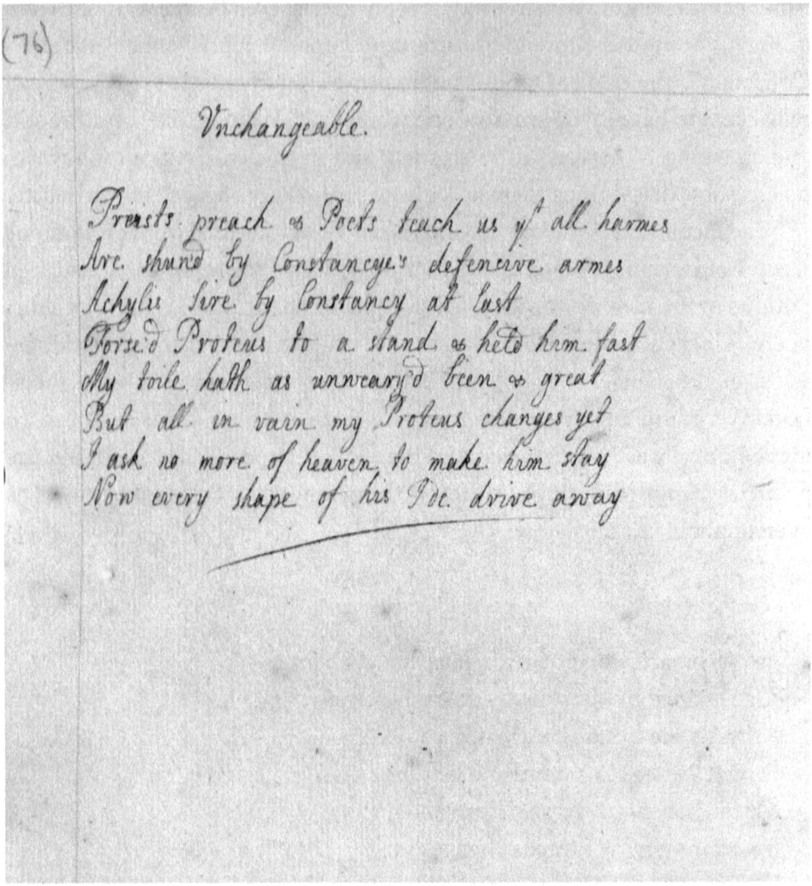

> (76)
>
> **Unchangeable.**
>
> Preists preach & Poets teach us y^t all harmes
> Are shun'd by Constancye's defensive armes
> Achylis Sire by Constancy at last
> Forse'd Proteus to a stand & held him fast
> My toile hath as unweary'd been & great
> But all in vain my Proteus changes yet
> I ask no more of heaven to make him stay
> Now every shape of his I'de drive away

FIGURE 8. Anne Wharton, "Unchangeable", Osborn MS b408, fol. 76, James Marshall and Marie-Louise Osborn Collection, Beinecke Rare Book and Manuscript Library, Yale University

rather captured Proteus. Moreover, he captured him in order to seize the secret of how to seduce Thetis. This male-preached constancy, then, is one which has sexual violence at its heart. And this is reflected in the final, enigmatic couplet: "I ask no more of heaven to make him stay / Now every shape of his I'd drive away". This may mean that the speaker wants to drive away her lover's other identities and forms, retaining only his true one. But it could also be read as a final rejection of her lover altogether: "Now every shape of his I'd drive away". Ultimately, her constancy does not win her lover's fidelity, but allows her to reject him.

In "Melpomene against Complaint", Wharton adopts the voice of the muse of tragedy. Here Melpomene reflects on complaint, as one of her own arts:

> In soft complaints no longer ease I find,
> That latest refuge of a tortured mind;
> Romantic heroes may their fancy please
> In telling of their Griefs to senseless trees.
> 'Tis now to me no pleasure to rehearse
> A doleful tale in melancholy verse!
> Men are more deaf than trees, more wild than seas:
> Complaints and tears will sooner storms appease,
> Than draw soft pity from a human breast.[92]

Lynn Enterline has adopted Katherine Rowe's elegant term "emotion scripts", for the way in which Ovid (in particular) provided models for the articulation of female woe.[93] Here Wharton adopts Ovid's "emotion scripts", while deviating from them. She develops the lamenting style of the Roman poet's influential *Heroides* but for her own female speaker: Melpomene was not a wronged heroine but a muse. This is also a poem of criticism: a complaint poem *about* complaint. The poem opens with "soft complaint" and closes with "soft pity". But the trajectory between poetic mode and emotional affect is not straightforward. Melpomene, complaining "against complaint", opens by rejecting it on two related accounts. First, she finds no "ease" in lament; it is not cathartic. Second, she argues that complaint has no effect. This goes to the heart of early modern complaint and its efficacy. And Wharton's answer is striking: she implies that complaint fails when its audience is not "soft" enough. Soft complaint should generate soft pity, but it fails to have any effect on those who are as unlistening as trees, waves and storms. While initially Melpomene's target seems gendered—"*Men* are more deaf than trees"—at the close of the poem it becomes more universal—"a *human* breast". Receptiveness, responsiveness, pity, softness, then, are qualities which Melpomene seeks in all her listeners. We might recall Behn's sardonic Lucretian idea that women are made of "feebler seeds"; Burnet's grudging, double-edged praise of Behn as "tender"; and a history of medieval and early modern examples of women being affiliated with softness and therefore fickleness. Here Wharton challenges that misogynistic tradition, implying that women's malleability might actually make them emotionally superior, and better readers of poems, because they are receptive to their affective effects. It is not just the lamenting speaker in "Melpomene against Complaint" who is female, but also the poet, and the ideal audience.

The poetic style of complaint is "soft" and it also has a greater effect (affect) on soft bodies and minds.

These poems of and about complaint also represent further dialogue with Behn. We saw earlier that Wharton defined Behn's own writing as crucially "soft". Aminta, the name of Wharton's speaker in "The inconstancy of Woman Kind", is also the name of the imagined lover in Behn's poem "The Dream", and a character in Behn's "Voyage to the Isle of Love" (in which Aminta is described, after her death, as a "yielding maid"). Moreover, Behn also wrote female-voiced complaints, and Gillian Wright has argued for the importance of these to her career.[94] Ovidian complaint, as authored by men, had become an elite poetic mode. Publishing her own Ovidian complaints, especially her paraphrase on *Oenone to Paris* (1680), was part of Behn's career-defining strategy. These complaint poems, then, were Behn's and Wharton's bid for a place in elite poetic culture; they were also, I have argued, a challenge to the male ventriloquism of complaining women. Wharton's little-known poems redefine the form, foregrounding its female speakers as both pitiful and, crucially, more able to feel pity. In short, women are not just appropriate subjects of complaint but better readers and writers of complaint. If Wharton's complaint and anti-complaint poems aimed at career definition, like Behn's, then it is striking and poignant that of the three discussed here, only "Melpomene against Complaint" has ever been published. But by reading them now we can see how her critical complaints change our history of the form, and of the vexed principle of poetic softness more broadly. Wharton's critical complaint poems reshape softness and tenderness from a position of bodily weakness to one of admired emotional sensitivity and career-defining strength.

Smoothness was a category of style defined both with and against the female body, through the seventeenth century. By tracing the relationship of smooth with its antonyms (rough, rugged, strong) and associated terms (soft, sweet, tender) we can trace a changing landscape of poetic criticism in which women both challenge and define the critical terms of their age. The idea of smoothness as an aesthetic quality had multiple inflections in the seventeenth century: it could connote craft and artistry, as a stone or sculpture is polished into a smooth, crafted surface; tactile in a quite different way, it could be closer to softness, a female or effeminate bodily smoothness which is also soft, malleable, and thus associated with a morally problematic changeability. It could be used alongside sweet, with that word's ever-multiplying connotations of either moral virtue or sensuous vice.

I have shown for the first time that women poet-critics challenged these meanings and developed others of their own. Smoothness was a crucial part of the rhetoric by which women poets sought to redefine the practice and criticism of poetry. Anne Southwell and Lucy Hutchinson overturn an association of smoothness with femininity. Both poets condemn smoothness as politically and morally dubious and themselves claim a roughness that is pious and honest. When Southwell claims her verse is "rugged", then, this is no mere modesty topos. Lucy Hutchinson's rejection of smoothness has both specific and wide ramifications: in "To Mr Waller" she accuses Waller of complicity with Cromwell's betrayal of the republic, in his "smoothing up" of political disappointment in his triumphal panegyric on the Lord Protector. While Southwell and Hutchinson reject smoothness and embrace roughness, a group of later women poet critics redefined and championed smoothness. In the poetry and correspondence between Edmund Waller, Anne Wharton, Aphra Behn, and Gilbert Burnet, softness overtakes smoothness as a vexed and gendered critical term. Paula Loscocco has brilliantly shown how "softness" became a feminized and devalued principle (in contrast to a now masculine Restoration smoothness). Yet analysis of these little-known poems, especially a cluster of poems by Anne Wharton published here for the first time, reveals how women were writing against this development. Both Wharton and Behn were claiming softness as a strength: a term connoting not only deft aesthetic technique, but also a powerful sensitivity to poetic effect and affect. In both the roughness of Southwell and Hutchinson and the softness of Wharton and Behn, we find women challenging the famously dominant smoothness of male, royalist poets such as Edmund Waller and, in doing so, writing a different literary history.

Conclusion

A NEW HISTORY OF STYLE

THIS BOOK HAS SHOWN THAT women writers were foundational to the establishment of literary criticism as a practice and in shaping the key terms by which it came to operate, terms which are still used today to define literary value. It has shown that a new history of the development of early modern poetic style and criticism in English must both analyse the gender politics of key literary terms and also reveal women writers' part in defining these terms in their commentary and their poetry. By including women writers in histories of poetry and poetics, we can not only see women writers' compositional skill and theoretical sophistication, and the role they played in shaping early modern literary criticism itself, but also reveal the gendered presumptions underpinning many major literary critical terms, and the values they perpetuate.

In Chapter 1: Criticize, I offered six provocations which *Sex and Style* set out to articulate and investigate: (1) that the language of style has always been gendered; (2) that women's style has been read primarily through their bodies; (3) that early modern women weaponized the critical language used against them; (4) that women theorized literature as much as men did; (5) that women's poetic practice is also theory; and, finally, (6) that women shaped the debates we see as key to seventeenth-century poetics. We have seen how a cluster of key words for style—critical; feminine; original; irregular; smooth; soft—were at the centre of early modern debates around stylish and poetic language, and how women writers (often occluded from the history of such gendered terms) were central to determining their meaning and usage. These seemingly neutral literary terms are in fact heavily gendered and ideologically freighted in discussions and definitions by male writers, both then and often now. Initiating a series of case studies for this phenomenon, Chapter 2 showed that the gendering of feminine rhyme has often been used to devalue either women, or feminine rhyme, or both, but that writers such as Anne Southwell and Hester Pulter used this rhyme technique in novel ways to demonstrate and even showcase their poetic skill and inventiveness. Chapter 3 argued that male writers excluded women from positions of literary influence by isolating them through a discourse of uniqueness that women writers such as Margaret Cavendish and Lucy Hutchinson then adapted into strong claims for the originality of their inspirations, sources, and compositions. Chapter 4 showed how male critics interpreted metrical irregularity as error or flaw in women's verse but as purposeful and artful in men's poems. It then showed writers such as Hutchinson and Philips intentionally deploying metrical irregularity in epics and Pindaric odes to reinforce their poetic meaning. Chapter 5 charted the developing ideas of "smooth" and "soft" versification across the seventeenth century, terms that are increasingly gendered so that "soft," in particular, becomes feminized. Women writers were foundational to this gendering, and responded to its inherent misogyny: mid-century women poets critique men for soft and smooth styles, while by the late Restoration we see women claiming and weaponizing a "soft poetics" as a formulation of their superior creativity.

Each chapter has untangled the complicated literary critical history of a term and then revealed women's reinvention of it, as they countered or adapted male writers' gendered assumptions in their own, highly distinctive, ideas and compositions. Women writers critically intervened in debates over the gendered meaning of these terms, using their own theories and verse to reorientate both the concepts themselves and the practice of them. These critical interventions often showcased women poets' formal artistry and theoretical complexity, such as in Pulter's and Southwell's use of what I have called virtuosic feminine rhyme, or Hutchinson's purposeful irregularity. In every chapter we have seen that women's poetic theory is found in their practice; and their practice often represents theoretical intervention. In Chapter 4: Irregular, for instance, I argued that reading women's poetic irregularity as error rather than as style (as readers have done since the seventeenth century) profoundly and inaccurately devalues their verse, and removes them from certain genealogies of poetic development which have endured in modern criticism. If we read women's writing for innovation rather than error, as this book aims to do, we can see a new literary history of style emerging. This is a history both of the gendered, ideological meanings and effects of style, and of its practice by male and female poets. Throughout the book, we have seen women writers engaged in writing what I call critical poetics, that is, poetry which is informed by current theoretical debates, and in turn develops its own. The critical poetics of Pulter, Southwell, Cavendish, Hutchinson, Philips, Wharton, Behn and others thus brought together style and literary criticism, and showed how they form one another.

This book has asked the question throughout: how has poetic style been gendered? In his *Timber, or Discoveries*, Ben Jonson identified (and critiqued) feminine and masculine styles. He depicts poetic masculinity and femininity both as styles to avoid. Having critiqued "women's poets" for their shallow smoothness, as we saw in Chapter 5, he turns to a different kind of stylistic affectation:

> Others that in composition are nothing but what is rough and broken [...] And if it would come gently, they trouble it of purpose. They would not have it run without rubs, as if that style were more strong and manly, that struck the ear with a kind of unevenness. These men err not by chance, but knowingly and willingly; they are like men that affect a fashion by themselves, have some singularity in a ruff, cloak, or hatband, or their beards specially cut to provoke beholders and set a mark upon themselves. They would be reprehended, while they are looked on. And this vice, one that is in authority with the rest, loving, delivers over to them to be imitated; so that oft-times the faults which he fell into, the others seek for: this is the danger, when vice becomes a precedent.[1]

Here Jonson attacks not men but a particular performance of masculinity: a style that is adopted, not inherent, like a particular cloak or haircut. In mapping rough and smooth onto masculine and feminine styles, Jonson clearly genders these styles, but not according to the sex of the author. Both are bad models of male authorship: an excessively macho, intentionally rough style versus an excessively smooth one, lacking depth. The latter might be writing *for* women ("women's poets") but these are probably male authors. Writing of another passage from *Timber*, Colby Gordon teases out Jonson's anxious movement from the style itself to the writer who produces it, "at first, the tirade analogizes 'witty' language to cosmetic adornment, but over the course of a few sentences this manner of speech comes to characterize the excessively feminine 'Gallant' Jonson sets himself to browbeating, bedecked in fussy outfits and embroidered sweet-bags until he is just as soft and effeminate ('*mollibus et effoeminatis*') as the verse he produces".[2] Soft, smooth, sweet: Jonson suggests that these poets lack depth. There is no difficulty to tussle with in poetry that seems to be generated by sliding, smooth running, though equally there may be no semantic or true difficulty underlying the wilful unevenness of excessively masculine style which is more the performance of difficulty than the thing itself.

While Jonson depicted both excessively masculine and excessively feminine poetry as styles to avoid, either too difficult or too easy to read, Thomas Sprat's portrait of Cowley's style (published some fifteen years later) represented both as desirable:

> there is a kind of variety of sexes in poetry as well as in mankind: that as the peculiar excellence of the feminine kind, is smoothness and beauty: so strength is the chief praise of the masculine.[3]

The relationship between gendered styles and authors here is not straightforward. Strength is masculine and smooth beauty is feminine, but both styles are embodied by Cowley; a male poet can adopt "a variety of sexes in poetry". And indeed Sprat calls upon this mixture of gendered styles to explain the difficulty of Cowley's poetry, specifically his Pindaric odes (as we saw in Chapter 4: Irregular). Without wanting to claim Cowley or Sprat as champions of either women's or queer style, Sprat's characterization of gendered styles untethered to bodies does seem to allow more possibility than Jonson's anxious attack on "Gentlemen" and "Gallants" whose writing is not masculine enough.

This kind of feminine style, that of "smoothness and beauty", often described as ease, was one that poets were more willing to endorse, as long as it was practised by male poets. William Davenant's introduction to his play *Gondibert* championed "easy plainness":

> And it appears that poesy hath for its natural prevailings over the understandings of men (sometimes making her conquests with easy plainness, like native country beauty) been very successful in the most grave, and important occasions that the necessities of states or mankind have produced.[4]

In this introduction, which became so much of a critical work in its own right that it was published separately to the play, Davenant writes of "native country beauty" here, feminine through association with "poesy" who makes "her" conquests. "Native" and "country" suggest familiar, yet complex and troubling associations, as female beauty has to be innate rather than cultivated, rustic not sophisticated, and to possess the inalienable rights of Englishness which Davenant, writing from continental exile during the civil war, nostalgically promotes.

This book has asked the question, how can we read the history of style differently, with the women in the foreground? As so often, if we look for women interlocutors to Jonson and Hobbes, we find Margaret Cavendish. Her essay 'Of the Labyrinth of Fancy', also takes on the question of the values and risks of different styles:

> The reason why men run in such obscure conceits, is, because they think their wit will be esteemed, and seem more when it lies an odd and unusual way, which makes their verse not like a smooth running stream; but as if they were shelves of sand, or rocks in the way, and though the water in those places goeth with more force, and makes a greater sound: yet it goeth hard and uneasy. As if to express a thing hard, were to make it better, but the best poetry is plain to the understanding, of easy expressions, and full of fresh and new conceits: like a beauty that every time it is looked upon discovers new graces; besides they do not only move passions, but make passions, for a right poetical wit turns hard and rough nature, to a soft, gentle, and kind disposition: for verses are fine fancies, which are spun in the imagination to a small and even thread, but some are worse spinsters then others.[5]

Cavendish's terms overlap with Jonson's ("smooth running stream") and "plain" is the same word as Davenant. Here, as more broadly in her works, Cavendish claims an untutored, aristocratic, natural ease that dovetails with feminine plainness. It also allows her, as we saw in Chapter 3, to claim a distinctively feminine originality. Cavendish returns to the question of what makes good style in multiple essays in the same volume. In 'Of Eloquence, art, and speculation', she considers the perception of eloquence, and its reality:

> Many do seem to admire those writings, whose styles are eloquent and through ignorance takes it for eloquence, commending the method, instead of the matter, the words instead of the sense, the paint instead of the face; the garb instead of the person, but hard and unusual phrases, are like a constraint behaviour, it hath a set countenance, treads nicely, taking short steps, and carries the body so stiff, and upright, as it seems difficult, and uneasy: like those that think it a part of good breeding to eat their meat by rule, and measure; opening the mouth at a just, and certain wideness; grinding the meat betwixt their teeth, like a clock with so many strokes as make an hour, so many bits makes a swallow; so likewise if the little finger be not bowed short, and by degrees all their fingers to be jointed until the forefinger, and the thumb, meets in a round circle, they think all other vulgarly bred.[6]

In this single virtuosic sentence, Cavendish both adapts and rejects many contemporary understandings of literature. In her list of pairs, valuing matter over method and sense over words, she is in line with views that will develop around experimental science, culminating in Sprat's history of the Royal Society, despite her antipathy to the Society's experimentalism. And with her rejection of "the paint instead of the face; the garb instead of the person", Cavendish draws on a tradition of depicting elaborate style as cosmetics or clothing, voiced by writers from Dudley North to Anne Southwell and Ben Jonson. Cavendish portrays the effects of "hard and unusual phrases" with a striking personification. Hard phrases act, she says, "like a constraint behaviour", a person who carries themselves very stiffly, walking with small steps "as it seems difficult, and uneasy", and who eats "by rule, and measure", "grinding the meat between their teeth" in an unnatural and artificial manner. As I argued in Chapter 3, Cavendish's *The Worlds Olio* is an extended conversation with Ben Jonson's *Timber*. Jonson had taken on familiar Senecan and Horatian metaphors of poetic composition as digestion. In Adam Smyth's terms, Jonson represented "imperfect digestion of a source" as like a "bad meal", comparing an author who insufficiently adapted their source materials to "a creature that swallows what it takes in crude, raw, or indigested".[7] In this extraordinary essay, Cavendish gives these metaphors of gathering, consuming, and digesting her own distinctive twist, promoting originality over learning and satirizing status anxiety. Cavendish describes grotesque eating behavior, as someone opening their mouth only a "certain wideness", like the movements of hands on a clock face. Here she draws on the anthropomorphism of clocks, with their faces and hands- and even teeth, in their mechanism. And the comparison of the clock face to an uptight person, anxiously trying to demonstrate "good breeding", is grotesque and unnatural, keying into Cavendish's resistance to contemporary mechanistic hypotheses (that saw the body itself as a mechanism). She also promotes the natural over the mechanical:

> But nature is easy: and art hard, and what resembles nature nearest, is most to the life: and what is most to the life, is best; but art belongs more to the mechanics, and peasants, then to the noble and free.
>
> (*THE WORLDS OLIO*, P. 14)

This comparison also suggests class prejudice, a recurrent feature of discussions of stylistic ease.[8] Cavendish's assertion that art belongs to mechanics may sound egalitarian, but it probably plays on the term "mechanic arts" (OED I.1), relating to manual skill, in contrast to the liberal arts. Cavendish rejects both. She sees both mechanic and liberal arts as technical knowledge, from which women were excluded, while she possesses and produces natural knowledge.

Cavendish writes against a male-authored early modern poetics, in which femininity was often caught in a double bind of style: femininity was the opposite of difficult, but it was also the opposite of ease. Women themselves were not allowed to be intellectually difficult, nor were they credited with ease, at least not in the artful, refined sense that was promoted and valued in the later seventeenth century. Yet across this book we have seen a powerful countercurrent to this narrative. At the same time as Wallerian masculine smoothness was taking hold, we see women writing explicitly in an *un*smooth style, experimenting with non-couplet forms, roughness, and irregularity: Southwell's "rugged twine"; Pulter's sometimes jagged tercets and virtuosic rhyme; Cavendish's rebarbative plain style; Hutchinson's strategically irregular *De rerum natura* and *Order and Disorder*; Philips's irregular ode, so unexpected to a contemporary reader that they re-lineated it. It is precisely the roughness and experimentalism, by some criteria, the "masculinity" of women's poetry that has excluded it from later literary history, as critics like Atterbury and Pope promoted a different kind of masculinity, that of smoothness, refinement, and ease.

When any style is gendered feminine, this is usually a way of devaluing both it, and women poets. If the only gendered style that is aspirational is some kind of imagined true authentic masculinity (virile style, in Patricia Parker's influential formulation), any other inflection of gender is usually negative—feminine, effeminate, hermaphroditic—alongside the key terms of this book: feminine, original, irregular, smooth, soft. By reading women as both highly inventive stylists and critics, as I have done throughout this book, and their poetry as a form of critical poetics, we gain a more diverse, more historically accurate, and more complex, picture of the history of criticism. When women poets get to be difficult or easy, regular or irregular, smooth or rough, soft or hard, original or imitative, and get to define what those terms mean, then we will have a richer history of literary criticism, and one which is more inclusive in its definitions of literary value, and of whose opinions matter. We will have a history of literary criticism with the women put back in.

NOTES

1. Criticize

1. Anne Southwell, "Precept 4", BL Lansdowne MS 740, in *The Southwell-Sibthorpe Commonplace Book: Folger MS. V.b.198*, ed. Jean Klene, ll. 445–456, p. 156. All quotations from the Folger and Lansdowne manuscripts of Southwell's writings come from this edition. As throughout this book, I have modernized spelling and punctuation (see Note on the Text). On the compositional process and structure of the manuscript, see Jonathan Gibson, "Synchrony and Process".

2. Of dictionaries included in the "Lexicons of Early Modern English," ed. Ian Lancashire, "criticize" first appears as a headword in Benjamin Norton Defoe's *New English Dictionary* (1735) and then Samuel Johnson's *A Dictionary of the English Language* (1755).

3. Throughout this book, I use the term "woman" inclusively, responding to a writer's own formulation of their gender (where present) and attending to the gendering of language and identity in ways which I hope reveal both the prejudices of premodern understandings of sexuality and gender identity and its possibilities. Here I draw on many foundational works in queer and trans philology, including Jeffrey Masten's *Queer Philologies* and Joseph Gamble's "Toward a Trans Philology", and all the essays in this special issue of *JEMCS* on "Early Modern Trans Studies".

4. Susan S. Lanser and Evelyn Torton Beck, "Why Are There No Great Women Critics and What Difference Does It Make?", in *The Prism of Sex*, ed. J. A. Sherman and E. Torton Beck.

5. Hazard Adams, ed., *Critical Theory Since Plato* (1971). The revised edition of 1992 adds eight women to complement the 109 men.

6. Lawrence Lipking, *Abandoned Women and Poetic Tradition*, p. 209.

7. *English Renaissance Literary Criticism*, ed. Brian Vickers; *Augustan Critical Writing*, ed. David Womersley. In his *A History of Modern Criticism, 1750–1950, vol. 1: The Later Eighteenth Century*, René Wellek discusses Germaine de Staël.

8. *Women Reading Shakespeare, 1660–1900*, ed. by Ann Thompson and Sasha Roberts has one pre-1800 writer (Margaret Cavendish); *Women Critics 1660–1820*, ed. by Folger Collective on Early Women Critics has three. Jane Donawerth's rich collection, *Rhetorical Theory by Women before 1900*, is the exception, with nine pre-1800 writers from Aspasia to Astell.

9. Michel de Montaigne, "Of three commerces or societies", in *Essays written in French*, trans. John Florio, p. 461.

10. See Danielle Clarke, *The Politics of Early Modern Women's Writing*, p. 27.

11. Sasha Roberts, "Women's Literary Capital in Early Modern England", p. 248. On other European developments see, for instance, Julie Campbell, *Literary Circles and Gender in Early Modern Europe* and Diana Robin, *Publishing Women*.

12. See also Clarke, *Politics*, pp. 28–29, on Puttenham's discussion of women writing in sections on either vice or ornament.

13. George Puttenham, *The Art of English Poesy*, ed. Frank Whigham and Wayne A. Rebhorn, p. 336.

14. Clarke, *Politics*, pp. 27–28.

15. Jeff Dolven, *Senses of Style*, p. 48.

16. Ellen Rooney, "Foreword: An Aesthetic of Bad Objects", to Naomi Schor, *Reading in Detail*, p. xxx. On excess, see Karen Jackson Ford, *Gender and the Poetics of Excess*.

17. Margaret Cavendish, "To All Noble, and Worthy Ladies", *Poems, and Fancies*, sig. A3r.

18. As Juliet Fleming argues, "women were interpellated as users of hard word lists not because they cared to ascertain the correct use of English, but because they could be used to represent its problems", "Dictionary English and the Female Tongue", in *Privileging Gender in Early Modern England*, ed. Jean R. Brink, p. 181.

19. Patricia Parker, *Literary Fat Ladies*, p. 104.

20. Patricia Parker, "Virile Style", in *Premodern Sexualities*, ed. Louise Frandenburg and Carla Freccero with the assistance of Kathy Lavezzo, p. 199.

21. Dudley Fenner, *The Artes of Logike and Rethorike*, sig. D1v. See also Parker, *Literary Fat Ladies*, p. 108.

22. Lorna Hutson, "Civility and Virility in Ben Jonson". See also Clarke, *Politics*.

23. Katharine Craik, *Reading Sensations in Early Modern England*, p. 44.

24. Joseph Gamble, "Toward a Trans Philology", p. 39.

25. Joan Kelly, "Did Women have a Renaissance?"; Lara Dodds and Michelle M. Dowd, "Happy Accidents", p. 170.

26. For recent analyses of the relationship between PCRS and early modern women's writing, see Joyce MacDonald, "How Race Might Help Us Find 'Lost' Women's Writing", and Bernadette Andrea, "Early Modern Women, Race, and Writing Revisited". Andrea traces an influential intellectual genealogy through the work of Kim F. Hall, Margo Hendricks and Joyce Green MacDonald.

27. Gavin Alexander, ed., *Sidney's "The Defence of Poesy" and Selected Renaissance Literary Criticism*, p. lxxvii.

28. Fleming, "Dictionary English", p. 191. "During the elevation of the vernacular at the turn of the century it does seem that, briefly retaining their association with English, women found themselves at the center of the nation's new cultural enterprise. It was of course a promotion that was circumscribed in scope, and of brief duration . . . But this is a coincidence that may lead us to suspect that the masculinity that became a hallmark of British high culture was in part designed to contain, and in part produced itself in the act of containing, the epiphenomenon of Queen Anne's influence on the arts."

29. The Lansdowne manuscript now in the British Library seems to have been intended for presentation to the king, but as its date is uncertain, debate remains as to which monarch she was writing under and therefore whether she intended it for James or Charles. See Klene "Introduction" (*Southwell-Sibthorpe Commonplace Book*); Elizabeth Clarke, "Anne Southwell and the Pamphlet Debate", in *Debating Gender in Early Modern England, 1500–1700*, ed. Cristina Malcolmson and Mihoko Suzuki; Erica Longfellow, *Women and Religious Writing in Early Modern England*, especially p. 105; Gillian Wright, *Producing Women's Poetry, 1600–1730*, p. 47.

30. Danielle Clarke and Marie-Louise Coolahan, "Gender, Reception, and Form", in *The Work of Form*, ed. by Elizabeth Scott-Baumann and Ben Burton.

31. Klene, ed., *Southwell-Sibthorpe Commonplace Book*, p. 5–6.

32. Abraham Cowley, "Upon Mrs. K. Philips her Poems", in Katherine Philips, *Poems by the most deservedly admired Mrs. Katherine Philips, the matchless Orinda*, sig. c1r.

33. Thompson and Roberts, *Women Reading Shakespeare*, p. 12, of Cavendish's Letter CXXII. See also in this book, Chapter 3: Original.

34. Katherine Philips, *The Collected Works of Katherine Philips*, ed. Patrick Thomas, 3 vols, Vol ii: Letters, Letter XXXVI, pp. 101–104.

35. Alexander, ed., *Sidney's "The Defence of Poesy"*, p. xiv.

36. Anne Southwell, 'To my worthy muse', in Klene, ed., *The Southwell-Sibthorpe Commonplace Book*, pp. 4–5.

37. Samuel Daniel, *Poems and A Defence of Ryme*, ed. Arthur Colby Sprague, p. 139.

38. Klene, ed., *The Southwell-Sibthorpe Commonplace Book*, p. 4.

39. Puttenham opens his *Art* with the analogy between poetry and God's creation (p. 93). Cf. Sidney, in *Sidney's "The Defence of Poesy"*, ed. Alexander, pp. 8–9.

40. Daniel, *Defence*, p. 138.

41. Daniel, *Defence*, p. 138.

42. Alexander, ed., *Sidney's "The Defence of Poesy"*, p. 9.

43. "[T]he holy David's Psalms are a divine poem" (Alexander, ed., *Sidney's "The Defence of Poesy"*, p. 7), and see Hannibal Hamlin, "'The Highest Matter in the Noblest Form'".

44. Puttenham, *Art*, p. 164. Southwell's immersion in both the theory and poetry of England in the 1590s might seem a little odd given her manuscript's date of 1626 and connection with her time in Ireland. But the notebook seems to incorporate work composed over some decades, and Southwell may have written the letter defence to her friend Lady Ridgeway in the early years of the seventeenth century, before she moved to Ireland. See Marie-Louise Coolahan, *Women, Writing, and Language in Early Modern Ireland*, pp. 180–218; especially p. 187.

45. Clarke and Coolahan, "Gender, Reception, and Form"; Coolahan, *Early Modern Ireland*, p. 148.

46. See also Clarke and Coolahan, "Gender, Reception, and Form".

47. See Sasha Roberts, *Reading Shakespeare's Poems in Early Modern England*, pp. 44–5.

48. Roland Greene, *Five Words*, in his book's subtitle: *Critical Semantics in the Age of Shakespeare and Cervantes*.

49. Patricia Akhimie, *Shakespeare and the Cultivation of Difference* and "Cultivating expertise"; Nandini Das et al., *Keywords of Identity, Race, and Human Mobility in Early Modern England*; Kim F. Hall, *Things of Darkness* and all Hall's subsequent articles; Masten, *Queer Philologies*; and—although not exclusively early modern—Paisley Currah and Susan Stryker eds., *TSQ: Transgender Studies Quarterly* 1, no. 1–2 (2014), *Key Concepts for a Twenty-First-Century Transgender Studies*.

50. Masten, *Queer Philologies*, p. 221.

51. Brian Cummings, "Philosophical Poetry", in *Fulke Greville and the Culture of the English Renaissance*, ed. Russ Leo et al., and David Scott Wilson-Okamura, "The French Aesthetic of Spenser's Feminine Rhyme".

158   NOTES TO CHAPTER 2

52. Walter Charleton, in *Letters and Poems In Honour of the Incomparable Princess, Margaret, Dutchess of Newcastle*, pp. 117–18. I have modernized the spelling in all quotations from early modern texts, or used modernized editions where available.

53. Margaret Cavendish, *Philosophical and Physical Opinions*, p. 171.

54. Munro, "Mrs Lucie Hutchinson's Translation of Lucretius", p. 52.

55. Jenny C. Mann, "Marlowe's 'Slack Muse'"; Jenny C. Mann, *The Trials of Orpheus*.

56. Clarke and Coolahan, "Gender, Reception, and Form", p. 149.

57. In admiring homage to Jeffrey Masten's alternative contents page for *Queer Philologies*, "Contents (Q)", p. xi–xii.

2. Feminine

1. John Harington, trans., *Orlando furioso in English heroical verse*. All further references are to this edition.

2. William Shakespeare, *The Complete Poems of Shakespeare*, ed. Cathy Shrank and Raphael Lyne. All further references are to this edition.

3. Anne Southwell, "Thou shalt keep holy the sabbath day", version from Folger MS V.b.198, in Klene ed., *The Southwell-Sibthorpe Commonplace Book*, p. 72, ll. 407–412.

4. Reuven Tsur, "Masculine and Feminine Rhymes", p. 3.

5. For wider discussions of taste, history, and identity, see Gitanjali Shahani, *Tasting Difference*.

6. For sugar in wine specifically, see Tim Richardson, *Sweets*, p. 140; Sidney W. Mintz, *Sweetness and Power*, p. 136, both drawing on Fynes Morison, and Falstaff's protestation "If sack and sugar be a fault, God help the wicked!". For sweetness more broadly, see Elizabeth L. Swann, *Taste and Knowledge in Early Modern England*.

7. Shahani, "Sugar", in *Tasting Difference*; Hall, "Culinary spaces".

8. Daniel's *Defence* was attached to a panegyric to the king and a response to Thomas Campion's treatise in favor of classical meter (*Observations in the Art of English Poesie*, 1602), in *A panegyrike congratulatory deliuered to the Kings most excellent maiesty at Burleigh Harrington in Rutlandshire. By Samuel Daniel. Also certaine epistles. With a defence of ryme*.

9. Daniel, *Defence of Ryme*, sig. H6v–7r. See also Robert Stagg, "Rhyme's Voices: Hearing Gender in *The Taming of the Shrew*".

10. Christopher Warley, *Sonnet Sequences and Social Distinction in Renaissance England*; Wayne A. Rebhorn, *The Emperor of Men's Minds*; Frank Whigham, *Ambition and Privilege*; Richard Helgerson, "Barbarous Tongues", in *The Historical Renaissance*, ed. by Heather Dubrow and Richard Strier. Patricia Parker (*Literary Fat Ladies*) and Maureen Quilligan have discussed the gendered hierarchies promoted by these theories, and Quilligan has extended this question to feminine rhyme, in an essay to which I will return: "Feminine Endings: The Sexual Politics of Sidney's and Spenser's Rhyming".

11. Philip Sidney, *An Apologie for Poetrie*, sigs. K1r–v.

12. Quilligan, "Feminine Endings", p. 312.

13. Ann Thompson writes that Daniel "rewrote some of his sonnets in order to eliminate them. A notable example of this is his sonnet that begins 'The star of my mishap imposed this paining' in 1592 (Sonnet 27 in his *Delia* sequence), which is altered to 'The star of my mishap

imposed this pain' in 1594; a further six feminine rhymes in the poem are similarly revised [...] Joan Rees notes that Daniel altered thirty-seven feminine endings in revisions of his poems between 1594 and 1601, having become convinced that they were a blemish on his work". Ann Thompson, "A Lingering Farewell", in *The Sonnets: The State of Play*, ed. Hannah Crawforth et al., p. 125. See Joan Rees, *Samuel Daniel: A Critical and Biographical Study*, p. 21 and Edward Haviland Miller, "Samuel Daniel's Revisions in *Delia*".

14. Philip Sidney, *Defence of Poesy*, sig. K1v.

15. Jonson, *Timber* in *The Cambridge Edition of the Works of Ben Jonson*, vol. 7, ll. 513–519 Nota 5.

16. Richard Dutton suggests Jonson might have Daniel in mind as the target of "women's poets", *Ben Jonson*, p. 133; see also Hutson, ed., *Cambridge Edition of the Works of Ben Jonson*, vol. 7, notes to lines 515–17, p. 524.

17. See Cummings, "Philosophical Poetry' and Wilson-Okamura, "The French Aesthetic of Spenser's Feminine Rhyme".

18. Cummings, "Philosophical Poetry", p. 33.

19. Cummings, "Philosophical Poetry", p. 33.

20. Wilson-Okamura, "The French Aesthetic", p. 360.

21. Quilligan, "Feminine Endings".

22. Helen Vendler, *The Art of Shakespeare's Sonnets*, p. 381; Michael Schoenfeldt, *The Cambridge Introduction to Shakespeare's Poetry*, p. 91.

23. Stagg, "Rhyme's Voices", p. 332: "it is likely that Shakespeare knew of Daniel's anxieties about the feminine rhyme and then made those anxieties central to some of his own verse. Shakespeare's Sonnet 20 could be read as, among other things, an early response to Daniel's fretting over feminine rhyme."

24. Colby Gordon, "A Woman's Prick", in *Shakespeare / Sex: Contemporary Readings in Gender and Sexuality*, ed. Jennifer Drouin.

25. Ben Jonson, "Song. That women are but men's shadows", ed. by Colin Burrow, *The Cambridge Edition of the Works of Ben Jonson*, vol. 5, pp. 224–25.

26. The origin point of "weak" rhyme as an alternative to "feminine' rhyme is hard to trace. OED gives a quotation from Jonson's *English Grammar* for "weak" referring to a sound, but not specifically word ending or rhyme.

27. "Informations to William Drummond of Hawthornden", ed. Ian Donaldson, in *The Cambridge Edition of the Works of Ben Jonson*, vol. 5, pp. 359–91. "Pembroke and his lady discoursing, the Earl said the women were men's shadows, and she maintained them. Both appealing to Jonson, he affirmed it true; for which my Lady gave a penance to prove it in verse, hence his epigram" (ll. 282–84, p. 377). In Drummond's account, this comes just after Jonson's comment that "My Lord Lisle's daughter, my Lady Wroth, is unworthily married on a jealous husband" (ll. 275–76).

28. *The Poems of Sir Philip Sidney*, ed. by William A. Ringler, p. lvi.

29. Ben Jonson, "A Sonnet: To the Noble Lady, the Lady Mary Wroth", ed. Colin Burrow, *The Cambridge Edition of the Works of Ben Jonson*, vol. 7, p. 142–43.

30. Though if it was intended as a dedicatory poem, it was one that didn't make it into the published work. See Michael Brennan, "'A SYDNEY though un-named'".

31. Alexander argues "This is at least a wrong reading of *Pamphilia to Amphilanthus*, the rhetoric of which is arguably directed from one fictional (or semi-autobiographical) character to

another, and if it is directed at another reader intends to witness to love and not to stir it". *Writing After Sidney*, p. 284.

32. This poem's use of ostentatious feminine rhymes is accentuated by the subsequent poem in Jonson's *Underwood* collection, "A Fit of Rhyme against Rhyme", which yokes rhymes such as "letters/fetters" to represent the aesthetically, and even ideologically, damaging effects of (feminine) rhyme.

33. The text of both "hermaphrodite poems" is taken from *Mary Wroth's Poetry: An Electronic Edition*, ed. Paul Salzman.

34. See J.S.P. Tatlock, "The Siege of Troy in Elizabethan Literature, Especially in Shakespeare and Heywood", p. 679 (f.n. 3); J.S.P. Tatlock, "The Hermaphrodite Rime".

35. "We might well ask what impact this programmatic cultural gendering of rhyme could have had on actual women", Quilligan, "Feminine Endings", p. 320.

36. From Wroth, Song 5, *Pamphilia to Amphilanthus*. Modernized version of Folger MS,V.a.104, taken from *Mary Wroth's Poetry*.

37. Southwell, "An Elegy written by the Lady A. S. to the Countess of London Derry supposing her to be dead by her long silence", in Klene ed., *The Southwell-Sibthorpe Commonplace Book*, pp. 24–27.

38. Southwell, "An Epitaph upon Cassandra MackWilliams wife to Sir Thomas Ridgway Earl of London Derry, By the Lady A.S.", in Klene ed., *The Southwell-Sibthorpe Commonplace Book*, pp. 27–28, ll. 1–2.

39. Southwell, "Precept 4", version from British Library Lansdowne MS 740, in Klene ed., *The Southwell-Sibthorpe Commonplace Book*, p. 151 ll. 289–94.

40. Southwell, "Precept 4", version from British Library Lansdowne MS 740, in Klene ed., *The Southwell-Sibthorpe Commonplace Book*, p. 156, ll. 289–94 445–50.

41. Southwell, "Thou shalt keep holy the sabbath day", version from Folger MS V.b.198, in Klene ed., *The Southwell-Sibthorpe Commonplace Book*, p. 72, ll. 407–11.

42. Southwell was not alone in mentioning grammatical gender as a point of frustration. *OED* cites Philip Sidney's *Apologie for Poetrie*: "Those cumbersome differences of cases, genders, moods, and tenses, which I think was a piece of the Tower of Babylon's curse." (*OED*, Gender, noun, 1.a.).

43. See Elizabeth Scott-Baumann, "'crittickize uppon the smallest word'".

44. See Elizabeth Scott-Baumann, "Hester Pulter's Well-Wrought Urns' and Frances E. Dolan, "Hester Pulter's Dunghill Poetics".

45. All Pulter poems are taken from *The Pulter Project*, ed. Leah Knight and Wendy Wall.

46. Dianne Mitchell, "Lyric Backwardness", in *The Oxford Handbook of Early Modern Women's Writing in English, 1570–1700*, ed. by Elizabeth Scott-Baumann et al.,p. 189; see also Dolan, "Hester Pulter's Dunghill Poetics".

47. Philips, *The Collected Works of Katherine Philips*, ii, p. 64.

48. Paul Trolander and Zeynep Tenger, *Sociable Criticism in England 1625–1725*, p. 47.

49. "as for the words *heaven and power*, I am of your opinion too, especially as to the latter; for the other may, I think be sometimes so placed, as not to offend the ear, when it is used in two syllables" (*The Collected Works of Katherine Philips*, ii, p. 70).

50. George Gascoigne, "Certayne Notes of Instruction", in *A Hundreth Sundrie Flowres*, ed. G. W. Pigman III, p. 459.

51. See *The Collected Works of Katherine Philips*, ii, p. 112. Letter dated 26th October, 1663.

52. The translation includes several feminine rhyme pairs (divided/decided; season/reason; obligation/nation) so it seems likely that these are what Philips saw as "frequent". The term "double rhyme" was sometimes used to mean internal rhyme (see also my note 55 on Wesley).

53. Roberts comments that "Philips's attention to 'the Ear' echoes the concern with sound that is commonly voiced in treatises of formal composition", "Women's Literary Capital in Early Modern England", p. 255.

54. Preface to *Annus Mirabilis*, 1667.

55. Samuel Wesley, "An epistle to a friend concerning poetry by Samuel Wesley", p. 16. In this poem Wesley refers to "double rhyme", meaning internal rhyme, separately to feminine rhyme. He also condemns double rhyme as "*antiquated* grown, / Or us'd in *Satyr* or *Burlesque* alone".

56. Wilson-Okamura, "The French Aesthetic", p. 362.

57. Anne Southwell, "Thou shalt keep holy the sabbath day", version from Folger MS V.b.198, in Klene ed., *The Southwell-Sibthorpe Commonplace Book*, p. 72, ll. 407–410.

3. Original

1. Sarah Kunjummen, "Reading Milton Like a Woman", p. 75.

2. Charleton, *Letters and Poems*, pp. 117–8.

3. Mary Sidney Herbert is "peerless" (Edmund Spenser, "Ruines of Time", l. 317, *Complaints*, 1591); Katherine Philips is "matchless" (Title of posthumous *Poems by the most deservedly admired Mrs. Katherine Philips, the matchless Orinda*, 1667) and "incomparable" (Preface, *Poems*, 1667); Margaret Cavendish was "*Margaret* the First" (Charleton, *Letters and Poems*, p. 152, echoing back her own self-characterisation in the preface to *The Blazing World*, 1666; "singular" (Evelyn diary, William Bray ed., *Diary and Correspondence of John Evelyn*, 4 vols, vol ii, 27 April 1667, p. 23) and "incomparable" (Title of *Letters and Poems*); Bradstreet has "sprung up" (title, *The Tenth Muse Lately Sprung up in America*, 1650).

4. Alexander, "Introduction", *Sidney's "The Defence of Poesy"*, p. xxxiii.

5. Alexander, *Sidney's "The Defence of Poesy"*, p. xxxiii; David Quint, *Origin and Originality in Renaissance Literature*.

6. Margaret J. M. Ezell, "The Laughing Tortoise", p. 335.

7. Charleton, *Letters and Poems*, pp. 117–18.

8. Dolven, *Senses of Style*, p. 39.

9. Jane Stevenson, "Inventing Fame", in *A History of Early Modern Women's Writing*, ed. by Patricia Phillippy, p. 349.

10. Philips. *Poems*, sig. ar [sic].

11. Jonson, "CV. To Mary Lady Wroth", *Epigrams*, in *The Cambridge Edition of the Works of Ben Jonson*, vol. 5, pp. 171–72.

12. "To the right Honorable, the Lord Vi-count LISLE, and his most vertuous Lady: To Sir Robert SIDNEY, Knight, their Hopefull Sonne: To the most Worthy Lady WROTH, with the rest of their right vertuous Daughters: & To all the Noble SIDNEYS & SEMI-SIDNEYS.", from Joshua Sylvester, *All the small vvorkes of that famous poet Iosuah Siluester Gathered into one volume*, sig. Y1r.

13. Quint, *Origin and Originality*.

14. Alexander, *Sidney's "The Defence of Poesy"*, p. xiv.

15. Charleton, *Letters and Poems*, pp. 116–18.

16. Mary Evelyn, in *Diary and Correspondence of John Evelyn*, iv, p. 9.

17. See Patricia Pender, *Early Modern Women's Writing and the Rhetoric of Modesty*, which shows that modesty was often a rhetorical strategy used by women to gain access to literary culture, as much as to acknowledge their exclusion from it.

18. Anne Bradstreet, "The Prologue", ll. 31–48, from *Women Poets of the English Civil War*, ed. Sarah C. E. Ross and Elizabeth Scott-Baumann.

19. See Trevor Ross, *The Making of the English Literary Canon*, p. 297.

20. Cavendish, *Philosophical and Physical Opinions*, sig. A1v.

21. Cavendish, *The Worlds Olio*, sig. H3r.

22. Catherine Gallagher, "Embracing the Absolute", p. 30.

23. Scott-Baumann, *Forms of Engagement*, especially Chapter 2 "Margaret Cavendish as Editor and Reviser", pp. 60–80.

24. This engraving, by Abraham van Diepenbeeck, was included in certain editions of Cavendish's works during her lifetime and afterwards. It is quoted here from the British Library copy of *The Worlds Olio* (London: 1671), shelfmark 8407.h.11.

25. See, for example, Lara Dodds, *The Literary Invention of Margaret Cavendish* and Lisa T. Sarasohn, *The Natural Philosophy of Margaret Cavendish*.

26. Cavendish, *Philosophical and Physical Opinions*, p. 171.

27. OED 6.b.; OED 1.a.

28. Cavendish, *Poems, and Fancies*, sig. A5v.

29. Jonson does not name his addressee. As Jonson's patron, a father of two sons, William Cavendish is often assumed to be the addressee. See Tom Rutter, "The Cavendishes and Ben Jonson", in *A Companion to the Cavendishes*, ed. Lisa Hopkins and Tom Rutter.

30. See Greene, *Five Words*; Hannah Crawforth, *Etymology and the Invention of English*, p. 72.

31. Colin Burrow, *Imitating Authors: Plato to Futurity*, p. 254.

32. Lorna Hutson, "Introduction" to *Timber, or Discoveries*, in *The Cambridge Edition of the Works of Ben Jonson*, vol. 7, p. 483.

33. See Lorna Hutson, "Civility and Virility in Ben Jonson", p. 10.

34. Parker, "Virile Style".

35. Jonson, *Timber*, l. 166 and ll. 266–7; Hutson "Introduction", *Timber* in *The Cambridge Edition of the Works of Ben Jonson*, vol. 7, p. 490.

36. Mihoko Suzuki, "The Essay Form as Critique".

37. Elizabeth Scott-Baumann, "'Bake'd in the Oven of Applause': The blazon and the body in Margaret Cavendish's Fancies", *Women's Writing*, 15 (2008), 86–106.

38. Susan Du Verger, *Du Vergers humble reflections vpon some passages of the Right Honorable the Lady Marchionesse of Nevvcastles Olio, or, An appeale from her mes-informed, to her ovvne better informed iudgement*, (London: 1657), unpaginated prefatory "Epistle to the Right Honorable the Marchioness of Newcastle". The rest of the work focuses on rebutting Cavendish's anti-Catholicism.

39. Cavendish, *The Worlds Olio*, p. 5.

40. Hutson "Introduction", *Timber* in *The Cambridge Edition of the Works of Ben Jonson*, vol. 7, p. 495.

41. Hutson "Introduction", *Timber* in *The Cambridge Edition of the Works of Ben Jonson*, vol. 7, p. 493.
42. Hutson "Introduction", *Timber* in *The Cambridge Edition of the Works of Ben Jonson*, vol. 7, p. 493.
43. Jonson, *Timber* in *The Cambridge Edition of the Works of Ben Jonson*, vol. 7, ll. 502–512, Nota 4.
44. Cavendish, "To the Reader", *The Worlds Olio*, sig. A6r
45. Hutson "Introduction", *Timber* in *The Cambridge Edition of the Works of Ben Jonson*, vol. 7, p. 491.
46. Cavendish, "The Epistle", *The Worlds Olio*, p. 178.
47. Jonson, *Timber* in *The Cambridge Edition of the Works of Ben Jonson*, vol. 7, ll. 89–91, translating Vives.
48. Swinburne, *A Study of Ben Jonson* (1889), p. 132, quoted in *Timber* in *The Cambridge Edition of the Works of Ben Jonson*, vol. 7, p. 503, n. 91.
49. Cavendish, "The Epistle", *The Worlds Olio*, p. 178.
50. For a different approach to Cavendish and Ovid, see G. Gabrielle Starr, "Cavendish, Aesthetics, and the Anti-Platonic Line", *Eighteenth-Century Studies* 39 (2006), pp. 295–308. Starr argues that women sometimes turned to Ovid and Lucretius as anti-Platonic writers.
51. From *Women Poets of the English Civil War*, p. 218, ll. 1–4.
52. Quint, *Origin and Originality*.
53. OED C1, "oily-tongued".
54. Dodds, *Literary Invention*, p. 2.
55. Debapriya Sarkar, *Possible Knowledge*, p. 127.
56. "Change in Nature", *The Worlds Olio*, p. 162.
57. "wit is the child of nature", *The Worlds Olio*, p. 6; "I am a Legitimate Poetical Child of Nature", *Sociable Letters*, Letter 146, p. 301.
58. See OED "brownetta" (n.) and "brunette" (n. & adj.)
59. Cavendish, *Sociable Letters*, Letter 146, p. 301. For a rich analysis of Cavendish and race, focusing on other works, see Sujata Iyengar, "Royalist, Romancist, Racialist: Rank, Gender and Race in the Science and Fiction of Margaret Cavendish", *English Literary History* 69 (2002), 649–72.
60. *Sociable Letters*, Letter 146, p. 304. On this letter, see also Jessie Hock, *The Erotics of Materialism*, especially pp. 166–7.
61. *Sociable Letters*, Letter 123, p. 246.
62. Edward Young, *Conjectures on Original Composition*, p. 80. As Lucy Newlyn puts it, "[Young] makes the century's clearest and loudest claim for originality as the first requisite of 'genius' and the paramount concern of poetry. It brings into focus, as an aesthetic issue, the author's claim to 'ownership' of his own ideas", Lucy Newlyn, *Paradise Lost and the Romantic Reader*, p. 48. See also Ian Donaldson, *Ben Jonson*, p. 436, "As *originality* was increasingly promoted throughout the eighteenth century as the hallmark of genius, so Jonson's reputation began quite rapidly to decline".
63. Thompson and Roberts, *Women Reading Shakespeare*, p. 12.
64. On gender in early modern responses to the *Heroides*, see Danielle Clarke, "'Signifying, but not sounding'", in *Renaissance Paratexts*, ed. Helen Smith and Louise Wilson. Cavendish, though, focuses not on the *Heroides* but *Metamorphoses*. She may have been interested in Ovid's

status as a political exile, like herself. On Cavendish and exile, see Emma L. E. Rees, *Margaret Cavendish* and Anna Battigelli, *Margaret Cavendish and the Exiles of the Mind*.

65. See Paul Hammond, *Dryden and the Traces of Classical Rome*, pp. 208–9.

66. Victoria Moul, "The Transformation of Ovid in Cowley's Herb Garden", in *The Afterlife of Ovid*, ed. by Peter Mack and John North, p. 231, "In the course of book 2, as the debate about the purpose of menstruation unfolds, a woman's essential power of transformation is progressively re-defined: from the destructive and magical power of menstrual blood, to 'change' (that is, erode or destroy)[232] almost anything with which it comes into contact, according to Dittany (and Pliny); to a mocking Ovidian reprise of this idea in Rose's poem, followed by a stress upon the miraculous transformation of blood into milk; and finally a claim that menstruation is all that prevents a woman actually becoming a man." See also Mairéad McAuley, "Matermorphoses".

67. See, for instance, Leah DeVun, *The Shape of Sex*.

68. Mairéad McAuley, *Reproducing Rome*, pp. 117–18.

69. Lucy Hutchinson, *The Works of Lucy Hutchinson, vol. 1: The Translation of Lucretius*, ed. by Reid Barbour and David Norbrook, with Latin text by Maria Cristina Zerbino. 24 is my own count, including Hutchinson's prefatory material and arguments to each book.

70. Norbrook and Barbour, eds, *The Works of Lucy Hutchinson* p. 462 note to l. 67 of the "Dedication"; Norbrook and Barbour, eds, *The Works of Lucy Hutchinson*, "Introduction", p. 72.

71. Jake Arthur, "'The stuffe not ours'", pp. 190–204.

72. See especially the Introduction to *The Works of Lucy Hutchinson*, vol. 1; Jonathan Goldberg, "Lucy Hutchinson Writing Matter"; Cassandra Gorman, *The Atom in Seventeenth-Century Poetry*.

73. "Preface" to *Order and Disorder* from *Women Poets of the English Civil War*.

74. Hutchinson, "Dedication" to *De rerum natura*, pp. 7–8.

75. Hutchinson, "Preface" to *Order and Disorder*, p. 296.

76. Hutchinson, "Dedication" to *De rerum natura*, p. 9.

77. Hutchinson, "Dedication" to *De rerum natura*, p. 15.

78. Scott-Baumann, *Forms of Engagement*, "Afterword", pp. 202–209.

79. John Florio, in preface to Montaigne, described translations as "reputed femalls, delivered at second hand", Michel de Montaigne, *The essayes or morall, politike and millitarie discourses* [...], trans. by John Florio, sig. A2r. Neil Rhodes extrapolates from this to portray early modern perceptions of translation as "reproductive" and therefore suitable for women, Neil Rhodes, *Common*, pp. 120–22. For a challenge to this, see Arthur, "'The stuffe not ours'".

80. Klene ed., *The Southwell-Sibthorpe Commonplace Book*, p. 4.

81. Mary Evelyn, in *Diary and Correspondence of John Evelyn*, iv, p. 9.

82. Burrow, *Imitating Authors*, p. 237.

83. Quint, *Origin and Originality*.

4. Irregular

1. H.A.J. Munro, "Mrs Lucie Hutchinson's Translation of Lucretius", p. 132.

2. Mary Wollstonecraft, *Thoughts on the Education of Daughters* (1787), in *The Works of Mary Wollstonecraft*, 7 vols, eds Janet Todd and Marilyn Butler, vol 4, p. 21.

3. *The Works of Lucy Hutchinson*, vol. 1, hereafter *Lucretius*, p. 7.

4. Munro, "Mrs Lucie Hutchinson's Translation of Lucretius", p. 132.

5. See David Norbrook, *Writing the English Republic*, p. 225 on "Milton's republican sublimity", and on Payne Fisher's ode to Cromwell "the metre is highly irregular, perhaps to give a sense of sublime breaking of forms", p. 234. See also p. 135 on a kind of "anti poetics" in which Milton "constantly presents the truth he is uttering as breaking out of the constraints of the tract's formal structures".

6. Wollstonecraft, *Thoughts on the Education of Daughters*, in *The Works of Mary Wollstonecraft*, vol. iv, p. 21.

7. Here describing "brutish" men in "To all Ingenious Ladies", preface to *The Ladies Defense*, in *The Poems and Prose of Mary, Lady Chudleigh*, ed. Margaret J. M. Ezell, p. 5.

8. William Davenant, *A discourse upon Gondibert an heroick poem [...]*, p. 37; 59.

9. Harington, "A Preface, or rather a Briefe Apologie of Poetrie", *Orlando furioso*, unnumbered page.

10. Aphra Behn, *The Luckey Chance*, sig. A4v (unpaginated).

11. See DeVun, *The Shape of Sex*, p. 85 and throughout.

12. See Sara Read, *Menstruation and the Female Body in Early Modern England* and Jenni Nuttall, *Mother Tongue*, pp. 55–57.

13. See, for instance, Rush, *The Fetters of Rhyme*; Andrea Brady, "Silken Fetters", in *Poetry and Bondage*; Susan Stewart, "Rhyme and Freedom" in *The Sound of Poetry / The Poetry of Sound*, ed. by Marjorie Perloff and Craig Dworkin, pp. 29–48.

14. Rosalie Colie, *The Resources of Kind*, p. 1.

15. Richard Strier, "Bondage and the Lyric", in *The Work of Form*, p. 87.

16. Brady, *Poetry and Bondage*, p. 359. Also James Kuzner, "Metaphysical Freedom"; Strier, "Bondage and the Lyric".

17. John Milton, *Paradise Lost*, 5, ll. pp. 618–27, ed. Alastair Fowler.

18. Nathaniel Lee, "To Mr. Dryden, on his Poem of Paradise", prefacing John Dryden, *The state of innocence and fall of man an opera*, sig. A4r, ll. 1–4.

19. Rowan Ricardo Phillips, *When Blackness Rhymes with Blackness*, p. 21. Phillips is describing Phyllis Wheatley and eighteenth-century poetic culture: "She was, in this sense, a real poet of the eighteenth century, when poetry was practically synonymous with frill and code. How far toward a rebellious African heart that code may have swung we will never know."

20. See Rush, *The Fetters of Rhyme*; J. Paul Hunter, "Form as Meaning: Pope and the Ideology of the Couplet".

21. Barbara Herrnstein Smith, *Poetic Closure*; Stephen Guy-Bray, *Line Endings in Renaissance Poetry*.

22. Gathered and foregrounded by Norbrook in several articles and the multi-volume *The Works of Lucy Hutchinson*, eds Reid Barbour and David Norbrook, and many articles and books, including (to name just a few) Shannon Miller, *Engendering the Fall*; Sarah C.E. Ross, *Women, Poetry, and Politics in Seventeenth- Century Britain*; Penelope Anderson, *Friendship's Shadows*; Jessie Hock, *The Erotics of Materialism*.

23. Julie Crawford, "Transubstantial Bodies in Paradise Lost and Order and Disorder", p. 82.

24. Jonathan Goldberg, *The Seeds of Things*, pp. 172–73.

25. Hutchinson, *Order and Disorder*, p. 3.

26. As shown in the commentary to the new Oxford edition by Norbrook and Barbour, *The Works of Lucy Hutchinson*, pp. xcvi–cv, hereafter *Lucretius*, and previously discussed in Hugh de Quehen, "Ease and Flow in Lucy Hutchinson's Lucretius".

27. *Lucretius*, p. 7.

28. On the complexities of this prefatory image, see Norbrook and Barbour, *Introduction*, pp. xciv–xcv. On gendered images of needlework and writing more widely, see Susan Frye, *Pens and Needles*; Michele Osherow, "'At My Petition'", in *The Oxford Handbook of Early Modern Women's Writing in English*.

29. Munro, "Mrs Lucie Hutchinson's Translation of Lucretius", p. 132.

30. See especially Goldberg, "Lucy Hutchinson Writing Matter"; *The Works of Lucy Hutchinson*; Hock, *The Erotics of Materialism*, p. 135.

31. *Lucretius*, p. xcix.

32. De Quehen, "Ease and Flow"; Norbrook, "Milton, Lucy Hutchinson and the Lucretian Sublime".

33. De Quehen defends Hutchinson as a pre-Augustan poet, Norbrook sees her as an anti-Augustan one. See De Quehen, "Ease and Flow"; Lucy Hutchinson, "To Mr Waller upon his Panegyric to the Lord Protector", text attached to David Norbrook, "Lucy Hutchinson versus Edmund Waller" and *Lucretius*, p. xcvii.

34. Hutchinson, *Order and Disorder*, p. 3.

35. Gore Vidal, *Palimpsest: A Memoir*, p. 417.

36. Hutchinson, *Lucretius*, pp. 9–15

37. Hutchinson, *Order and Disorder*, p. 3.

38. Norbrook, "Milton, Lucy Hutchinson and the Lucretian Sublime".

39. Goldberg, "Lucy Hutchinson Writing Matter"; David Norbrook, "John Milton, Lucy Hutchinson, and the Republican Biblical Epic"; Norbrook, "Milton, Lucy Hutchinson and the Lucretian Sublime".

40. Rogers, *The Matter of Revolution*; Norbrook, "Milton, Lucy Hutchinson and the Lucretian Sublime".

41. Norbrook, "John Milton, Lucy Hutchinson, and the Republican Biblical Epic", p. 43.

42. Hutchinson, *Order and Disorder*, 19, l. 409, in Osborn MS fb 100.

43. Norbrook and Barbour point out that she uses the word "congression" five times, note to 5.192.

44. *Lucretius*, p. 323.

45. Hutchinson, "To Mr Waller upon his Panegyric to the Lord Protector", ll. 173–6, from *Women Poets of the English Civil War*.

46. Waller, "A Panegyric to my Lord Protector", ll.173–6, Waller's poem taken from David Norbrook, "Lucy Hutchinson versus Edmund Waller". Modernization my own.

47. See work such as John Creaser, "Service is Perfect Freedom" and Creaser, "Prosodic Style and Conceptions of Liberty in Milton and Marvell" and Sharon Achinstein, "Milton's Spectre in the Restoration". See also John Leonard on the history of disputes over the form of *Paradise Lost*, Leonard, *Faithful Labourers*, Chapter 1 "Sound and Sense: 1667–1800".

48. An anonymous *TLS* review of E. M. W. Tillyard's 1929 edition, quoted in Susanne Woods, "Inventing English Verse", pp. 1–14; Ruth Ahnert, *The Rise of Prison Literature in the Sixteenth Century*, p. 70, and see also Chapter 5, "Liberating the Text?", pp. 144–92; Powell, "Editing Wyatts", pp. 96–7.

49. Leonard, *Faithful Labourers*, pp. 45–6.

50. While an earlier phase of scholarship (including of course Barthes's "The Death of the Author") seemed to dismantle intentionality, in recent decades questions of identity around

sexuality, race, class, and gender have changed the stakes: if our priorities as critics include social justice, the identities and even intentions of both writer and reader are not aspects we would seek to exclude from analysis; indeed, they may often be fundamental to criticism of a text, however ineluctable from its aesthetic properties, and even contributing to these. In some ways, this has put critical study of gender, as well as race, at odds with other parts of the field; as Lara Dodds and Michelle Dowd succinctly put it, "the death of the author coincided almost exactly with the ascendancy of literary recovery projects aiming to draw attention to women's writing". Dodds and Dowd, "Happy Accidents", p. 174.

51. See Julia Flanders, "'A Telescope for the Mind'", in *The Oxford Handbook of Early Modern Women's Writing in English*; Margaret J. M. Ezell, "The Laughing Tortoise".

52. Powell, "Editing Wyatts", p. 102. On the challenges of reading a major poetic manuscript which shows no sign of circulation or reading, for instance, see *Poems, Emblems, and The Unfortunate Florinda*, ed. Alice Eardley.

53. Wyatt, for instance, was probably edited to comply with a developing taste to which his editor Tottel was marketing; Gabriel Harvey corrected the meter of his king's poems at times seemingly to bring them into line with the rules of James's own poetic treatise, but at times going against these rules. Jennifer Richards shows that "Harvey tests and extends the king's laws for rhyming iambic meter; at no point does he ever just obey them [. . .] In this poem Harvey also adapts the meter; he changes the opening stress pattern of every second line from an iamb to a spondee, and he introduces a rhyme scheme not used by James", Jennifer Richards, "Gabriel Harvey, James VI, and the Politics of Reading Early Modern Poetry", p. 319.

54. Aston Cokain, "To my ingenuous Friend Mr. Alexander Brome on his Essay to translate Lucretius", in Aston Cokain, *Small poems of divers sorts*, sig. 204 (labeled p. 204 but page numbers not all sequential).

55. As David Norbrook has shown, including in *Lucretius*, p. xxiii-xxiv.

56. This poem accompanies Cowley's essay on the same topic. "Ode. Upon liberty", *Works*, 1668, *Essays*, p. 90, sig. M1v.

57. Abraham Cowley, *Poems written by A. Cowley*, labeled sig. b^r..

58. Congreve, "Discourse on the Pindarique Ode", 1706, in *Complete Works of William Congreve*, 4 vols, ed. Montague Summers vol. 4: 82–6.

59. Samuel Johnson, *The Lives of the Poets: A Selection*, ed. Roger Lonsdale, introduction by John Mullan, p. 40

60. See Annabel Patterson, *Censorship and Interpretation*; Joshua Scodel, "The Cowleyan Pindaric ode and sublime diversions", in *A Nation Transformed: England after the Restoration*, ed. by Alan Houston and Steve Pincus; Stella P. Revard, *Politics, Poetics, and the Pindaric Ode: 1450–1700*. For the politics of the Pindaric ode beyond Cowley, see Victoria Moul, *Jonson, Horace and The Classical Tradition*.

61. Susan Stewart, "What Praise Poems Are For", p. 236.

62. See Scott-Baumann, *Forms of Engagement*, p. 107.

63. Rush, *Fetters of Rhyme*, p. 149.

64. Rush, *Fetters of Rhyme*, p. 150.

65. *The Collected Works of Katherine Philips*, ii, Letter XXXVI, pp. 101–104, 17 September 1664.

66. Philips, "Upon Mr Abraham Cowley's Retirement. Ode.", from *Women Poets of the English Civil War*.

67. Bodleian Rawl Poet MS 90. Peter Beal dates it to the late seventeenth-century, Falconer Madan's summary catalogue to the first half of the eighteenth century. Peter Beal, *Index of Literary Manuscripts*, 4 vols; Falconer Madan, et al., *A summary catalogue of western manuscripts in the Bodleian Library at Oxford*, 7 vols., in vol. 8 [sic].

68. See Anderson, *Friendship's Shadows*; Elizabeth H. Hageman and Andrea Sununu, "New Manuscript Texts of Katherine Philips"; Hageman and Sununu, "More copies of it abroad than I could have imagin'd".

69. Paula Loscocco has written eloquently about how Philips's reception history illuminates shifting poetic tastes, identifying around the Restoration a move towards much more explicitly gendered ideas about smoothness and softness. This manuscript witness might take its place in such a history. See Paula Loscocco, "'Manly Sweetness'".

70. Cowley, "Ode. Upon Liberty", *The Works of Mr. Abraham Cowley*, sig. M1v (p. 90 within the pagination of *Several Discourses by Way of Essayes, In Verse and Prose*).

71. [anon], 'The Answer to the Emulation. A Pindarick Ode', *Triumphs of Female Wit* (1683), p. 6. The extraordinary title to this collection deserves quoting in full, as it indicates the explicit aim to exclude women from writing or theorizing poetry, while also showcasing claimed women poets: *Triumphs of female wit, in some pindarick odes, or, The emulation together with an answer to an objector against female ingenuity, and capacity of learning: also, a preface to the masculine sex by a young lady*. Stella P. Revard also suggests that one possible object of the poem's critique, beyond the anonymous female poet(s) of the preface and female-voied poems, might be Aphra Behn. Stella P. Revard, "Katherine Philips, Aphra Behn, and the Female Pindaric", in *Representing Women in Renaissance England*, eds Claude J. Summers and Ted-Larry Pebworth.

72. Thomas Sprat preface to Abraham Cowley, *Works*, 1668, sig. b2v.

73. Chris Beyers, *A History of Free Verse*, p. 70

74. Behn, "To Mr. Creech (under the Name of *Daphnis*) on his Excellent Translation of *Lucretius*", *Poems upon several occasions*, pp. 51–2.

75. Philips, *The Collected Works of Katherine Philips*, vol. ii, pp. 101–104.

5. Smooth/Soft

1. John Florio, *Queen Anna's New World of Words* (1611), p. 322.

2. Gilbert Burnet, letter to Anne Wharton, 14 December 1682, *Surviving Works of Anne Wharton*, eds Greer and Hastings, p. 351.

3. Florio, *Queen Anna's New World of Words*. The definition here is slightly expanded from that in the 1598 edition. Glossed by the OED (1) as "Lifelike delicacy in flesh tints".

4. Indeed, Juliet Fleming has shown that addresses to women in dictionaries often served to identify women as the lawless language users which those books sought to regulate, Judith Fleming, "Dictionary English and the Female Tongue".

5. William Scott, *The Model of Poesy*, ed. Gavin Alexander, p. 65.

6. Mann, "Marlowe's 'Slack Muse'"; Jessie Hock, "Voluptuous Style".

7. Jonson, *Timber* in *The Cambridge Edition of the Works of Ben Jonson*, vol. 7, ll. 513–519 Nota 5.

8. Puttenham, *The Art of English Poesy*, Book 3, Chapter 2, p. 333.

9. Henry Vaughan, "To the most Excellently accomplished, Mrs. K. Philips", *Olor Iscanus*, p. 28.

10. Loscocco, "'Manly Sweetness'".

11. Cowley, "Upon Mrs K. Philips her poems", in *Poems by the most deservedly admired Mrs. Katherine Philips*, sig. c1r

12. Andrew Carpenter has argued that "Philo-Philippa" was a male poet, "Katherine Philips, 'Philo-Philippa' and Restoration Dublin". If the poet was male, different yet equally revealing insights can be gleaned from his ventriloquism of a woman's voice to praise a woman's voice.

13. Philo-Philippa, "To the Excellent Orinda", *Poems by the most deservedly admired Mrs. Katherine Philips*, sig. d2r.

14. DeVun, *The Shape of Sex*; see also Colby Gordon, "A Woman's Prick".

15. See Miles P. Grier, "Black / White", in *Shakespeare/text*, ed. Claire M.L. Bourne, pp. 319–42.

16. Alexander Pope, *Essay on Criticism* (London: 1711; here quoted from 1749), p. 51, ll. 360–1.

17. Alexander Pope, "Epistle to Augustus", in *Poems of Alexander Pope*, ed. by John Butt, ll. 265–9.

18. Thomas Kaminski, "Waller's Easy Style and the Heroic Couplet". See also Robin Sowerby, *The Augustan Art of Poetry*, esp. Chapter 2 "The Augustan Ideal: Rhyme and Refinement", pp. 62–143; Helgerson, "Barbarous Tongues". For prosodic development, see Eric Weiskott. *Meter and Modernity in English Verse, 1350–1650*; Stagg, "Rhyme's Voices"; Marina Tarlinskaja, *Shakespeare and the Versification of English Drama, 1561-1642*.

19. Warren L. Chernaik, *The Poetry of Limitation*, p. 205.

20. George Gilfillan ed., *The Poetical Works of Edmund Waller and Sir John Denham*, p. viii.

21. Loscocco, "Manly Sweetness", p. 266

22. Loscocco, "Manly Sweetness", p. 266.

23. Southwell, "Precept 4", in Klene ed., *The Southwell-Sibthorpe Commonplace Book*, ll. 283–94.

24. On "fair" more broadly see Kim F. Hall, *Things of Darkness: Economies of Race and Gender in Early Modern England*, and Sujata Iyengar, *Shades of Difference: Mythologies of Skin Color in Early Modern England*.

25. On the broader questions of whitening cosmetics see Farah Karim-Cooper, *Cosmetics in Shakespearean and Renaissance Drama*, and on the materials and technologies of print in relation to race, see Grier, "Black / White".

26. Hutson, "Introduction" to Timber, *Cambridge Works of Ben Jonson*, vol. 7, p. 17.

27. Anne Southwell, "The First commandment", Klene ed., p. 45, ll. 31–36.

28. Southwell, "Precept 4", Klene ed., p. 152, l. 307.

29. Southwell, "Precept 4", Klene ed., p. 152, ll. 307–12.

30. Epistle to the "Waldegrave" Manuscript (Stonyhurst MS A.v.27), from *The Collected Poems of S. Robert Southwell*, ed. Peter Davidson and Anne Sweeney, p. 1. Anne Southwell's father, Sir Thomas Southwell, was Robert Southwell's nephew. See Erica Longfellow, "Lady Anne Southwell's Indictment of Adam", in *Early Modern Women's Manuscript Writing*, ed. Victoria E. Burke and Jonathan Gibson, pp. 111–33.

31. See Nuttall, *Mother Tongue*, p. 244.

32. Masten, *Queer Philologies*, p. 221

33. On other politicized uses of false etymology, see Crawforth, *Etymology and the Invention of English in Early Modern* Literature, including the sexualized false etymological connection

suggested by Milton between "whore" and "abhor", p. 151, and woman as a deriving from "she who brought woe to men", p. 176.

34. *POEMS &c. By JAMES SHIRLEY*, p. 9.

35. Diana Henderson, "Female Power and the Devaluation of Renaissance Love Lyrics", in *Dwelling in Possibility*, eds Yopie Prins and Maeera Shreiber, p. 50. See also Kristen Olson, "*Semper Eadem*", in *The Shakespearian International Yearbook*, ed. Graham Bradshaw et al.

36. Anne Southwell, "Thou shalt not commit Adultery", Folger MS V.b.198, fol. 51v, quoted from Klene ed., *The Southwell-Sibthorpe Commonplace Book*, p. 83, ll. 251–56.

37. Wright, *Producing Women's Poetry*, p. 56.

38. Cassandra Gorman, "Universal Verse".

39. BL MS ADD 17, 018 fols. 213–17. David Norbrook first published it in an article in 1996, Norbrook, "Lucy Hutchinson versus Edmund Waller".

40. See Norbrook, "Lucy Hutchinson versus Edmund Waller" and Timothy Raylor, "Waller's Machiavellian Cromwell".

41. Raylor, "Waller's Machiavellian Cromwell", p. 387.

42. Waller, "A panegyrick to my Lord Protector", ll.1–4, Waller's poem taken from Norbrook, "Lucy Hutchinson versus Edmund Waller". Modernization my own.

43. Hutchinson, "To Mr Waller", ll.1–4, from *Women Poets of the English Civil War*.

44. Margaret Cavendish, *Orations of divers sorts*, unpaginated recto before sig. a1r.

45. Norbrook, "Lucy Hutchinson versus Edmund Waller", p. 65.

46. Francis Atterbury, preface to *The Second Part of Mr Waller's Poems*, from Womersley, *Augustan Critical Writing*, p. 121. Atterbury is not named as author to this preface, but it has been assumed to be his.

47. Germaine Greer and Susan Hastings, "Introduction", *Surviving Works of Anne Wharton*.

48. For a recent account of Wharton's life that explores these inaccuracies, see Orlando Project: "Women's Writing in the British Isles from the Beginnings to the Present", <https://web.archive.org/web/20240726155417/https://orlando.cambridge.org/profiles/wharan> [accessed 26 November 2024].

49. ODNB; Introduction to Greer and Hastings, *Surviving Works of Anne Wharton*.

50. Margaret Ezell describes this phenomenon, of being saved and condemned by association with a famous man, in the cases of Anne Killigrew and Damaris Masham, see, for example, Margaret J. M. Ezell, "'Household Affairs Are the Opium of the Soul': Damaris Masham and the Necessity of Women's Poetry", in *Write or Be Written*, eds Barbara Smith and Ursula Appelt, pp. 49–65.

51. I am using the term "soft poetics" in dialogue with Jenny C. Mann, "Marlowe's 'Slack Muse'". Mann argues that Marlowe, in translating and in dialogue with Ovid's Elegies, develops the idea of a creative poetics of softness, in contrast to the dominant association of softness with effeminacy and failure.

52. Edward Young, *The Idea of Christian Love being a Translation*.

53. Anne Wharton, "To Mr Waller", *Surviving Works of Anne Wharton*, ed. by Germaine Greer and Susan Hastings, pp. 182–183, ll. 28–31; 56–58.

54. Edmund Waller, "Of Divine Poesy", *Surviving Works of Anne Wharton*, ed. by Germaine Greer and Susan Hastings, p. 287, ll. 9–10.

55. "twist", verb, OED II.3.a. and also "twist", noun II.4.a.

56. Anne Wharton, "To Mr Waller", *The Gentleman's Magazine*, 85, pt. i (June 1815), p. 493.

57. Greer and Hastings, "Introduction" to *Surviving Works of Anne Wharton*, p. 81. They also describe his letters as "a repulsive mixture of servility, trepidation and bland impudence", p. 83. This is perhaps characteristic of Burnet who had once, unwisely, counselled no less than Charles II to change his behaviour. Martin Greig, "Gilbert Burnet" (1643–1715) ODNB.

58. Greer and Hastings, eds, *Surviving Works of Anne Wharton*, p. 356. Later in the letters he comments of another poem "both in this and in your Despair, you say some things so like the language of the Atheists concerning the next state, as doubting of it, and hinting as if the soul were dissolved, that I am confident, when you reflect on this, you will watch over such passages, if they chance to spring in your fancy at any time hereafter", pp. 356–7.

59. Chernaik, *The Poetry of Limitation* (title and throughout).

60. Aphra Behn, "On the Death of the Late Earl of Rochester", in *Miscellany, being a collection of poems by several hands; together with Reflections on morality, or, Seneca unmasqued*, p. 45.

61. Wharton, "To Mrs. A. Behn, On what she Writ of the Earl of Rochester", *Surviving Works of Anne Wharton*, eds Greer and Hastings, p. 143; ll. 1–2.

62. Abraham Cowley, *The third part of the works of Mr. Abraham Cowley being his Six books of plants never before printed in English*, p. 143.

63. I am indebted in my discussion to two unpublished works which discuss these poems: Katherine Smith, "Ovidian Female-Voiced Complaint Poetry in Early Modern England" and a conference paper shared kindly by Gillian Manning, "Translation matters".

64. *Miscellany, being a Collection of Poems*, pp. 212–13.

65. In her unpublished conference paper, "Translation Matters", Manning says "my view is that in 'Sapho to Phaon', Wharton was consciously heterosexualizing/'normalizing' her given materials by introducing the then popularly received view of Sappho as suffering unrequited desire for her male lover, Phaon. This version of the Sappho myth may also perhaps have held a personal appeal for Wharton, in view of her own well-documented, unhappy marriage."

66. "Verses made by Sappho, done from the Greek by Boyleau, and from the French by a Lady of Quality", in *Miscellany, being a Collection of Poems*, pp. 212–213.

67. Manning, "Translation Matters".

68. Loscocco, "'Manly Sweetness'", p. 266.

69. Behn, "To Mrs. W. On her Excellent Verses (Writ in Praise of some I had made on the Earl of Rochester) Written in a Fit of Sickness", *Poems upon several occasions*.

70. Janet Todd, *Aphra Behn* (Fenton Press, London, 2017, [1996]), p. 269

71. Ros Ballaster, "Rochester, Behn and Enlightenment liberty", in *Lord Rochester in the Restoration World*, ed. Matthew C. Augustine and Steven N. Zwicker, p. 207.

72. Ballaster, "Rochester, Behn and Enlightenment liberty", p. 214.

73. Aphra Behn, "On the Death of the Late Earl of Rochester", ll. 36–38.

74. James Turner, *Schooling Sex*, p. 376.

75. Gilbert Burnet, letter to Anne Wharton, 14 December 1682, *Surviving Works of Anne Wharton*, eds. Greer and Hastings, p. 351–2.

76. OED, 8.a.

77. OED, A.I.1.a.

78. OED, II.3.a.

79. Shakespeare, *Cymbeline*, ed. J. M. Nosworthy (London: Arden Bloomsbury, 2014 [1955]) Act 5, Scene 5, p. 186.

80. "To Mrs Wharton", eds Greer and Hastings, *Surviving Works of Anne Wharton*, pp. 292–3.

81. "To Mrs Wharton", eds Greer and Hastings, *Surviving Works of Anne Wharton*, pp. 293–4. He writes a third poem about Wharton addressing her as "Orinda", aligning her with Katherine Philips who was also often used as a virtuous counterpoint to Behn's libertinism.

82. Greer and Hastings, "Introduction", *Surviving Works of Anne Wharton*, p. 19; p. 63.

83. Todd, *Aphra Behn*, p. 270.

84. Behn, "To Mr. *Creech* (under the Name of *Daphnis*) on his Excellent Translation of *Lucretius*", *Poems upon several occasions*, pp. 51. See discussion in Revard, "Katherine Philips, Aphra Behn, and the Female Pindaric".

85. On this poem, see Sophie Tomlinson, "'A Woman's Reason'". On Lucretius and gender, amongst others, see S. Georgia Nugent, "Mater *Matters*", p. 205, for the more negative view of Lucretius and the female; for a more positive see Martha Nussbaum, *The Therapy of Desire*; against heteronormative readings of Lucretian materialism, see Goldberg, "Lucy Hutchinson Writing Matter".

86. BL Add. MS 28104. fols. 6–7. Peter Davidson reads "hayvinesse" rather than "hayrinesse" here but I follow Jill Woodberry's reading of "hayrinesse" arguing that "the repetition three times of the word 'smooth', as a desirable quality which Fanshawe judges to have been achieved by Evelyn as a refinement of Lucretius, suggests that Fanshawe has in mind the Latin words *hispidus* or *horridus* to describe the original text, both of which can mean 'hairy', but with the sense 'bristly', 'tangled' or 'rough'", and also the key opposition between "hairy" and "smooth" between Esau and Jacob. Peter Davidson ed. *The Poems and Translation of Sir Richard Fanshawe*, vol. 1, p. 333. See Jill Woodberry, PhD in progress (University College London), "Horace in England, 1620–1640", especially Chapter 1, Section 2, "Early translators of Horatian lyric".

87. Sarah C. E. Ross and Rosalind Smith eds., *Early Modern Women's Complaint*, and the Early Modern Women's Complaint Poetry Index <https://cems.anu.edu.au/complaintindex/> [accessed 16 December 2024] by the project team Ross, Smith, O'Callaghan, Arthur, Whitelaw.

88. As far as I know, this poem appears only in Beinecke Library's Osborn MS b408, p. 77. I have modernized and punctuated, in line with my Note on the Text.

89. In what remains the only extended study of Wharton's complaint poems, Katherine Smith's PhD thesis argues for Wharton's authorship. Smith, "Ovidian Female-Voiced Complaint Poetry in Early Modern England". Smith also mentions Germaine Greer's suggestion (in personal correspondence) that "Unchangeable" and "The inconstancy of Woman Kind" might have been generated in a poetic game or exchange, and therefore not necessarily both by Wharton pp. 239. Certainly the opening of Wharton's poem, and the name Aminta, evoke Behn's "The Dream".

90. Edmund Spenser, "Sonnet LXXV", *Amoretti and Epithalamion* (London: 1595), [unnumbered page].

91. As far as I know, this poem appears only in Beinecke Library's Osborn MS b408, p. 76. I have modernized and punctuated, in line with my Note on the Text.

92. Wharton, "Melpomene against Complaint", Osborn MS b408, pp. 65–6; also published as Wharton's in "To Melpomene against Complaint. By the same Author" in *A Collection of Poems By Several Hands*, (1693).

93. Lynn Enterline, "'Past the help of law'", in *Early Modern Women's Complaint*, p. 316. Enterline's usage draws on Rowe in Gail Kern Paster, Katherine Rowe, and Mary Floyd-Wilson, eds. *Reading the Early Modern Passions* which in turn draws upon Anna Wierzbicka, "Emotion, Language, and Cultural Scripts", in *Emotion and Culture*, ed. by Shinobu Kitayama and Hazel Rose Markus.

94. Gillian Wright, "Aphra Behn's 'Oenone to Paris', John Dryden, and the Ovidian Complaint in Restoration Literary Culture", in *Early Modern Women's Complaint*.

Conclusion. A new history of style

1. Jonson, *Timber* in *The Cambridge Edition of the Works of Ben Jonson*, vol. 7, 502–512 Nota 4.

2. Colby Gordon, 'Lyly's Trans Style: Natural Transitioning in *Galatea*', in *Early Modern Trans Drama*, eds. Simone Chess and Sawyer Kemp (ACMRS Press, forthcoming 2025).

3. [Thomas Sprat], Preface, *The Works of Mr. Abraham Cowley* (London: 1668), sig. b2v.

4. Davenant, *A discourse upon Gondibert*, p. 108.

5. Cavendish, "Of the Labyrinth of Fancy", *The Worlds Olio*, p. 10.

6. Cavendish, "Of Eloquence, art, and speculation", *The Worlds Olio*, p. 14.

7. Adam Smyth, *Material Texts in Early Modern England* (Cambridge: Cambridge University Press, 2018), p. 174.

8. See Sarasohn, *The Natural Philosophy of Margaret Cavendish*.

BIBLIOGRAPHY

Primary Texts

A Collection of Poems By Several Hands. (London: 1693).
Triumphs of female wit, in some pindarick odes. (London: 1683).
Behn, Aphra. *Poems upon several occasions: with, A voyage to the island of love.* (London: 1684).
———. *The Luckey Chance.* (London: 1687).
Behn, Aphra, ed. *Miscellany, being a collection of poems by several hands; together with Reflections on morality, or, Seneca unmasqued.* (London, 1685).
Bradstreet, Anne. *The Tenth Muse Lately Sprung up in America.* (London: 1650).
Campion, Thomas. *Observations in the Art of English Poesie.* (London: 1602).
Cavendish, Margaret. *Poems, and Fancies.* (London: 1653).
———. *Philosophical and Physical Opinions.* (London: 1655).
———. *Sociable Letters.* (London: 1664).
———. *Observations upon Experimental Philosophy to which is Added the Description of a New Blazing World.* (London: 1666).
———. *Orations of divers sorts.* (London: Anna Maxwell, 1668).
———. *The Worlds Olio.* (London, 1655; London, 1671).
Cawdrey, Robert. *A Table Alphabetical, Containing and Teaching the Understanding of Hard Usual English Words.* (London: 1617).
Charleton, Walter. *Letters and Poems in Honour of the Incomparable Princess, Margaret Cavendish* (London: Thomas Newcombe, 1676).
Chudleigh, Mary. *The Poems and Prose of Mary, Lady Chudleigh,* edited by Margaret J. M. Ezell. (Oxford and New York: Oxford University Press, 1993).
Cokain, Aston. *Small poems of divers sorts.* (London: 1658).
Congreve, William. *Complete Works of William Congreve,* 4 vols, ed. by Montague Summers. (London: Nonesuch Press, 1923).
Cowley, Abraham. *Poems written by A. Cowley.* (London: Humphrey Moseley, 1656).
———. *The Works of Mr. Abraham Cowley.* (London: 1668).
———. *The third part of the works of Mr. Abraham Cowley being his Six books of plants never before printed in English.* (London: 1689).
Daniel, Samuel, *A panegyrike congratulatory deliuered to the Kings most excellent maiesty at Burleigh Harrington in Rutlandshire. By Samuel Daniel. Also certaine epistles. With a defence of ryme.* (London: 1603).

———, *Poems and A Defence of Ryme*, edited by Arthur Colby Sprague. (Cambridge, MA: Harvard University Press, 1930).

Davenant, William, *A discourse upon Gondibert an heroick poem written by Sr. William D'Avenant; with an answer to it, by Mr. Hobbs.* (Paris: Mattieu Guillemot, 1650).

de Montaigne, Michel. *The essayes or morall, politike and millitarie discourses* [. . .]. Translated by John Florio. (London: Valentine Sims, 1603).

———. *Essays written in French by Michael Lord of Montaigne, Knight of the Order of S. Michael, gentleman of the French Kings chamber*, translated by John Florio. (London: 1613).

Dryden, John. *The Rival Ladies.* (London: 1664).

———. *The state of innocence and fall of man an opera.* (London: 1677).

———. *Annus Mirabilis.* (London: 1667).

Du Verger, Susan. *Du Vergers humble reflections vpon some passages of the Right Honorable the Lady Marchionesse of Nevvcastles Olio, or, An appeale from her mes-informed, to her ovvne better informed iudgement.* (London: 1657).

Early Modern Women's Complaint Poetry Index <https://cems.anu.edu.au/complaintindex/> [accessed 16 December 2024].

Evelyn, John. *Diary and Correspondence of John Evelyn*, 4 vols. Edited by William Bray (London: Henry Colburn, 1850).

Fenner, Dudley. *The Artes of Logike and Rethorike.* (London: 1584).

Florio, John. *Queen Anna's New World of Words.* (London: 1611).

Gascoigne, George. *A Hundreth Sundrie Flowres.* Edited by G. W. Pigman III. (Oxford: Clarendon Press, 2000).

Gilfillan, George. *The Poetical Works of Edmund Waller and Sir John Denham. With memoir and critical dissertation.* (Edinburgh: James Nichol, 1857).

Harington, John, trans. *Orlando furioso in English heroical verse.* (London: 1591).

Hutchinson, Lucy. *The Works of Lucy Hutchinson, vol. 1: The Translation of Lucretius*, edited by Reid Barbour and David Norbrook, with Latin text by Maria Cristina Zerbino. (Oxford: Oxford University Press, 2012).

———. *Order and Disorder*, edited by David Norbrook. (Oxford: Blackwell, 2001 [1679]).

Johnson, Samuel. *The Lives of the Poets: A Selection*. Edited by Roger Lonsdale, introduction by John Mullan. (Oxford: Oxford University Press, 2009).

Jonson, Ben, *Workes.* (London: 1616).

———. *Cambridge Edition of the Works of Ben Jonson*, 7 vols. Edited by David Bevington, Martin Butler, Ian Donaldson. (Cambridge: Cambridge University Press, 2012).

Letters and Poems In Honour of the Incomparable Princess, Margaret, Dutchess of Newcastle. (The Savoy: Thomas Newcombe, 1676).

Milton, John. *Paradise Lost.* Edited by Alastair Fowler. (Harlow: Longman, 1998).

Orlando Project: Women's Writing in the British Isles from the Beginnings to the Present, <https://orlando.cambridge.org/>[accessed 16 December 2024].

Philips, Katherine. *Poems by the most deservedly admired Mrs. Katherine Philips, the matchless Orinda.* (London: 1667).

———. *The Collected Works of Katherine Philips: The Matchless Orinda*, 3 vols. Edited by Patrick Thomas. (Stump Cross, Essex: Stump Cross Books, 1990).

Pope, Alexander. *Poems of Alexander Pope.* Edited by John Butt. (New Haven, CT: Yale University Press, 1963).

——. *An Essay on Criticism*. With notes by Mr. Warburton. (London: 1749) [1711]).
Pulter, Hester. *The Pulter Project*. Edited by Leah Knight and Wendy Wall, <https://pulterproject.northwestern.edu/> [accessed 24 November 2024].
Puttenham, George. *The Art of English Poesy*. Edited by Frank Whigham and Wayne A. Rebhorn. (Ithaca, NY: Cornell University Press, 2007).
Ross, Sarah C. E., and Elizabeth Scott-Baumann, eds. *Women Poets of the English Civil War*. (Manchester: Manchester University Press: 2017).
Rymer, Thomas. *A short view of tragedy its original, excellency and corruption: with some reflections on Shakespear and other practitioners for the stage*. (London: 1693).
Scott, William. *The Model of Poesy*. Edited by Gavin Alexander. (Cambridge: Cambridge University Press, 2013).
Shakespeare, William. *Shake-speares Sonnets*. (London: 1609).
——. *Cymbeline*. Edited by J. M. Nosworthy. (London: Arden Bloomsbury, 2014 [1955]).
——. *The Complete Poems of Shakespeare*. Edited by Cathy Shrank and Raphael Lyne. (Abingdon: Routledge, 2018).
Shirley, James. *POEMS &c. By JAMES SHIRLEY*. (London: Humphrey Moseley, 1646).
Sidney, Philip. *An Apologie for Poetrie*. (London: 1595).
——. *The Poems of Sir Philip Sidney*. Edited by William A. Ringler. (Oxford: Clarendon Press, 1962).
Spenser, Edmund. *Complaints*. (London: 1591).
——. *Amoretti and Epithalamion* (London: 1595).
Southwell, Anne. *Miscellany of Lady Anne Southwell, ca. 1587–1636*. Folger Shakespeare Library, MS V.b.198
——. *The Southwell-Sibthorpe Commonplace Book: Folger MS. V.b.198*. Edited by Jean Klene. (Tempe, AZ: Medieval & Renaissance Texts & Studies, 1997).
Southwell, Robert. *The Collected Poems of S. Robert Southwell*. Edited by Peter Davidson and Anne Sweeney. (Manchester: Carcanet Press, 2007).
Sylvester, Josuah. *All the small workes of that famous poet Iosuah Siluester Gathered into one volume*. (London: Humphrey Lownes, 1620).
Vaughan, Henry. *Olor Iscanus*. (London: 1651).
Wesley, Samuel. "An epistle to a friend concerning poetry by Samuel Wesley." (London: 1700).
Wharton, Anne. "[Poems]", Beinecke Library, Osborn MS b408.
——. "To Mr Waller", *The Gentleman's Magazine*, 85, pt. i (June 1815): 493.
——. *Surviving Works of Anne Wharton*. Edited by Germaine Greer and Susan Hastings. (Stump Cross, Essex: Stump Cross Books, 1997).
Wollstonecraft, Mary. *The Works of Mary Wollstonecraft*, 7 vols. Edited by Janet Todd and Marilyn Butler. (London: Routledge, 1989).
Wroth, Mary. *Mary Wroth's Poetry: An Electronic Edition*. Edited by Paul Salzman. <http://wroth.latrobe.edu.au/> [accessed 3 December 2024]
Young, Edward. *Conjectures on Original Composition*. (London: 1759).
——. *The Idea of Christian Love being a Translation [...] with a Large Paraphrase on Mr. Waller's Poem of Divine Love; to which are Added some Copies of Verses from that Excellent Poetess Mrs. Wharton, with Others to Her*. (London: 1688).

Secondary Texts

Achinstein, Sharon. "Milton's Spectre in the Restoration: Marvell, Dryden, and Literary Enthusiasm", *Huntington Library Quarterly* 59, no.1 (1996): 1–29.
Adams, Hazard, ed. *Critical Theory Since Plato*. (New York, NY: Harcourt Brace Jovanovich, 1971).
Ahnert, Ruth. *The Rise of Prison Literature in the Sixteenth Century*. (Cambridge: Cambridge University Press, 2013).
Akhimie, Patricia. *Shakespeare and the Cultivation of Difference: Race and Conduct in the Early Modern World*. (New York: Routledge, 2018).
——. "Cultivating expertise: Glossing Shakespeare and race", *Literature Compass* 18, no. 10, (2021): article #e12607.
Alexander, Gavin, ed. *Sidney's "The Defence of Poesy" and Selected Renaissance Literary Criticism*. (London: Penguin, 2004).
——. *Writing After Sidney: The Literary Response to Sir Philip Sidney, 1586–1640*. (Oxford: Oxford University Press, 2006).
Anderson, Penelope. *Friendship's Shadows: Women's Friendship and the Politics of Betrayal in England, 1640–1705*. (Edinburgh: Edinburgh University Press, 2012).
Andrea, Bernadette. "Early Modern Women, Race, and Writing Revisited", in *The Oxford Handbook of Early Modern Women's Writing in English, 1540–1700*. Edited by Elizabeth Scott-Baumann, Danielle Clarke, and Sarah C. E. Ross. (Oxford: Oxford University Press, 2022): 703–16.
Arthur, Jake, "'The stuffe not ours': The work of derivation in early modern Englishwomen's writing". (Oxford DPhil thesis, 2022): 190–204.
Ballaster, Ros. "Rochester, Behn and Enlightenment liberty", in *Lord Rochester in the Restoration World*. Edited by Matthew C. Augustine and Steven N. Zwicker. (Cambridge: Cambridge University Press, 2015): 207–30.
Battigelli, Anna. *Margaret Cavendish and the Exiles of the Mind*. (Lexington, KY: University Press of Kentucky, 1998).
Beal, Peter. *Index of Literary Manuscripts*, 4 vols. (London: Mansell Publishing Ltd, 1987).
Beyers, Chris. *A History of Free Verse*. (Fayetteville, AR: University of Arkansas Press, 2001).
Brady, Andrea. *Poetry and Bondage: A History and Theory of Lyric Constraint*. (Cambridge: Cambridge University Press, 2021).
Brennan, Michael. "'A SYDNEY though un-named': Ben Jonson's Influence in the Manuscript and Print Circulation of Mary Worth's Writings", *Sidney Journal* 17 (1999): 31–52.
Burrow, Colin. *Imitating Authors: Plato to Futurity*. (Oxford: Oxford University Press, 2019).
Campbell, Julie. *Literary Circles and Gender in Early Modern Europe: A Cross-Cultural Approach*. (Aldershot: Ashgate, 2006).
Carpenter, Andrew. "Katherine Philips, 'Philo-Philippa' and Restoration Dublin", *Eighteenth-Century Ireland / Iris an dá chultúr*, 33 (2018): 11–32.
Chernaik, Warren L. *The Poetry of Limitation: A Study of Edmund Waller*. (New Haven, CT: Yale University Press, 1968).
Clarke, Danielle. *The Politics of Early Modern Women's Writing*. (Harlow: Longman, 2001).
——. "'Signifying, but not sounding': Gender and paratext in the complaint genre", in *Renaissance Paratexts*. Edited by Helen Smith and Louise Wilson. (Cambridge: Cambridge University Press, 2011): 133–49.

Clarke, Danielle, and Marie-Louise Coolahan. "Gender, Reception, and Form: Early Modern Women and the Making of Verse", in *The Work of Form: Poetics and Materiality in Early Modern Culture*, edited by Elizabeth Scott-Baumann and Ben Burton. (Oxford: Oxford University Press, 2014): 144–61.

Clarke, Elizabeth. "Anne Southwell and the Pamphlet Debate: The Politics of Gender, Class, and Manuscript", in *Debating Gender in Early Modern England, 1500–1700*. Edited by Cristina Malcolmson and Mihoko Suzuki (Basingstoke: Palgrave Macmillan, 2002): 37–53.

Colie, Rosalie. *The Resources of Kind: Genre Theory in the Renaissance*. (Berkeley, CA: University of California Press, 1973).

Coolahan, Marie-Louise. *Women, Writing, and Language in Early Modern Ireland*. (Oxford: Oxford University Press, 2010).

Craik, Katharine. *Reading Sensations in Early Modern England*. (Basingstoke: Palgrave Macmillan, 2007).

Creaser, John. "'Service Is Perfect Freedom': Paradox and Prosodic Style in Paradise Lost", *The Review of English Studies* 58, no. 235 (2007): 268–315.

———. "Prosodic Style and Conceptions of Liberty in Milton and Marvell", *Milton Quarterly* 34, no. 1 (2000): 1–13.

Crawford, Julie. "Transubstantial Bodies in *Paradise Lost* and *Order and Disorder*", *Journal for Early Modern Cultural Studies* 19, 4 (2019): 75–93.

Crawforth, Hannah. *Etymology and the Invention of English*. (Cambridge: Cambridge University Press, 2013).

Cummings, Brian. "Philosophical Poetry: Greville and the Feminine Ending", in *Fulke Greville and the Culture of the English Renaissance*, edited by Russ Leo, Katrin Röder, and Freya Sierhuis (Oxford: Oxford University Press, 2018): 29–46.

Currah, Paisley, and Susan Stryker, eds. *TSQ: Transgender Studies Quarterly* 1, no. 1–2 (2014).

Das, Nandini, João Vicente Melo, Haig Smith, and Lauren Working, *Keywords of Identity, Race, and Human Mobility in Early Modern England*. (Amsterdam: University of Amsterdam Press, 2021).

Davidson, Peter, ed. *The Poems and Translation of Sir Richard Fanshawe*, vol. 1. (Oxford: Oxford University Press, 1997).

de Quehen, Hugh. "Ease and Flow in Lucy Hutchinson's Lucretius", *Studies in Philology* 93, no. 3 (1996): 288–303.

DeVun, Leah. *The Shape of Sex: Nonbinary Gender from Genesis to the Renaissance*. (New York, NY: Columbia University Press, 2021).

Dodds, Lara. *The Literary Invention of Margaret Cavendish*. (Pittsburgh, PA: Duquesne University Press, 2013).

Dodds, Lara, and Michelle M. Dowd, "Happy Accidents: Critical Belatedness, Feminist Formalism, and Early Modern Women's Writing", *Criticism* 62, no. 2 (2020): 169–93.

Dolan, Frances E. "Hester Putler's Dunghill Poetics", *Journal for Early Modern Cultural Studies* 20, no. 2 (2020): 16–42.

Dolven, Jeff. *Senses of Style: Poetry Before Interpretation*. (Chicago: Chicago University Press, 2017).

Donaldson, Ian. *Ben Jonson: A Life*. Oxford: Oxford University Press, 2011.

Donawerth, Jane, ed. *Rhetorical Theory by Women before 1900: An Anthology*. (Lanham, MD: Rowman & Littlefield, 2002).

Dutton, Richard. *Ben Jonson: Authority: Criticism*. (Basingstoke: Macmillan, 1996).

Eardley, Alice, ed. *Poems, Emblems, and The Unfortunate Florinda*. (Toronto: Iter, Centre for Reformation and Renaissance Studies, 2014).

Enterline, Lynn. "'Past the help of law': Epyllia and the Female Complaint", in *Early Modern Women's Complaint: Gender, Form, and Politics*. Edited by Sarah C. E. Ross and Rosalind Smith. (New York: Palgrave Macmillan, 2020): 315–27.

Ezell, Margaret J. M. "'Household Affairs Are the Opium of the Soul': Damaris Masham and the Necessity of Women's Poetry", in *Write or Be Written: Early Modern Women Poets and Cultural Constraints*. Edited by Barbara Smith and Ursula Appelt. (Aldershot: Ashgate, 2001): 49–65.

———. "The Laughing Tortoise: Speculations on Manuscript Sources and Women's Book History", *English Literary Renaissance*, 38, no.2 (2008): 331–55.

Flanders, Julia. "'A Telescope for the Mind': Digital Modelling and Analysis of Early Modern Women's Writing", in *The Oxford Handbook of Early Modern Women's Writing in English, 1540–1700*, edited by Elizabeth Scott-Baumann, Danielle Clarke, and Sarah C. E. Ross. (Oxford: Oxford University Press, 2022): 657–72.

Fleming, Judith. "Dictionary English and the Female Tongue", in *Privileging Gender in Early Modern England*. Edited by Jean R. Brink. (Kirksville, MO: Sixteenth Century Journal Publishers, 1993): 175–204.

Folger Collective on Early Women Critics, ed. *Women Critics 1660–1820: An Anthology*. (Bloomington, IN: Indiana University Press, 1995).

Ford, Karen Jackson. *Gender and the Poetics of Excess: Moments of Brocade*. (Jackson: University of Mississippi Press, 1997).

Frye, Susan. *Pens and Needles: Women's Textualities in Early Modern England*. (Philadelphia, PA: University of Pennsylvania Press, 2010).

Gallagher, Catherine. "Embracing the Absolute: Margaret Cavendish and the Politics of the Female Subject in 17th Century England", *Genders*, 1 (1988): 24–39.

Gamble, Joseph. "Toward a Trans Philology", *Journal for Early Modern Cultural Studies*, 19 (2019): 26–44.

Gibson, Jonathan. "Synchrony and Process: Editing Manuscript Miscellanies." *Studies in English Literature*, 52 (2012): 85–100.

Goldberg, Jonathan. "Lucy Hutchinson Writing Matter", *English Literary History* 73 (2006): 275–301.

———. *The Seeds of Things: Theorizing Sexuality and Materiality in Renaissance Representations*. (New York, NY: Fordham University Press, 2009).

Gordon, Colby. "A Woman's Prick: Trans Technogenesis in Sonnet 20", in *Shakespeare / Sex: Contemporary Readings in Gender and Sexuality*, edited by Jennifer Drouin (Bloomsbury: London, 2020): 268–88.

———. 'Lyly's Trans Style: Natural Transitioning in *Galatea*', in *Early Modern Trans Drama*, edited by Simone Chess and Sawyer Kemp (ACMRS Press, forthcoming 2025).

Gorman, Cassandra, *The Atom in Seventeenth-Century Poetry* (Woodbridge, UK: Boydell and Brewer, 2021)

———. "Universal Verse: The Cosmological Poetics of Anne Southwell", *Parergon* 40, no. 2 (2023): 87–107

Greene, Roland. *Five Words: Critical Semantics in the Age of Shakespeare and Cervantes* (Chicago, IL: Chicago University Press, 2013).

Greig, Martin. "Burnet, Gilbert (1643–1715), bishop of Salisbury and historian." *Oxford Dictionary of National Biography*. 23 September 2004. <doi.org/10.1093/ref:odnb/4061>
Grier, Miles P. "Black / White", in *Shakespeare/text: Contemporary readings in textual studies, editing and performance*, edited by Claire M.L. Bourne (London: The Arden Shakespeare, 2021): pp. 319–42.
Guy-Bray, Stephen. *Line Endings in Renaissance Poetry* (New York, NY: Anthem Press, 2022)
Hageman, Elizabeth H., and Andrea Sununu. "New Manuscript Texts of Katherine Philips, the 'Matchless Orinda'", *English Manuscript Studies 1100–1700*, 4 (1993): 174–219.
———. "'More Copies of it abroad than I could have imagin'd': Further Manuscript Texts of Katherine Philips, 'the Matchless Orinda'", *English Manuscript Studies 1100–1700*, 5 (1995): 127–69.
Hammond, Paul. *Dryden and the Traces of Classical Rome* (Oxford: Oxford University Press, 1999).
Hamlin, Hannibal. "'The Highest Matter in the Noblest Form': The Influence of the Sidney Psalms", *Sidney Journal*, 23 (2005): 133–57
Hall, Kim F. "Culinary spaces, Colonial Spaces: The Gendering of Sugar in the Seventeenth Century", in *Feminist Readings of Early Modern Culture: Emerging Subjects*, edited. by Valerie Traub, M. Lindsay Kaplan and Dympna Callaghan (Cambridge: Cambridge University Press, 1996).
———. *Things of Darkness: Economies of Race and Gender in Early Modern England*. (Ithaca, NY: Cornell University Press, 1996).
Helgerson, Richard. "Barbarous Tongues: The Ideology of Poetic Form in Renaissance England", in *The Historical Renaissance: New Essays on Tudor and Stuart Literature and Culture*, edited by Heather Dubrow and Richard Strier (Chicago: University of Chicago Press, 1988): 273–92.
Henderson, Diana. "Female Power and the Devaluation of Renaissance Love Lyrics", in *Dwelling in Possibility: Women Poets and Critics on Poetry*, edited by Yopie Prins and Maeera Shreiber. (Ithaca, NY: Cornell University Press, 1997): 38–59.
Hock, Jessie. *The Erotics of Materialism: Lucretius and Early Modern Poetics*. (Philadelphia: University of Pennsylvania Press, 2021).
———. "Voluptuous Style: Lucretius, Rhetoric, and Reception in Montaigne's 'Sur des vers de Virgile'", *Modern Philology* 118 (2021): 492–514.
Hunter, J. Paul, 'Form as meaning: Pope and the Ideology of the Couplet', *The Eighteenth Century* 37 (1996): 257–70.
Hutson, Lorna. "Civility and Virility in Ben Jonson", *Representations* 78 no. 1 (2002): 1–27.
Iyengar, Sujata, "Royalist, Romancist, Racialist: Rank, Gender and Race in the Science and Fiction of Margaret Cavendish", *English Literary History* 69 (2002): 649–72.
———. *Shades of Difference: Mythologies of Skin Color in Early Modern England*. (Philadelphia, PA: University of Pennsylvania, 2005).
Kaminski, Thomas. "Waller's Easy Style and the Heroic Couplet", *SEL: Studies in English Literature 1500–1900* 55 (2015): 95–123.
Karim-Cooper, Farah. *Cosmetics in Shakespearean and Renaissance Drama*. (Edinburgh: Edinburgh University Press, 2006).
Kelly, Joan. "Did Women have a Renaissance?", in *Becoming Visible: Women in European History*, ed. by Renate Bridenthal and Claudia Koonz. (Boston, MA: Houghton Mifflin, 1977): 137–61.

Kramnick, Jonathan Brody. "The Making of the English Canon", *PMLA*, 112 (1997): 1087–1101.

Kunjummen, Sarah. "Reading Milton Like a Woman", *Criticism* 63, no. 1–2 (2021): 75–85.

Kuzner, James. "Metaphysical Freedom", *Modern Language Quarterly* 74 (2013), 465–92.

Lancashire, Ian, ed. "Lexicons of Early Modern English." Toronto: University of Toronto Press, 2018. <http://leme.library.utoronto.ca> [accessed 16 December 2024].

Lanser, Susan S., and Evelyn Torton Beck. "Why Are There No Great Women Critics and What Difference Does It Make?", in *The Prism of Sex: Essays in the Sociology of Knowledge*, edited by J. A. Sherman and E. Torton Beck. (Madison, WI: University of Wisconsin Press, 1979): 79–91

Le Dœuff, Michèle. *The Sex of Knowing*. (New York, London: Routledge, 2003).

Leonard, John, *Faithful Labourers: A Reception History of Paradise Lost, 1667–1970*. (Oxford: Oxford University Press. 2013).

Lipking, Lawrence. *Abandoned Women and Poetic Tradition*. (Chicago, IL: University of Chicago Press, 1988).

Longfellow, Erica. *Women and Religious Writing in Early Modern England*. (Cambridge: Cambridge University Press, 2004).

———. "Lady Anne Southwell's Indictment of Adam", in *Early Modern Women's Manuscript Writing: Selected Papers from the Trinity/Trent Colloquium*, edited by Victoria E. Burke and Jonathan Gibson. (Aldershot: Ashgate, 2004): 111–33.

Loscocco, Paula. "'Manly Sweetness': Katherine Philips among the Neoclassicals", *Huntington Library Quarterly* 56, no. 3 (1993): 259–79.

MacDonald, Joyce, "How Race Might Help Us Find 'Lost' Women's Writing", *Criticism*, 63 (2021): 45–53.

Madan, Falconer, et al. *A summary catalogue of western manuscripts in the Bodleian Library at Oxford*, 7 vols (Oxford: Clarendon Press, 1980 [1895–1953]).

Mann, Jenny C. "Marlowe's 'Slack Muse': All Ovids Elegies and an English Poetics of Softness", *Modern Philology* 113, no. 1 (2015): 49–65.

———. *The Trials of Orpheus: Poetry, Science, and the Early Modern Sublime*. (Princeton: Princeton University Press, 2021).

Manning, Gillian. "Translation matters: Wharton, Sappho, Boileau & Behn" (unpublished)

Masten, Jeffrey. *Queer Philologies: Sex, Language, and Affect in Shakespeare's Time*. (Philadelphia, PA: University of Pennsylvania Press, 2016).

McAuley, Mairéad. "Matermorphoses: Motherhood and the Ovidian Epic Subject", *Eugesta* 2 (2012): 123–68.

———. *Reproducing Rome: motherhood in Virgil, Ovid, Seneca, and Statius* (Oxford: Oxford University Press, 2016), 117–18.

Merchant, Carolyn. *The Death of Nature: Women, Ecology and the Scientific Revolution*. (San Francisco, CA: Harper and Row, 1983).

Miller, Edward Haviland. "Samuel Daniel's Revisions in *Delia*", *The Journal of English and Germanic Philology* 53, no. 1 (1954): 58–68.

Miller, Shannon. *Engendering the Fall: John Milton and Seventeenth-Century Women Writers*. (Philadelphia: University of Pennsylvania Press, 2008).

Mintz, Sidney W. *Sweetness and Power: The Place of Sugar in Modern History*. (New York: Penguin, 1985).

Mitchell, Dianne. "Lyric Backwardness", in *The Oxford Handbook of Early Modern Women's Writing in English, 1540–1700*, edited by Elizabeth Scott-Baumann, Danielle Clarke, and Sarah C. E. Ross. (Oxford: Oxford University Press, 2022): 189–202.

Moul, Victoria. *Jonson, Horace and The Classical Tradition*. (Cambridge: Cambridge University Press, 2010).

———. "The Transformation of Ovid in Cowley's Herb Garden: Books 1 and 2 of the Plantarum Libri Sex (1668)", in *The Afterlife of Ovid*, edited by Peter Mack and John North. (London: Institute of Classical Studies, University of London, 2015): 221–34.

Munro, H.A.J. "Mrs Lucie Hutchinson's Translation of Lucretius", *Journal of Classical and Sacred Philology* 4 (1858): 121–39.

Newlyn, Lucy. *Paradise Lost and the Romantic Reader*. (Oxford: Oxford University Press, 1991).

Norbrook, David. "Lucy Hutchinson versus Edmund Waller: An Unpublished reply to Waller's 'A Panegyrick to my Lord Protector'", *The Seventeenth Century*, 11 (1996): 61–86.

———. *Writing the English Republic: Poetry, Rhetoric and Politics, 1627–1660*. (Cambridge: Cambridge University Press, 1999).

———. "John Milton, Lucy Hutchinson, and the Republican Biblical Epic", *Milton and the Grounds of Contention*, edited by Mark R. Kelley, Michael Lieb and John T. Shawcross. (Pittsburgh: Duquesne University Press, 2003): 37–63.

———. "Milton, Lucy Hutchinson and the Lucretian Sublime", *Tate Papers*, 13 (2010). <https://www.tate.org.uk/research/tate-papers/13/milton-lucy-hutchinson-and-the-lucretian-sublime> [accessed December 6 2024].

Nugent, S. Georgia. "Mater *Matters*: The Female in Lucretius' De Rerum Natura", *Colby Quarterly* 30, no. 3 (1994): 179–205.

Nussbaum, Martha. *The Therapy of Desire: Theory and Practice in Hellenistic Ethics*. (Princeton, NJ: Princeton University Press, 1994).

Nuttall, Jenni. *Mother Tongue: The Surprising History of Women's Words*. (London: Virago, 2023).

Olson, Kristen. "*Semper Eadem*: The Paradox of Constancie in Shakespeare's *Phoenix and the Turtle*", in *The Shakespearian International Yearbook*, edited by Graham Bradshaw, Top Bishop, and Tetsuo Kishi. (Aldershot: Ashgate Publishing, 2007): 92–123.

Osherow, Michele. "'At My Petition': Embroidering Esther", in *The Oxford Handbook of Early Modern Women's Writing in English, 1540–1700*, edited by Elizabeth Scott-Baumann, Danielle Clarke, and Sarah C. E. Ross. (Oxford: Oxford University Press, 2022): 67–82.

Parker, Patricia. *Literary Fat Ladies: Rhetoric, Gender, Property*. (London and New York, NY: Methuen, 1987).

———. "Virile Style", in *Premodern Sexualities*, edited by Louise Frandenburg and Carla Freccero with the assistance of Kathy Lavezzo. (New York, NY and London: Routledge, 1996): 199–222.

Paster, Gail Kern, Katherine Rowe, and Mary Floyd-Wilson, eds. *Reading the Early Modern Passions: Essays in the Cultural History of Emotion*. (Philadelphia, PA: University of Pennsylvania Press, 2004).

Patterson, Annabel. *Censorship and Interpretation: The Conditions of Writing and Reading in Early Modern England*. (Madison, WI: University of Wisconsin Press, 1984).

Pender, Patricia. *Early Modern Women's Writing and the Rhetoric of Modesty*. (Basingstoke: Palgrave Macmillan, 2012).

Phillips, Rowan Ricardo. *When Blackness Rhymes with Blackness*. (Champaign, IL: Dalkey Archive Press, 2010).

Powell, Jason. "Editing Wyatts: Reassessing the Textual State of Sir Thomas Wyatt's Poetry," *Poetica* 71 (2009): 93–104.

Quilligan, Maureen. "Feminine Endings: The Sexual Politics of Sidney's and Spenser's Rhyming", in *The Renaissance Englishwoman in Print: Counterbalancing the Canon*, edited by Anne M. Haselkorn and Betty S. Travitsky. (Boston: University of Massachusetts Press, 1990): 311–26.

Quint, David. *Origin and Originality in Renaissance Literature: Versions of the Source*. (New Haven, CT: Yale University Press, 1983).

Raylor, Timothy. "Waller's Machiavellian Cromwell: The Imperial Argument of *A Panegyrick to My Lord Protector*", *RES*, 56 (2005): 386–411.

Read, Sara. *Menstruation and the Female Body in Early Modern England*. (London: Palgrave Macmillan, 2013).

Rebhorn, Wayne A. *The Emperor of Men's Minds: Literature and the Renaissance Discourse of Rhetoric*. (Ithaca, NY: Cornell University Press, 1995).

Rees, Emma L. E. *Margaret Cavendish: Gender, Genre, Exile*. (Manchester: Manchester University Press, 2003).

Rees, Joan. *Samuel Daniel: A Critical and Biographical Study*. (Liverpool: Liverpool University Press, 1964).

Revard, Stella P. "Katherine Philips, Aphra Behn, and the Female Pindaric", in *Representing Women in Renaissance England*, edited by Claude J. Summers and Ted-Larry Pebworth. (Columbia: University of Missouri Press, 1997): 227–41.

———. *Politics, Poetics, and the Pindaric Ode: 1450–1700*. (Tempe, AZ: Arizona Center for Medieval and Renaissance Studies, 2009).

Rhodes, Neil. *Common: The Development of Literary Culture in Sixteenth-Century England*. (Oxford: Oxford University Press, 2018): 120–22.

Richards, Jennifer. "Gabriel Harvey, James VI, and the Politics of Reading Early Modern Poetry", *Huntington Library Quarterly* 71, no.2 (2008): 303–21.

Richardson, Tim. *Sweets: The History of Temptation*. (London: Bantam Press, 2003).

Roberts, Sasha. *Reading Shakespeare's Poems in Early Modern England*. (Basingstoke: Palgrave Macmillan, 2003).

———. "Women's Literary Capital in Early Modern England: Formal Composition and Rhetorical Display in Manuscript and Print", *Women's Writing* 14 (2007): 246–69.

Robin, Diana. *Publishing Women: Salons, the Presses, and the Counter Reformation in Sixteenth-Century Italy*. (Chicago, IL: University of Chicago Press, 2007).

Rogers, John. *The Matter of Revolution: Science, Poetry and Politics in the Age of Milton*. (Ithaca, NY: Cornell University Press, 1996).

Ross, Sarah C. E. *Women, Poetry, and Politics in Seventeenth- Century Britain*. (Oxford: Oxford University Press, 2015).

Ross, Sarah C. E., and Rosalind Smith, eds. *Early Modern Women's Complaint: Gender, Form, and Politics* (Basingstoke: Palgrave Macmillan, 2020).

Ross, Trevor. *The Making of the English Literary Canon: From the Middle Ages to the Late Eighteenth Century*. (Montreal: McGill-Queen's University Press, 1998).

Rush, Rebecca M. *The Fetters of Rhyme: Liberty and Poetic Form in Early Modern England*. (Princeton, NJ: Princeton University Press, 2021).

Rutter, Tom. "The Cavendishes and Ben Jonson", in *A Companion to the Cavendishes*, edited by Lisa Hopkins and Tom Rutter. (Kalamazoo, MI: Arc Humanities Press, 2020): 107–26.

Sarasohn, Lisa T. *The Natural Philosophy of Margaret Cavendish: Reason and Fancy during the Scientific Revolution*. (Baltimore: Johns Hopkins University Press, 2010).

Sarkar, Debapriya. *Possible Knowledge: The Literary Forms of Early Modern Science*. (Philadelphia, PA: University of Pennsylvania Press, 2023).

Schoenfeldt, Michael. *The Cambridge Introduction to Shakespeare's Poetry*. (Cambridge: Cambridge University Press, 2010).

Schor, Naomi. *Reading in Detail: Aesthetics and the Feminine*. (Oxford and New York: Routledge, 2007).

Scodel, Joshua. "The Cowleyan Pindaric ode and sublime diversions", in *A Nation Transformed: England after the Restoration*, edited by Alan Houston and Steve Pincus. (Cambridge: Cambridge University Press, 2001): 180–210.

Scott-Baumann, Elizabeth. "'Baked in the Oven of Applause': The blazon and the body in Margaret Cavendish's Fancies", *Women's Writing*, 15 (2008): 86–106.

———. *Forms of Engagement: Women, Poetry and Culture, 1640–1680*. (Oxford University Press, 2013).

———. "Hester Pulter's Well-Wrought Urns: Early Modern Women, Sonnets, and the New Criticism", *Journal for Early Modern Cultural Studies* 20, no. 2 (2020): 118–43.

———, "'crittickize upon the smallest word': Anne Southwell and the place of gender in early modern criticism", in *The Places of Early Modern Criticism*, edited. by Gavin Alexander, Emma Gilby and Alexander Marr. (Oxford University Press, 2021): 143–57.

Shahani, Gitanjali. *Tasting Difference: Food, Race, and Cultural Encounters in Early Modern Literature*. (Ithaca, NY: Cornell University Press, 2020).

Smyth, Adam. *Material Texts in Early Modern England*. Cambridge: Cambridge University Press, 2018.

Smith, Barbara Herrnstein. *Poetic Closure*. (Chicago: University of Chicago Press, 1968).

Smith, Katherine. "Ovidian Female-Voiced Complaint Poetry in Early Modern England". PhD thesis, Warwick University, 2017. <https://wrap.warwick.ac.uk/id/eprint/95225/1/WRAP_Theses_Smith_2016.pdf> (accessed 16 December 2024)

Sowerby, Robin. *The Augustan Art of Poetry: Augustan Translation of the Classics*. (Oxford: Oxford University Press, 2006).

Spencer, Jane. *The Rise of the Woman Novelist: From Aphra Behn to Jane Austen*. (Oxford: Blackwell, 1986).

Stagg, Robert. "Rhyme's Voices: Hearing Gender in *The Taming of the Shrew*", *Studies in Philology* 119, no.2 (2022): 323–46.

Starr, G. Gabrielle. "Cavendish, Aesthetics, and the Anti-Platonic Line", *Eighteenth-Century Studies* 39 (2006): 295–308.

Stevenson, Jane. "Inventing Fame", in *A History of Early Modern Women's Writing*, edited by Patricia Phillippy. (Cambridge: Cambridge University Press, 2018): 348–63.

Stewart, Susan. "What Praise Poems Are For", *PMLA*, 120, no. 1 (2005): 235–45.

———. "Rhyme and Freedom", in *The Sound of Poetry / The Poetry of Sound*, edited by Marjorie Perloff and Craig Dworkin. (Chicago: University of Chicago Press, 2009): 29–48.

Strier, Richard. "Bondage and the Lyric: Philosophical and Formal, especially Renaissance", in *The Work of Form: Poetics and Materiality in Early Modern Culture*, edited by Ben Burton and Elizabeth Scott-Baumann. (Oxford: Oxford University Press, 2014): 73–87.

Suzuki, Mihoko. "The Essay Form as Critique: Reading Cavendish's *The World's Olio* through Montaigne and Bacon (and Adorno)", *Prose Studies* 22 (1999): 1–16.

Swann, Elizabeth L. *Taste and Knowledge in Early Modern England*. (Cambridge: Cambridge University Press, 2020).

Swinburne, Algernon Charles. *A Study of Ben Jonson*. (London: 1889).

Tarlinskaja, Marina. *Shakespeare and the Versification of English Drama, 1561-1642*. (Farnham: Ashgate, 2014).

Tatlock, J. S. P. "The Siege of Troy in Elizabethan Literature, Especially in Shakespeare and Heywood", *PMLA* 30, 4 (1915): 673–770.

———. "The Hermaphrodite Rime", *MLN*, 32 (1917).

Thompson, Ann, and Sasha Roberts, eds. *Women Reading Shakespeare, 1660–1900: An Anthology of Criticism*. (Manchester: Manchester University Press, 1997).

———. "A Lingering Farewell: Sonnet 87", in *The Sonnets: The State of Play*, edited by Hannah Crawforth, Elizabeth Scott-Baumann and Clare Whitehead. (London: Bloomsbury Arden Shakespeare, 2017): 117–35.

Todd, Janet. *Aphra Behn: A Secret Life*. (London: Fenton Press, 2017 [1996]).

Tomlinson, Sophie. "'A Woman's Reason': Aphra Behn Reads Lucretius", *Intellectual History Review* 22, no. 3 (2012): 355–72.

Trolander, Paul, and Zeynep Tenger. *Sociable Criticism in England 1625–1725*. (Newark: University of Delaware Press, 2007).

Tsur, Reuven. "Masculine and Feminine Rhymes: Their Structural Effect", *Style*, 47 (2013): 1–24.

Turner, James. *Schooling Sex: Libertine Literature and Erotic Education in Italy, France, and England 1534–1685*. (Oxford: Oxford University Press, 2003).

Vendler, Helen. *The Art of Shakespeare's Sonnets*. (Cambridge, MA: Harvard University Press, 1997).

Vickers, Brian, ed. *English Renaissance Literary Criticism*. (Oxford: Clarendon Press, 1999).

Vidal, Gore. *Palimpsest: A Memoir*. (New York: Random House, 1995).

Warley, Christopher. *Sonnet Sequences and Social Distinction in Renaissance England*. (Cambridge: Cambridge University Press, 2005).

Weiskott, Eric. *Meter and Modernity in English Verse, 1350-1650*. (Philadelphia: Pennsylvania University Press, 2021).

Wellek, René. *A History of Modern Criticism, 1750–1950*. (Cambridge: Cambridge University Press, 1981 [1955]).

Whigham, Frank. *Ambition and Privilege: The Social Tropes of Elizabethan Courtesy Theory*. (Berkeley, CA: University of California Press, 1984).

Wierzbicka, Anna. "Emotion, Language, and Cultural Scripts", in *Emotion and Culture: Empirical Studies of Mutual Influence*, edited by Shinobu Kitayama and Hazel Rose Markus. (Washington, DC: American Psychological Association, 1994).

Wilson-Okamura, David Scott. "The French Aesthetic of Spenser's Feminine Rhyme", *Modern Language Quarterly*, 68 (2007): 345–62.

Womersley, David, ed. *Augustan Critical Writing*. (London: Penguin, 1987).
Woodberry, Jill. "Horace in England, 1620–1640: English and Latin interpretations, with special reference to Richard Fanshawe and Mildmay Fane" PhD in progress, University College London.
Woods, Susanne. "Inventing English Verse", in *Early Modern English Poetry: A Critical Companion*, edited by Patrick Cheney, Andrew Hadfield, and Garrett A. Sullivan, Jr. (New York and Oxford: Oxford University Press, 2007): 1–14.
Wright, Gillian. *Producing Women's Poetry, 1600–1730*. (Cambridge: Cambridge University Press, 2013).
——. "Aphra Behn's 'Oenone to Paris', John Dryden, and the Ovidian Complaint in Restoration Literary Culture", in *Early Modern Women's Complaint: Gender, Form, and Politics*, edited by Sarah C. E. Ross and Rosalind Smith. (Basingstoke: Palgrave Macmillan, 2020): 205–23.

INDEX

Akhimie, Patricia, 19
Alexander, Gavin, 8, 14, 49–50, 53, 159n31
Andrea, Bernadette, 7, 156n26
Ariosto, Ludovico, 28
Arthur, Jake, 68
Atterbury, Francis, 119, 123, 133, 170n46
Atwood, William, 137–38
Aubrey, John, 111, 118

Bacon, Francis, 58
Ballaster, Ros, 134
Barbour, Reid, 67
Barthes, Roland, 166n50
Behn, Aphra, 77, 102–4, 120, 131; Burnet on, 105, 136–37, 139, 145; Cokain on, 100; Ovid and, 146; on Rochester, 133–35; soft style of, 12, 21, 121, 138–39; tenderness of, 135–40; Wharton and, 130–40, 146, 147
Beyers, Chris, 101–4
Blount, Thomas, 42
Boileau, Nicolas, 132
Bradstreet, Anne, 20, 53–55
Brady, Andrea, 78
Brome, Alexander, 91, 92
Bullokar, John, 77, 80
Burke, Edmund, 76
Burnet, Gilbert, 134, 147; on Behn, 105, 136–37, 139, 145; Wharton and, 120, 121, 125–27, 135–37
Burrow, Colin, 73–74
Burton, Robert, 1

Campion, Thomas, 158n8
Carpenter, Andrew, 169n12
Cavendish, Margaret, 149–54; Charleton on, 20, 49–50, 53, 72–73; Hutchinson and, 70; Jonson and, 57–63, 72, 153; on originality, 15, 20, 55–57, 61–67, 72–74, 84; Ovid and, 62–67, 74, 116, 163n50, 163n64; Toppe on, 56–57; on writing style, 5, 12, 60–61, 152–54; works of: "An Epistle to justify the Lady Newcastle . . .", 55; "Of Eloquence, art, and speculation", 152–53; "On the Labyrinth of Francy", 152; *Poems, and Fancies*, 62–63, 65; "The Purchase of Poets", 62–64, 66–67; *Sociable Letters*, 13; "To all Noble, and Worthy Ladies", 65; *The Worlds Olio*, 57–62, 66, 70, 153
Cavendish, William, 118, 162n29
Cervantes, Miguel de, 50
Chakravarty, Urvashi, 7
"changeable", 18; Behn on, 139; Cavendish on, 66; Wharton on, 140–43
Charles I of Great Britain, 117
Charles II of Great Britain, 117, 171n57
Charleton, Walter, 20, 49–50, 53, 72–73
Chernaik, Warren, 127
Chudleigh, Mary, 77
Cicero, 6, 11, 72
Clarke, Danielle, 4, 18
Cokain, Aston, 91–92, 100, 102, 139
complaint poems, 140–46, 172n89
"copy", 19; Cavendish on, 56, 73; Evelyn on, 53, 73; Hutchinson on, 68; Philips on, 51

Corneille, Pierre, 13, 45, 95, 104
Cotterell, Charles, 44–46, 95
couplet styles, 81
Cowley, Abraham, 8, 109; Johnson on, 94; Milton and, 101; on Ovid, 67; Philips and, 12, 94, 104, 109, 112; Pindaric odes of, 93–94, 98, 100, 108, 151; Sprat and, 93, 100–101, 108, 112, 151; works of: *Davideis*, 85; *Sylva*, 132; "Upon Liberty", 93, 98, 167n56
Craik, Katharine, 6
Crawford, Julie, 82
Creech, Thomas, 102–3, 139
"critic" (term), 10–11, 148–49
critical poetics, 16, 140, 149–50
critical semantics, 19
"criticism" (term), 1–2, 23
criticism (subject), 13; amendment, 45; origins of, 15; Pope's essay on, 110; as tool of oppression, 2. *See also* literary criticism
Cromwell, Oliver, 89, 117–19, 147, 165n5
Cummings, Brian, 32–33

Daniel, Samuel, 2, 16; *Defence of Rhyme*, 8, 15, 29–31; on feminine rhyme, 29–32, 45–48, 158n13; originality of, 49–50; Shakespeare and, 159n23
Danvers, Henry, 120
Das, Nandini, 19
Davenant, William, 8, 77, 151
Davidson, Peter, 172n86
Decalogue poetry, 9
Denham, John, 85, 110
Denny, Edward, 20, 37–38, 47–48
de Quehen, Hugh, 85, 166n33
devotional poetry, 18, 22, 71, 113
DeVun, Leah, 110
Dickinson, Emily, 78
Dodds, Lara, 7, 64, 167n50
Dolven, Jeff, 4, 50, 73
Donne, John, 90, 143
double rhyme, 46, 47, 161n52, 164n55
Dowd, Michelle, 7, 167n50

Drummond, William, 35–36
Dryden, John, 8, 46, 67; Pope on, 110, 111; *The State of Innocence and Fall of Man*, 79–80
Du Verger, Susan, 58

elegy, 130
Enterline, Lynn, 145
epistolary literature, 13
epyllia, erotic, 17–18
Erasmus, Desiderius, 58
erotic poetry, 115
Evelyn, John, 70, 139
Evelyn, Mary, 53, 73
"exceptional", 19, 20, 50, 55; Charleton on, 72, 73; Evelyn on, 53
"excessive", 19, 26; Cavendish on, 5, 62, 66; Daniel on, 29
Ezell, Margaret, 50, 56

Falkland, Lord, 11
Fanshawe, Richard, 139
female-authored theory, 44
"feminine", 18–48, 148–49, 154
feminine rhyme, 15, 20, 26–48, 149; in Daniel, 29–32, 45–48, 159n23; in Denny, 20, 37–38, 47–48; in Greville, 32–33; in Harington, 26–32, 46–48; in Jonson, 20, 31–37, 46–48, 107; mosaic (multi-word), 34, 37, 42; Philips on, 45–46; in Pulter, 20, 38, 41–44, 48, 149; Quilligan on, 30, 32, 38; in Shakespeare, 20, 33–34, 47–48; in Sidney, 30–32, 33, 36; in Southwell, 20, 39–44, 48, 140; in Spenser, 33, 48; Wesley on, 46; in Wroth, 20, 32, 36, 38–39
feminine style, 12, 16–17, 99–100, 154; Cavendish on, 5, 12, 60–61, 154; Cowley on, 151; Dolven on, 4; Jonson on, 106–8, 150–51; Quintilian on, 6
Fenner, Dudley, 6
Fisher, Payne, 165n5
Fleming, Juliet, 5–6, 156n18, 156n28, 168n4
Florio, John, 71, 105, 136, 164n79

Ford, Karen Jackson, 5
"foreign", 19, 26, 31, 46, 47

Gallagher, Catherine, 56
Gamble, Joseph, 7
Gascoigne, George, 45
gendered language, 4, 12
gender politics, 7
genre, 16, 78
Goldberg, Jonathan, 83, 86
Gordon, Colby, 34, 150
grammar: Sidney on, 160n42; Southwell on, 15, 22
Greene, Roland, 19
Greer, Germaine, 121, 138
Greville, Fulke, 32–33

"hairy", 172n86
Hall, Kim F., 7, 19, 28
Harington, John, 77; on feminine rhyme, 26–32, 46–48; on masculine rhyme, 26, 28, 29; translation of Ariosto by, 28
Harvey, Gabriel, 167n53
Hendricks, Margo, 7
Herbert, William, 36, 37
"hermaphrodite", 37–38, 110
heroic couplets, 12, 20–21, 80–92
Hock, Jessie, 66, 85, 106
Homer, 63–64, 103
homophobia, 7, 58, 106, 107
Horace, 110, 153
humors (bodily), 15, 16, 72
Hutchinson, Lucy, 80–92; Cavendish and, 70; on Cromwell, 117–19, 147; irregularities in, 81–92, 101–4, 149; Munro on, 21, 75–76, 84; *Order and Disorder*, 68–72, 81–89, 117; on "original", 20, 67–72, 74, 149; on smoothness, 21, 117–19, 147; translation of Lucretius by, 20–21, 67–71, 81, 84–85, 88–92, 117, 139; Waller and, 89–90, 117, 121, 147
Hutson, Lorna, 6–8, 58, 59

"irregular", 18, 20–21, 75–104, 106, 148–49, 154; Milton on, 78–79; Sprat on, 100–101

irregularity, 16–17, 77; in Cowley, 93; in Donne, 90; in Hutchinson, 81–92, 101–4, 149; in Milton, 78–80, 82, 90; in Munro, 21, 75–76, 84, 102; in Philips, 92–104, 149; in Pindar, 93–94
irregular odes, 20–21, 77, 80, 92–104
Iyengar, Sujata, 7

James I of England, 10, 167n53
Johnson, Samuel, 94
Jonson, Ben, 6, 35–60, 153; Burrow on, 73; Cavendish and, 57–63, 72, 153; feminine rhyme in, 20, 31–37, 46–48, 107; on feminine style, 106–8, 150–51; Gordon on, 150; on masculine style, 6, 60, 106–8, 150–51; originality of, 51–52, 61, 73, 163n62; patron of, 162n29; Shakespeare and, 66; Sidney and, 35–36; Smyth and, 153; on women poets, 106–7; works of: "That women are but men's shadows", 34–36; *Timber, or Discoveries . . .* , 6, 31–32, 57–63, 106–7, 150; "To the Noble Lady, the Lady Mary Wroth", 36–37, 51–52

Kelly, Joan, 7
keywords, 19, 23–24
Kunjummen, Sarah, 49, 74

Lanser, Susan S., 3
"lawless", 6, 94, 168n4
Lee, Nathaniel, 79–80
Leonard, John, 90
"liberty": Cowley on, 93, 98, 167n56; Dryden on, 46; Hutchinson on, 89; Philips on, 13
Lipking, Lawrence, 3
literary criticism, 120, 148–50; Alexander on, 14; canon of, 22; history of, 2–9; Philips on, 44–47; Southwell on, 8–11, 14–18, 22–23. *See also* criticism
Longinus, 132
Loscocco, Paula, 109, 111–12, 133, 147, 168n69

Lucretius, 86, 163n50; Cokain on, 139; Creech's translation of, 139; Evelyn's translation of, 139; Hutchinson's translation of, 20–21, 67–71, 81, 84–85, 88–92, 117, 139; poetics of, 66, 106, 139; *primordia rerum* in, 67; Vidal on, 86

MacDonald, Joyce Green, 7
Machiavellianism, 117
Mann, Jenny C., 21, 106, 170n51
Manning, Gillian, 132, 171n63, 171n65
Marlowe, Christopher, 17; soft style of, 106, 170n51; Southwell on, 13, 18
Martial (Roman writer), 58
"masculine", 19, 21; Cokain on, 91–92; Craik on, 6; Dolven on, 4; Hutchinson on, 70; Parker on, 6, 58, 154
masculine rhyme, 19–20, 26–28, 45; in Daniel, 29–31, 45; in Harington, 26, 28, 29; in Jonson, 34–35, 150; in Philips, 45; in Pulter, 32, 41; in Sidney, 30, 32
masculine style, 19–20, 99–100; Cavendish on, 60–61; Cowley on, 151; Dolven on, 4; Jonson on, 6, 60, 106–7, 150–51; of Lucretius, 139; Parker on, 6, 58, 154; of Philips, 108–12; Quintilian on, 6; Scott on, 106; Sprat on, 108, 151; virile style and, 6, 58, 154
Masten, Jeffrey, 19, 115–16, 158n57
"matchless", 20, 49–55, 73, 131, 138. *See also* "original"
menstruation, 77, 164n66
metaphor: Brady on, 78; Fenner on, 6
Milton, John, 8, 68, 86, 94; Burrow on, 73–74; Cowley and, 101; *Eikonoklastes*, 1; *Paradise Lost*, 78–80, 82, 90, 101; "republican sublimity" of, 165n5; sublimity of, 75, 76, 86, 165n5; Wollstonecraft on, 75, 76
mimesis, 84–85
Minerva's owl, 9–10, 40
Mitchell, Dianne, 43
modesty: "matchless", 50–55; rhetoric of, 162n17; Southwell on, 115

Montaigne, Michel de, 3–4, 5, 58, 106
"morbidezza" (smoothness), 105, 136
mosaic (multi-word) rhyme, 34, 37, 42. *See also* feminine rhyme
"mulier", 115, 119, 136
Munro, Hugh, 21, 75–76, 84, 102

Newlyn, Lucy, 163n62
Ngai, Sianne, 64
Nochlin, Linda, 3
Norbrook, David, 67, 76, 85, 86, 118, 166n33
North, Dudley, 153

odes, 130; irregular, 20–21, 77, 80, 92–104; Pindaric, 93–94, 98–103, 149
"olio", 58
"original", 18, 49–75, 106, 148–50, 154; Cavendish on, 15, 20, 55–57, 61–67, 72–74, 84; Charleton on, 20, 49, 53, 72–73; Evelyn on, 53; Hutchinson on, 20, 67–72, 74; Jonson on, 51–52, 61, 73; Philips on, 51; Romanticism and, 163n62; as source, 63, 67; Southwell on, 15–16; synonyms of, 52–53, 161n3; Wroth as, 52. *See also* "matchless"
Ovid, 9–10, 106, 140; Behn and, 146; Cavendish and, 62–67, 74, 116, 163n50, 163n64; Cowley and, 67; Wharton and, 145

panegyric, 130
paradiastole, 65, 119
Parker, Patricia, 6–8, 11, 22–23, 58, 158n10
Persius (Roman satirist), 59–60
Philips, Katherine, 44–48, 75, 76; Cokain on, 100; Cowley and, 12, 94, 104, 109, 112; feminine-masculine styles of, 108–12; on feminine rhyme, 20, 45–46; irregularities of, 92–104, 149; literary criticism of, 44–47; pen name of, 51; Vaughan on, 108; works of: "In Praise of Country Life", 97–99, 99; "Ode upon retirement", 96–97; *Pompey*, 13, 45, 95
Phillips, Rowan Ricardo, 80

philology: queer, 19, 115–16, 158n57; trans, 7
Philo-Philippa (pseudonym), 109–10, 116, 169n12
Pindaric odes, 98–103, 149, 168n71; of Cowley, 93–94, 98, 100, 108, 151
plagiarism, 55
Plato, 63
Plutarch, 58
Pope, Alexander, 110–11, 154
Powell, Jason, 90, 91
praise poems, 119–30, 136, 138
Premodern Critical Race Studies (PCRS), 7, 156n26
profane/sacred, 69
Pulter, Hester, 20, 38, 41–44, 48, 148
Puttenham, George, 3–5, 107, 108
Pythagoras, 64–65

Queer Philologies (Masten), 19, 115–16, 158n57
Quilligan, Maureen, 30, 32, 38, 158n10
Quint, David, 50, 52, 63, 74
Quintilian, 6, 32, 58

race, 7, 66, 78, 110, 114–15
Raylor, Timothy, 117
"regular", 77, 80
Revard, Stella P., 168n71
rhetoric, 23; of modesty, 162n17; of originality, 55–56; sexualization of, 7
Rhodes, Neil, 164n79
Richards, Jennifer, 167n53
Ridgeway, Lady, 15–18, 40, 72, 157n44
Ringler, William, 36
Roberts, Sasha, 3
Rochester, Countess of (Anne Wilmot), 87, 91, 120
Rochester, Earl of (John Wilmot), 120–21, 130, 133–35, 138
Romanticism, 74, 163n62
Rooney, Ellen, 4–5
Ross, Trevor, 54
Rowe, Katherine, 145
Rush, Rebecca, 95

sacred/profane, 69
Samford, Hugh, 31
Sappho, 131–33, 135–38, 140, 171n65
Sarkar, Debapriya, 66
Schoenfeldt, Michael, 34
Schor, Naomi, 4–5
Scott, William, 106, 108
sdrucciola (slippery), 30, 32
Seneca, 153
Shahani, Gitanjali, 28
Shakespeare, William, 2; Daniel and, 159n23; feminine rhyme in, 20, 33–34, 47–48; Jonson and, 66; sister of, 3; Southwell on, 13, 18; works of: *Cymbeline*, 136; *A Lover's Complaint*, 140; "Sonnet 20", 26, 33–34, 65; *Venus and Adonis*, 17, 18
Shirley, James, 115
Sidney, Philip, 2; Jonson and, 35–36; on *sdrucciola*, 30, 32; Wroth and, 38–39; works of: *An Apologie for Poetrie*, 30–31, 160n42; *Certain Sonnets*, 32; *Defence of Poetry*, 17; *Old Arcadia*, 32
Smith, Katherine, 171n63, 172n89
"smooth/soft", 18–19, 21, 92, 105–47, 118, 149–50, 154; Behn on, 12, 21, 138–39; etymology of, 115; Florio on, 105; "hairy" and, 172n86; Jonson on, 32, 107, 150; Loscocco on, 112, 147; "strong" and, 112, 121, 146–47, 148–50; "sweet" and, 132–34, 146–47, 150; Waller and, 21, 92, 154
smooth/soft style, 21, 112–19, 146–47, 147; of Behn, 12, 21, 121, 138–39; of Hutchinson, 117–19, 147; of Marlowe, 106, 170n51; of Southwell, 113–15; of Waller, 117–18; of Wharton, 12, 21, 117–20, 121, 140–46, 154
Smyth, Adam, 153
Southwell, Anne, 153, 157n44; devotional poetry of, 18, 22, 40–41, 113; feminine rhyme in, 20, 39–44, 48, 149; on grammar, 15, 22, 160n42; literary criticism of, 8–11, 14–18, 22–23; on originality, 15–16; Pulter and, 38; on smoothness, 21, 113–16, 147; on writing styles, 40–41, 113–16; works of:

Southwell, Anne (*continued*)
"An Elegy . . . to the Countess of London Derry . . .", 39; "Epitaph", 40; "Precept", 1–2, 9–10, 22, 113; "Thou Shalt Keep Holy the Sabbath Day", 26, 48
Southwell, Robert, 169n30
Southwell, Thomas, 169n30
Spenser, Edmund, 33, 48, 141–42
Sprat, Thomas, 151; Cowley and, 93, 100–101, 108, 112, 151; history of Royal Society by, 153
sprezzatura, 84
Stevenson, Jane, 51
Stewart, Susan, 94, 98
"strong", 19, 27, 111; Behn on, 139; Cowley on, 109; Jonson on, 35, 60, 150; "smooth" and, 112, 121, 146–47; "sweet" and, 109–11; Wesley on, 46
Stuart, Mary, 115–16
sublimity, 75, 76, 86, 165n5
Suzuki, Mihoko, 58
"sweet", 19, 26, 47, 111; Behn on, 132–34; Cavendish on, 64; Cowley on, 109; Daniel on, 31; Harington on, 28–30, 47; Jonson on, 150; Loscocco on, 111; Pope on, 110; Quilligan on, 38, 111; Sidney on, 31; "soft" and, 132–34, 146–47, 150; Southwell on, 39; "strong" and, 109–11
Swinburne, Algernon, 61
Sylvester, Joshua, 52

Tate, Nahum, 123
tetracolon (patterns in fours), 16, 17
textual imagination, 22
Todd, Janet, 133, 138
Toppe, Elizabeth, 56–57
"trans philology" (Gamble), 7
"trans technogenesis" (Gordon), 34
tricolon (patterns in threes), 16, 17
Trolander, Paul, 45

Vaughan, Henry, 108
Vendler, Helen, 34
Vidal, Gore, 86
Virgil, 52, 63, 64, 72, 85, 103

"virile style", 6, 58, 154. *See also* masculine style
"virtuosa rhyme", 44
"voluptuous style", 106

Waller, Edmund, 45, 147; Atterbury on, 119, 123, 133; Aubrey on, 111; on Cromwell, 117–19; Hutchinson and, 89–90, 117–18; Pope on, 110–11; smooth style of, 21, 92, 117–20, 154; Wharton on, 120–29, 137–38
"weak", 19, 27, 159n26; Cavendish on, 63; Jonson on, 35; Shakespeare on, 115–16; Sidney on, 48; Southwell on, 40–41; Wesley on, 46; Wharton on, 146
Wesley, Samuel, 46
Wharton, Anne, 147; Atwood on, 137–38; Behn and, 130–40, 146, 147; Burnet and, 120, 121, 125–27, 135–36; death of, 137–38; marriage of, 120, 138, 171n65; Ovid and, 145; on Rochester, 138; on smooth style, 121; soft style of, 12, 21, 140–46; Waller and, 120–29, 137–38; works of: "Despair", 138; "The Inconstancy of Woman Kind", 140–43; "Melpomene against Complaint", 140, 145–46; "Unchangeable", 143–44, *144*
Wharton, Goodwin, 138
Wharton, Thomas, 120
Wheatley, Phyllis, 165n19
Williams, Raymond, 19
Wilmot, Anne. *See* Rochester, Countess of
Wilmot, John. *See* Rochester, Earl of
Wilson-Okamura, David Scott, 33
Wollstonecraft, Mary, 75, 76
Woodberry, Jill, 172n86
Wroth, Mary, 159n27; *The Countess of Montgomerie's Urania*, 37, 38; feminine rhyme in, 20, 32, 36, 38–39; Jonson's sonnet to, 36–37, 51–52; *Pamphilia to Amphilanthus*, 36–39, 156n31; Sidney and, 38–39; Sylvester on, 52
Wyatt, Thomas, 78, 90, 167n53

Young, Edward, 66

A NOTE ON THE TYPE

This book has been composed in Arno, an Old-style serif typeface in the classic Venetian tradition, designed by Robert Slimbach at Adobe.

GPSR Authorized Representative: Easy Access System Europe - Mustamäe tee
50, 10621 Tallinn, Estonia, gpsr.requests@easproject.com

www.ingramcontent.com/pod-product-compliance
Lightning Source LLC
Chambersburg PA
CBHW020901230426
43666CB00008B/1272